THE RESEARCH PROCESS IN SPORT, EXERCISE AND HEALTH

- What are the challenges and potential pitfalls of real research?
- What decision-making process is followed by active researchers?

The Research Process in Sport, Exercise and Health fills an important gap in the research methods literature. Conventional research methods textbooks focus on theory and descriptions of hypothetical techniques, while the peer-reviewed research literature is mainly concerned with discussion of data and the significance of results. In this book, a team of active researchers from across the full range of sub-disciplines in sport, exercise and health discuss real pieces of research, describing the processes they went through, the decisions they made, the problems they encountered and the things they would have done differently. As a result, the book goes further than any other in bringing the research process to life, helping students identify potential issues and problems with their own research right at the beginning of the process.

The book covers the whole span of the research process, including:

- identifying the research problem;
- justifying the research question;
- choosing an appropriate method;
- data collection and analysis;
- identifying a study's contribution to knowledge and/or applied practice;
- disseminating results.

Featuring real-world studies from sport psychology, biomechanics, sports coaching, ethics in sport, sports marketing, health studies, sport sociology, performance analysis, and strength and conditioning, the book is an essential companion for research methods courses or dissertations on any sport or exercise degree programme.

Rich Neil is a Senior Lecturer in Sport Psychology, former Discipline Director of Research Methods and current Programme Director of BSc Sport and Exercise Science at Cardiff Metropolitan University, UK. His research interests include the influence LIVERPOOL JMU LIBRARY behaviour, personality, reflective practice and sel

Sheldon Hanton is the Pro Vice-Chancellor and Director of Research for Cardiff Metropolitan University, UK. As Professor of Sport Psychology his subject expertise focuses around competition and organisational stress and anxiety, mental toughness, performance reflection and the psychology of injury. He has experience of qualitative and quantitative approaches to research, including intervention studies.

Scott Fleming is Professor of Sport and Leisure Studies and Director of Research at the Cardiff School of Sport, Cardiff Metropolitan University, UK. His research interests include ethnographies in sport, leisure and education, 'race relations', and research ethics. He is a former Chair of the Leisure Studies Association and is Chair of Cardiff Metropolitan University's Ethics Committee.

Kylie Wilson is an Applied Sport Psychologist working with Olympic athletes and coaches, and organisations at High Performance Sport New Zealand. Her research interests include athlete motivation, coach–athlete relationships, group dynamics and reflective practice.

THE RESEARCH PROCESS IN SPORT, EXERCISE AND HEALTH

Case studies of active researchers

*Edited by Rich Neil, Sheldon Hanton,
Scott Fleming and Kylie Wilson*

Routledge
Taylor & Francis Group

LONDON AND NEW YORK

First published 2014
by Routledge
2 Park Square, Milton Park, Abingdon, Oxon OX14 4RN

and by Routledge
711 Third Avenue, New York, NY 10017

Routledge is an imprint of the Taylor & Francis Group, an informa business

British Library Cataloguing in Publication Data
A catalogue record for this book is available from the British Library

Library of Congress Cataloging in Publication Data
The research process in sport, exercise, and health : case studies of active researchers / edited by Scott Fleming, Sheldon Hanton, Rich Neil, and Kylie Wilson.
    pages cm
    1. Physical education and training – Research – Methodology.
    2. Sports – Research – Methodology. 3. Health – Research –
    Methodology. I. Fleming, Scott, editor of compilation.
    II. Hanton, Sheldon, editor of compilation.
    GV361.R49 2014
    613.71072–dc23   2013018814

ISBN: 978-0-415-67343-3 (hbk)
ISBN: 978-0-415-67350-1 (pbk)
ISBN: 978-0-203-12639-4 (ebk)

Typeset in Bembo
by HWA Text and Data Management, London

Printed and bound by CPI Group (UK) Ltd, Croydon, CR0 4YY

CONTENTS

FIGURES

TABLES

CONTRIBUTORS

Stephen C. Bain PhD is Professor of Medicine (Diabetes), Director of Research and Development for ABM University Health Board and Clinical Lead for the Diabetes Research Network, Wales. Stephen was appointed to a newly created Chair in Medicine (Diabetes) in the University of Wales Swansea in 2005. His clinical interests include physical activity, the genetics of diabetic nephropathy, new therapies for diabetes and the provision of diabetes services within the community. Stephen is the Diabetes Lead Clinician for the ABM University Health Board, a member of the Wales Diabetes & Endocrine Society (WEDS) executive committee and sat on the Vascular Project Group established in 2009 by the Welsh Minister for Health and Social Services. He leads the new Clinical Research Facility being established in Swansea University and has a strong interest in the metabolic responses of diabetes patients to physical activity with a view towards improving their quality of life.

Jerry Bingham is the Research Manager at UK Sport. Jerry's research interests include the development of national elite sport systems; the impact of major sports events; the effectiveness of sport as a vehicle for international development; and ethical issues in sport.

Richard M. Bracken PhD is an Exercise Physiologist at the Sports and Exercise Science Research Centre, Swansea University. Richard is lead on the Physical Activity and Diabetes Research Development Group, part of the Diabetes Research Network, Cymru. He is a professional member of Diabetes UK, European Association for Study of Diabetes (EASD), Physiological Society, Welsh Endocrine and Diabetes Society (WEDS) and British Association for

Sports and Exercise Sciences (research accredited). He forms part of a productive multidisciplinary diabetes research team at Abertawe Bro Morgannwg University Health Board that examines the use of physical activity as a non-pharmacological therapy in diabetes.

Anna Campbell PhD is a Lecturer in Clinical Exercise Science at the University of Dundee. Anna's research interest is in the cellular and molecular, physical and psychological effects of exercise after a cancer diagnosis and evaluating the implementation and effectiveness of service delivery.

Scott Fleming PhD is Professor of Sport and Leisure Studies and Director of Research at the Cardiff School of Sport (Cardiff Metropolitan University). His research interests include ethnographies in sport, leisure and education, 'race relations', and research ethics. He is a former Chair of the Leisure Studies Association and is Chair of Cardiff Metropolitan University's Ethics Committee.

Marianne J. R. Gittoes PhD is a Senior Lecturer in Sports Biomechanics and Programme Director for the MSc in Sport and Exercise Sciences at the Cardiff School of Sport (Cardiff Metropolitan University). Marianne's research focuses on developing and applying a biomechanical modelling approach to develop understanding of the physical demands of potentially injurious impacts performed in sport and exercise.

Sheldon Hanton PhD is the Pro Vice-Chancellor and Director of Research for Cardiff Metropolitan University. As Professor of Sport Psychology his subject expertise focuses around competition and organisational stress and anxiety, mental toughness, performance reflection and the psychology of injury. He has experience of qualitative and quantitative approaches to research including intervention studies.

Nic James PhD is a Professor of Sport and Exercise Science, Programme Director for MSc Performance Analysis and Head of Research at the London Sport Institute, Middlesex University. Nic's research interests include profiling performance, momentum, performance indicators, reliability, automatic tracking of movement, situation awareness, anticipation, decision-making and motor skills. The main sports studied have been soccer, rugby, squash and golf with basketball and real tennis currently being investigated.

Carwyn Jones PhD is a reader in Sports Ethics at the Cardiff School of Sport, Cardiff Metropolitan University and President of the International Association of the Philosophy of Sport (2011–2013). Carwyn's research interests include all aspects of sports ethics, especially the development of moral character and issues of addiction and mental illness in sport.

Liam Kilduff PhD is a senior lecturer in Performance Physiology at Swansea University. His research interests focus on athlete preparation, athlete monitoring and recovery. Currently, he works with a number of national and international sporting bodies as a research consultant and is a member of the ESPRIT consortium.

Zoe Knowles PhD is a senior lecturer in Sport and Exercise Psychology in the School of Sport and Exercise Sciences, Liverpool John Moores University. Zoe's research interests include the utilisation of reflective practice with practitioners ranging from psychologists, sports scientists and coaches within the elite sport domain to early years practitioners facilitating active and natural play.

Stephen D. Mellalieu PhD is a Senior Lecturer in Sports Psychology at Swansea University. He is currently Associate Editor of the *Journal of Applied Sport Psychology* and a member of the Editorial Board for *The Sport Psychologist* journal. His research interests include the psychology of elite performers, competition and organisation stress in sport and psychological skills and behaviour change in individuals and high-performance teams. He has also co-edited several recent texts reviewing applied psychological theory and professional practice in sport including *Applied Sport Psychology Advances: A Review* (2009) and *Professional Practice in Sport Psychology: A Review* (2011). Stephen is an accredited sport and exercise psychologist with the British Association of Sport and Exercise Sciences (support and research), a chartered psychologist with the British Psychological Society (BPS) and a member of the health professions council (HPC).

Nanette Mutrie PhD is Professor of Physical Activity for Health at the University of Edinburgh and Director of the Scottish Physical Activity Research Collaboration (sparcoll.org.uk). Nanette is interested in how best to promote physical activity across the lifespan and for clinical populations and how best to raise the importance of the mental health benefits of activity.

Rich Neil PhD is a Senior Lecturer in Sport Psychology and Discipline Director of Research Methods at the Cardiff School of Sport (Cardiff Metropolitan University). His research interests include the influence of stress and emotions on behaviour, personality, reflective practice, and self-efficacy.

Geoff Nichols PhD is a Senior Lecturer in Sheffield University Management School, where he teaches modules on sport industry and sport policy. Geoff's major research interest over the last six years has been volunteers in sport.

Rita Ralston PhD is currently a Visiting Research Fellow having recently retired from working as a senior lecturer within the Department of Food and Tourism Management, Manchester Metropolitan University where her teaching was focused on tourism and event management. Rita was the Project Director of research conducted in co-operation with UK Sport, exploring the motivations, expectations and experience of event volunteering, with reference to the Manchester Commonwealth Games; with a view to establishing the volunteering and sports development implications of mega-events.

Martin J. Roderick PhD is a lecturer of sociology currently teaching in the School of Applied Social Sciences at Durham University. Martin has been involved in research focusing specifically on the management of injuries in professional football. His current research interests concern the issue of risk, pain and injury in physical activity; the problems associated with work and careers in professional sport; and the inter-connections among family life, issues of work–life balance and athletic careers.

Rob Shave is Professor of Sport and Exercise Physiology at the Cardiff School of Sport (Cardiff Metropolitan University). Rob's research focuses on the acute and chronic effects of exercise upon cardiac structure and function.

Simon Shibli PhD is Head of the Sport Industry Research Centre (SIRC) at Sheffield Hallam University where he is Professor of Sport Management. His research interests are centred around the application of techniques used in management accounting and economics to solve research questions in the sport and leisure industries.

Ross Wadey PhD is a Senior Lecturer in Sport and Exercise Psychology and Programme Coordinator for BSc Sport Psychology at the University of Roehampton. Ross's research interests focus on the biopsychosocial factors that prevent and promote recovery from injury, team and individual resilience, and personal and vicarious growth following adversity.

Daniel J. West PhD is an Exercise Physiologist at the Department of Sport and Exercise Science, Northumbria University. He is a professional member of Diabetes UK and the Physiological Society. Daniel is part of a multidisciplinary team at Northumbria University, where he conducts collaborative research in both clinical and athlete populations. He is also part of the Diabetes Research Group at the NIHR Clinical Research Facility, Newcastle Royal Victoria Infirmary, and his main research focus is to develop strategies that improve blood glucose control after exercise in people with Type 1 diabetes mellitus.

Kylie Wilson PhD is an applied sport psychologist working with Olympic athletes, and coaches, and organisations at High Performance Sport New Zealand. Her research interests include athlete motivation, coach–athlete relationships, group dynamics and reflective practice.

ACKNOWLEDGEMENTS

The following material is reproduced with permission.

Chapter 2

Tables 2.1 and 2.2 reproduced from the *British Medical Journal*, Nanette Mutrie, Anna M. Campbell, Fiona Whyte *et al.* (2007), vol. 334, 517–520, with permission from BMJ Publishing Group Ltd.

Chapter 3

Figures 3.4, 3.5, 3.6, 3.7 and Tables 3.1 and 3.3 reprinted by permission of the publisher from Shibli, S., & Bingham, J. (2008), 'A forecast of the performance of China in the Beijing Olympic Games 2008 and the underlying performance management issues', *Managing Leisure*, 13, 272–292, Taylor & Francis Ltd (http://www.tandf.co.uk/journals).

Chapter 4

Figures 4.1 and 4.2 reprinted by permission of the publisher from Emma Hart, Ellen Dawson, Peter Rasmussen *et al.* (2006), 'β-Adrenergic receptor desensitization in man: insight into post-exercise attenuation of cardiac function', *Journal of Physiology*, 717–725, John Wiley and Sons © 2006 the authors. Journal compilation © 2006 The Physiological Society.

Chapter 6

Figures 6.3, 6.4a and 6.4b reprinted from M.J.R. Gittoes and K.G. Kerwin (2009), 'Interactive effects of mass proportions and coupling properties on external loading in simulated forefoot impact landings', *Journal of Applied Biomechanics* 25(3): 238–246, Human Kinetics Inc.

Chapter 7

Figure 7.1 reprinted by permission of the publisher from Zoë Knowles, Gareth Tyler, David Gilbourne *et al.* (2006), 'Reflecting on reflection: exploring the practice of sports coaching graduates', *Reflective Practice,* 7, 2, 163–179, Taylor & Francis Ltd (http://www.tandf.co.uk/journals).

Chapter 8

Figure 8.1 reprinted by permission of the publisher from Liam P. Kilduff, Nick Owen, Huw Bevan *et al.* (2008), 'Influence of recovery time on post-activation potentiation in professional rugby players', *Journal of Sports Sciences,* 26, 8, 795–802, Taylor & Francis Ltd (http://www.tandf.co.uk/journals).

Chapter 9

Figures 9.1, 9.2 and Table 9.1 reprinted by permission of the publisher from Ross Wadey, Lynne Evans, Sheldon Hanton and Rich Neil (2011), 'An examination of hardiness throughout the sport injury process', *British Journal of Health Psychology* (2012), 17, 103–128, John Wiley and Sons © 2011 The British Psychological Society.

Chapter 10

Table 10.1 reprinted by permission of the publisher from Zar, Jerrold H., *Biostatistical Analysis*, 4th Edition © 1999 Reprinted by permission of Pearson Education, Inc., Upper Saddle River, NJ.

Chapter 12

Figures 12.3 and 12.4 reprinted by permission of the publisher from Daniel West, Richard Morton, Jeffrey Stephens *et al.* (2011), 'Isomaltulose Improves Postexercise Glycemia by Reducing CHO Oxidation in T1DM', *Medicine & Science in Sports & Exercise*, 43,2, 204–210, Wolters Kluwer Health.

Chapter 13

Figure 13.1 reprinted from *Psychology of Sport and Exercise*, vol. 12. ed. 4, Rich Neil, Sheldon Hanton, Stephen D. Mellalieu and David Fletcher, 'Competition stress and emotions in sport performers: The role of further appraisals,' 460–470 © 2011, with permission from Elsevier.

INTRODUCTION

Within many universities in the UK the teaching of research to undergraduate and postgraduate students has, traditionally, been through the delivery of *research methods* modules, where the focus has been on collecting and analysing data. Students learn about the importance of rigorous research designs and how to collect, interpret, analyse and present data. By focusing primarily on *methods*, there is often less of a feel for how to actually go through the whole *process* of doing research: from critiquing the relevant literature within a chosen subject field, to formulating a well-informed and focused research question that has the potential to further knowledge and practice, to then identifying appropriate and rigorous research designs, collecting and analysing data, representing the data in a format that is digestible to the reader, to, finally, emphasising the contribution to knowledge and impact on practice.

A few years ago we were afforded the opportunity to redevelop research methods modules at undergraduate level and, after much debate, decided that it would be more beneficial for students to experience the whole research process, that is, through experiential learning, guiding them through research processes similar to that described in the paragraph above. To complement this approach, we adopted some excellent books that give insight into doing research with consideration of each part of the process. At the time, these books included: Gratton and Jones (2004) *Research methods for sport studies* (2nd edition now available); Berg and Latin (2004) *Essentials of research methods in health, physical education, exercise science, and recreation* (3rd edition now available); Long (2007) *Researching leisure, sport and tourism: The essential guide*; and Thomas, Nelson, and Silverman (2005) *Research methods in physical activity* (6th edition now available). These and other adopted books provide insight into doing research, but they isolate each part of the process and do not follow a researcher's progress through it – therefore failing to give a real-life account of what researchers actually do. Indeed, no text – to the best of our knowledge – gives the reader a step-by-step description of what active researchers did and why they did it at each stage of the research process. Within this book, therefore, we aim to provide readers with a taste of the experiences of individuals actually doing research. We have attempted this by inviting a wide range of researchers from sport, exercise, and health disciplines to give a non-technical insight into what they did at each stage of the process and why they made those decisions.

The 13 chapters of this book are not presented in any particular order. In addition, the research process that each chapter contributor underwent may differ slightly to the process described earlier. This will become apparent from reading the chapters and does emphasise an important point – that the process of doing research may differ across disciplines and projects. *However, each chapter will begin by introducing the research article on which the chapter is based, and then discuss how the research was done, book-ended by personal prologues and reflections on the entire research process that was undertaken.*

The first chapter, by Carwyn Jones (sports ethics), provides insight into Carwyn's philosophical analysis of concepts at the heart of the coverage of professional athletes' misuse of alcohol. Some highlights of the process Carwyn underwent include the description of the philosophical method adopted to address each research question presented, along with Carwyn's reflection on the arguments he puts forward within the published manuscript.

In the second chapter (exercise and health), Nanette Mutrie and Anna Campbell describe the research process they pursued when exploring the psychological and physiological benefits of a 12-week supervised group exercise programme during treatment for early stage breast cancer. Highlights include their use, and explanation for the use, of a randomised controlled trial and why they chose both quantitative and qualitative measures of change.

In Chapter 3 (sports management), Simon Shibli and Jerry Bingham give insight into their experiences when developing a forecast of the number of gold medals that China would win as host nation at the Beijing 2008 Olympic Games. Key highlights include their progress towards the final, and fairly accurate, forecasting model and their user-friendly data presentation methods.

Rob Shave, in Chapter 4 (exercise physiology), provides an account of his and his research teams' progress towards identifying a mechanistic approach to understanding the influence of prolonged elevations in catecholamines (adrenaline and noradrenaline) upon the heart's ability to function following prolonged endurance exercise. Highlights here include the justification for research and the importance (and benefits) of collaborating with external partners.

In the fifth chapter (sociology of sport), Martin Roderick gives insight into his experience when exploring the uncertainty of footballers' workplace experiences. One of many research highlights is the struggle Martin had in developing his own personal research agenda – due to once being actively involved in the industry. In addition, a good account of the issues surrounding access and sampling is provided.

Marianne Gittoes, in Chapter 6 (sports biomechanics), details her experience when developing a biomechanical research approach to understand the influence of a sports performer's mass profile on the mechanical demands experienced in potentially injurious impact landings. Some of the highlights of this chapter include the rigorous model development and demonstration of what informed the discussion within the published article.

Chapter 7 (sports coaching) by Zoe Knowles, describes and justifies the process Zoe went through when examining the reflective practices deployed by six coaches. Research highlights include how the collected data was analysed and then represented to best address the generated research questions.

Chapter 8 (strength and conditioning) written by Liam Kilduff, gives insight into the research process he underwent to determine the recovery time required to observe enhanced muscle performance following a bout of heavy resistance training. Some of the highlights of the chapter include his journey towards the appropriate research question and the description and justification for data analysis.

In the ninth chapter (sports psychology), Ross Wadey provides details of his research into the effects of the personality type of hardiness on the prediction of, and athletes' responses to, sport injury. The highlights of this chapter include the justification for the measures used, along with the colloquial account of the findings presented.

Chapter 10 (performance analysis), by Nic James, describes Nic's progress towards the development of position specific performance indicators in rugby union. One highlight of the chapter is the approach adopted to transform data to account for differences in playing times of participants, while another point of interest is the described impact the study has on practice.

In Chapter 11 (sports development), Geoff Nichols and Rita Ralston describe the research process they conducted to examine the experiences of volunteers in a programme established as a legacy of the 2002 Manchester Commonwealth Games. Some of the research highlights include their experience of writing the paper for publication, and the process they underwent to get the paper to an accepted published format.

Richard Bracken, Dan West, and Stephen Bain, in Chapter 12 (exercise physiology), describe another example of an exercise physiology research process, specifically, the journey they underwent to compare the effects of ingesting high glycaemic index and low glycaemic index carbohydrates on metabolic and fuel oxidation responses before, during and after running with Type I Diabetic individuals. Research highlights include their coverage of ethical approval and their insight into the study's contribution to knowledge through a critical discussion.

In Chapter 13 we return to the discipline of sports psychology, where Rich Neil and Stephen Mellalieu give insight into their experiences when attempting to illuminate the stress and emotion process of elite and non-elite athletes. Highlights include why they focused on that particular research question, why they adopted interviews as the data collection approach and why single-case causal networks were used as modes of representation – alongside quotes and complementary text.

Given the different subject disciplines within sport, exercise, and health covered in the book, readers are guided to look first at those chapters (or subjects) of particular interest. However, given that the authors have attempted to write their chapters in a personal, non-technical manner, we recommend that you also look at other subject areas to broaden your horizons regarding conducting research. Indeed, the authors also provide justification for decisions made throughout the process – information that can prove valuable when going through your own research process. Where the authors' experiences complement those of the author(s) of another chapter, we have attempted to make this link explicit at the end of those chapters. Consequently, this may help you navigate the order in which you read the chapters.

Acknowledgements

We would like to first express our gratitude to the authors of each chapter for contributing to this book, and embracing the nature of the book. Our thanks also go to Routledge Publishing and the Sport and Leisure Studies section for their patience, guidance and support throughout, and to the publishers of the journal articles who granted permission for the reproduction of materials.

Finally, a dedication to our respective families for their continued love and support throughout the production of this book and our careers.

References

Berg, K.E. & Latin, R.W. (2004). *Essentials of research methods in health, physical education, exercise science, and recreation* (2nd edn). Baltimore, MD: Lippincott, Williams, & Wilkins.
Gratton, C. & Jones, I. (Eds.), (2004). *Research Methods for Sports Studies*. London: Routledge.
Long, J. (2007). *Researching Leisure, Sport and Tourism: The Essential Guide*. Sage: London.
Thomas, J., Nelson, J., & Silverman, S. (2005). *Research Methods in Physical Activity* (5th edn). Champaign, IL: Human Kinetics.

1

SPORTS ETHICS

Drunken role models: rescuing our sporting exemplars

Carwyn Jones

Article reference

Jones, C. (2011). Drunken role models: Rescuing our sporting exemplars. *Sport Ethics and Philosophy, 5,* 414–432.

Article summary

A number of the important and interesting questions about sport are ethical questions. They involve asking if it's fair, good, right, acceptable, desirable or valuable. The discipline of sports ethics employs philosophical methods to answer such ethical or moral questions which arise in our sporting practices and beyond. Unlike many other disciplines, ethics does not involve collecting data, but reflecting on data and asking what are its moral implications. The aim of the philosopher is to draw careful conclusions about moral questions using reason, critical thinking, analysis and logic. This chapter explains how philosophical methods are used to investigate the question: "Does sport provide good role models when it comes to alcohol related behaviour?" The chapter provides a step-by-step account of the stages of constructing a philosophical argument by identifying the basis of key claims and the structure of the important arguments.

Related author publications

Hardman, A., Jones, C., & Jones, R. (2010). Sports coaching, virtue ethics and emulation. *Physical Education and Sports Pedagogy, 15,* 345–359.

Fleming, S., Hardman, A., Jones. C., & Sheridan, H. (2005). Role models amongst elite young male rugby league players in Britain. *European Physical Education Review, 11,* 51–70.

Personal prologue

I became interested in sports ethics during my second year as an undergraduate on the Sport and Human Movement Studies degree course at Cardiff Metropolitan University (1991). It seemed to me that most of the interesting questions in relation to sport are moral or ethical in nature (or at least have a significant ethical dimension). The activities of two of sport's most infamous cheats, namely Ben Johnson and Diego Maradona, remained prominent in the public consciousness at the time and the opportunity to reflect debate, analyse and write about such events whilst learning more about the moral ideas embedded in such acts (justice, honesty, fairness, respect, truth, courage) appealed to me. I was fortunate to be given the opportunity to pursue a PhD in sports ethics under the tutelage of Mike McNamee and Jim Parry, pioneers of Sports Ethics in the United Kingdom, and embarked on a systematic and extensive ethical analysis of the concept of moral development. Scrutinising and analysing theories, ideas and methodologies which underpin "common sense" beliefs about sport and its role in developing good character was the focus of my thesis. During that time I read about some of the key ethical theories and accessed the thoughts of pre-eminent moral philosophers including Plato, Aristotle, Immanuel Kant, John Stuart Mill, John Rawls and Alasdair MacIntyre. I was very much taken by the depth and breadth of these writers' knowledge and their commitment to a philosophical method of solving problems and answering questions by reflecting on data as opposed to collecting data. Having completed my PhD I started examining a number of issues in sport from an ethical perspective. Sometimes these issues would be driven by a theoretical commitment, in other words I wanted to see what the application of ethical ideas would tell me about sport or physical education. At other times a particular incident or a pattern of behaviour in sport would trigger my interest and I attempted to improve my understanding of the issue by showing what moral philosophy might say about it. The particular research article discussed in this chapter is an example of the latter approach. During 2010–2011, I became interested in the newspapers' negative coverage of professional athletes (usually male team sports players) in relation to the misuse of alcohol (but also other behaviours such as gambling, sexual activity, drug taking and violence) and the sensationalisation and trivialisation of these behaviours. On the one hand I wanted to analyse certain concepts at the heart of the coverage (role models, addicts, vice, mental illness) from a moral philosophical perspective. On the other hand, having had some experience with people who misuse alcohol and other substances and being a citizen of an alcohol tolerant (or perhaps pro-alcohol) culture and a member of alcohol tolerant subcultures (sport), I wanted to evaluate critically a number of (sub)cultural ideas about our relationship with alcohol.

Key message: Your research question can reflect both your theoretical and your personal interests.

Moving from a research problem to a research question

Over the last few years the tabloid media in the United Kingdom have been pre-occupied by the private lives of elite sportsmen. In particular the escapades of professional football players and rugby players in relation to alcohol and sex have been "good copy". Exposing extra marital affairs, illicit liaisons, drink-fuelled parties, late-night disorder and all round bad behaviour have been staples of the tabloid press in particular and the media in general. Since writing the article, the English rugby team's antics at the Rugby World Cup is another high-profile example of the kinds of behaviour I'm interested in. The English rugby team engendered much criticism and vilification for their lack of professionalism, an indifference to the honour of representing one's country, indiscipline, intemperance, disrespect and gluttony in relation to their off-the-field behaviour. Somewhat ironically a year previously the press criticised the management of the English football team for not allowing the team to "relax" and "let their hair down" with a "few beers". There is much for sociologists and psychologists to get their teeth into in relation to elite sporting sub-cultures, but my interest in these types of events relates to the reasons given for condemning such behaviour. Having read a number of newspaper articles, listened to numerous "phone-ins", and looked at various websites, it was clear that there were a range of reasons given for condemning players' bad behaviour. Often these reasons are incoherent and confused, so the first task is to try and identify some core set of assumptions. This process is clearly informed by my beliefs which are based on my philosophical knowledge and understanding. To put it another way, the way I see the issues is informed by the theoretical perspective I have come to adopt over the years studying and reading about moral theory. My interpretations, therefore, are as Popper (in Magee 1982, p. 33) claims "interpretations in light of theories". The theoretical background or "moral tradition" which has informed my research during and after my PhD thesis can be described loosely as Virtue Ethics. I will say more about this later, but for now I will describe which research problem and which specific research questions became obvious in light of my philosophical/ethical beliefs.

It seemed to me that the condemnation of the elite athletes focused on a number of key ideas at the heart of virtue ethics. The first relates to vices. Players were condemned because their behaviour was a manifestation of a vice or set of vices. The second idea relates to role models. Their behaviour was criticised because it set a bad example for others, in particular children and young people. The research problem, therefore, is to do with the complex nature of the vices of excess in relation to alcohol consumption and the effect such vices have on the role model potential of professional sportsmen (the problem is not an exclusively male issue; the Canadian women's hockey team were condemned for their post-match celebration at the Vancouver winter Olympics 2010). From this rather general picture of the issues I wanted to explore a number of specific questions.

1   What, if anything, is morally wrong with young men overindulging in alcohol and behaving in a boisterous manner as long as no one else is harmed? (Is the action wrong?)
2   To what extent can we hold the individuals morally responsible for their actions; are there mitigating factors such as the culture (peer pressure), immaturity, ignorance or psychological problems?
3   Do young professional sportsmen have an obligation to be good role models, and if so why?
4   How good does a role model have to be?

These questions are philosophical questions. They cannot be answered by gathering data or talking to people. My primary focus as demonstrated by the questions above is not to find out what individuals or groups "feel" about these questions. Social Psychology might be interested in attitudes and perceptions towards alcohol and role models, but my interest is in the moral or ethical questions. The only methodological option open to me, therefore, is a philosophical approach.

Choice of method (Matching the method to the research question)

Often in philosophy it is not always easy to specify an end (answering a question), independently of the means of answering it (philosophical analysis). Yet, like other forms of good inquiry, philosophical research sets out to produce knowledge by answering a question or a set of questions. The kinds of questions moral philosophers try and answer are more often than not about good and bad, right and wrong, permissible and impermissible. Sometimes the questions might focus narrowly on rights and duties; for example "Should cyclists in the Tour de France refrain from taking EPO (Erythropoietin)"? The moral philosopher will set out to establish whether or not there are compelling reasons or obligations for the cyclist to refrain from taking the drug (Moller, 2010). Having examined the reasons, however, a moral philosopher might conclude that none of the reasons are individually necessary nor in combination sufficient to create a duty on the cyclist to refrain. In other words, they might conclude that the reasons are not sufficiently persuasive (clear, rigorous, logical, and substantiated) to support the injunction not to take EPO (Moller, 2010). Another way a moral philosopher might approach a question is to ask what is "valuable or worthwhile". For example one might ask what a "good" bike race might look like (fair, challenging, exciting, safe) or what type of cyclists would we admire (honest, just, courageous). In order to answer this type of question, philosophers will need to state clearly what they mean by certain key concepts. They cannot simply stipulate an "operational definition", because their account of say "cheating" must be clear, coherent, and consistent and must account for all incidents that we call cheating, whilst excluding incidents that are not cheating (McFee, 2004). For example, does the proposed account of cheating discriminate between accidental and intentional hand balls in football? The definition must also aim to generate a degree of consensus amongst other philosophers and the practice community and have common sense appeal. Importantly, philosophers are looking to do more than describe the way things are. It is a matter of fact that some professional footballers engage in acts aimed at deceiving referees in order to gain an advantage. It may even be a matter of fact that this has always been the case, will always be the case, and nothing can really be done about it. These facts are important, but the moral philosopher is looking to evaluate the facts. They are looking to produce a value (normative) judgement in relation to the facts. They are concerned with providing sound reasons why something is good/right or bad/wrong. To a certain extent any conclusion which might be reached is independent of what is custom and practice and may even be independent of certain rules and laws. The question about the use of EPO might be about whether there are good reasons for its use to be forbidden. We know it is forbidden, but ought it to be? Are there sufficiently convincing reasons for EPO to be banned? The discussion is likely to involve reference to important moral values and principles like fairness, harm, justice, freedom and autonomy. Philosophers will use various analogies, comparisons, hypothetical examples and thought experiments to help come to a conclusion. It involves a very careful and thorough critical and analytical process.

Philosophers are not left to fumble around in the dark trying to weave arguments from thin air. Like all the other academic disciplines, philosophers work within a tradition which provides a rich source of knowledge which informs their reflection. This knowledge is captured in a wealth of published work. In fact there is a history of over 2,000 years of philosophical reflection and writing about some of the concepts central to human existence. A significant portion of this writing is dedicated to questions about the good life and how human beings should conduct themselves. In other words there is a subsection of philosophy called Ethics. Within the sub-discipline of ethics there are countless different approaches to answering questions like "why should one be good?" or "do we have moral duties?" Certain distinct approaches have emerged over the centuries which share some basic ideas about how to answer these questions. I will discuss three of these approaches very briefly. *Utilitarianism* is a theoretical approach which identifies happiness or pleasure as the *telos* (goal) of human life. Increasing overall happiness and reducing pain and suffering is seen as the most important consideration. Questions about morality are therefore answered in relation to this goal. Good and right actions are actions that produce the greatest balance of pleasure over pain. A good person is a person who is able to act in such a way that they achieve this goal fairly consistently (see McNamee et al., 2007, pp. 34–37). *Deontology* on the other hand describes the idea that there are some actions which are intrinsically bad, such as torture, and ought never to be pursued regardless of any good consequences that might arise from it. Good people are those who can recognise and act according to their moral duties to be honest, just, fair and respectful (see McNamee et al., 2007, pp. 37–39). Another approach often contrasted with utilitarianism and deontology is *virtue ethics*. Virtue ethics focuses on character and the balance of virtues over vices. A good person has good character and acts in the right way at the right time and for the right reasons. They do so because living a genuinely good life consists of being just, honest, courageous, fair and honourable (see McNamee et al., 2007, pp. 39–40). Each of these approaches is far more complex than can be explained here, and the differences between them are not always clear cut. Nevertheless, in ethics textbooks one might reasonably expect to find these theories under different chapters. Moral theoretical approaches are not exhausted by these three either, but it is reasonable to say that most moral arguments draw upon one or more of these theories as their basis.

It is important to note that the particular moral theory one adopts does not commit one to a particular view on the issue. It would be wrong to say that utilitarians would come to one conclusion, deontologists to another and virtue theorists to another. The difference between them is their focus. All will consider the question carefully, weigh relevant considerations and attempt to construct an argument that supports a conclusion one way or another. This pattern is repeated with other questions, for example the issue of doping in sport. Tamburrini (2000) takes a utilitarian approach and favours a lifting of the prohibition on drugs. The lifting of the ban, he argues would increase good consequences and reduce bad ones. Good consequences include better conditioned athletes and a greater spectacle; bad consequences include a restriction of the liberty and privacy of athletes subjected to the World Anti-Doping Agency's (WADA) anti-doping policies including the whereabouts rules. McNamee (2008) supports the ban on drugs from a virtue theoretical approach, arguing that those who seek to use drugs are seeking to take short cuts and lack virtues such as integrity and courage. Fraleigh (1984), amongst others, argues that drug taking is in breach of fundamental moral principles like fairness. A person and an organisation have a duty to uphold fundamental moral principles; therefore they must neither sanction nor use methods to enhance performance which undermine such principles. As I said earlier, however, one's theoretical commitments do not necessarily point in one direction. The implications of theory must be analysed in relation to a particular example.

Addressing the research questions

Having given a very brief overview of the philosophical method in general and of the moral philosophical method in particular, I will now illustrate how I went about addressing each of the questions I identified earlier. This should both clarify some points about the general methodological approach and show how I used the method in answering these specific questions.

What, if anything, is morally wrong with young men overindulging in alcohol and behaving in a boisterous manner as long as no one else is harmed? (Is the action wrong?)

Heavy drinking and partying is seen as a right of passage in British society. Getting drunk and associated behaviour is central part of British youth culture. Town centres on weekends are inundated with drunken men and women "enjoying themselves", and during the summer resorts across the Mediterranean are a favoured location of young British citizens binge drinking. Promiscuity, violence, injury and health risks go hand in hand with this culture. Although there are increasing concerns about the effect of this culture on the health of youngsters, it is not immediately clear what the moral issue might be. Intuitively I feel that there is something problematic with this type of behaviour. Perhaps it shows disrespect for other citizens, property, the law, other party goers, and maybe disrespect for oneself (deontological considerations). Or perhaps the issue might relate to a misguided set of values and a failure to appreciate that these behaviours inhibit genuine flourishing for a whole host of reasons (virtue theory considerations). Perhaps it might be that the cost of binge drinking to society in terms of cleaning, policing, acute and chronic medical care, days lost at work and all sorts of other related expense means that we would be better off in lots of ways without it (utilitarian considerations). My feelings and opinions about these possibilities are important, but what are required are sound reasons for my beliefs. Given what I said in the prologue, the obvious choice for me was to look to virtue theoretical ideas to back up my intuitions that there is something morally problematic about the behaviour of professional athletes (and others) who drink excessively. The task therefore is to construct an argument that the behaviour in question is a vice or a collection of vices. I won't rehearse the arguments in detail here (you can see these in the paper) but simply sketch the process through the following steps.

Step 1. Setting the scene

I tried to argue that alcohol is a potentially hazardous drug, despite its legal and cultural status. To do this I conducted a search for evidence. This search took in government reports, World Health Organisation reports and reports from other organisations like Alcohol Concern. I also searched for peer reviewed academic journal articles on the subject as well as using academic books and other media sources. Using this evidence I tried to demonstrate that alcohol consumption has significant risks when ingested in greater volume than recommended by government advisors (as emphasised in the following claim).

Claim 1: Alcohol *causes* a wide range of harms when used excessively (empirical/factual claim).

Step 2. Excessive consumption as vice

Having gathered good evidence that excessive alcohol consumption has potentially harmful effects, I needed to argue that these harms were morally significant. In other words, the harms were not just a matter for the individual, but had wider moral significance. The way I did this was to argue that those who drank excessively exemplified vice, or a range of vices. This is a controversial claim, especially given the extent of excessive alcohol consumption in British culture. Using ideas from moral philosophers and more empirical data I argued that the behaviour in question did exemplify certain vices like deceptiveness, insensitivity, and disrespect for others and oneself, weakness of will, and so on. Importantly, I tried to argue that those who drank excessively failed in their "duty of care" for themselves and others. In the article, this argument involved the careful application of the ideas of philosophers such as Aristotle, MacIntyre (1985), McNamee (2008) and Pincoffs (1986). Of course, some will disagree with my argument for many reasons, and in fact in the peer review process, the anonymous reviewers asked for more careful and critical arguments in this section. This entails applying the method described earlier more carefully, looking for more compelling reasons, better evidence, constructing the argument more carefully and explaining some of the concepts more clearly (as emphasised in the following claim).

Claim 2: The excessive consumption of alcohol and associated anti-social behaviour *are* examples of vice (value judgement/moral claim).

To what extent can we hold the individuals morally responsible for their actions; are there mitigating factors such as the culture (peer pressure), immaturity, ignorance or psychological problems?

This question is crucial with respect to our moral evaluations. One might agree with all the arguments about vice and so forth, but it is a separate matter to apportion blame or culpability. It could be argued that all individuals who behave in a morally problematic way are not equally responsible for their actions, or not fully culpable. This is a central issue in moral philosophy. We may agree that certain *actions* are bad, but evaluate *agents* differently. The paradigm example might be when a child commits a heinous crime. There is no doubt that the act is bad, but we may temper our evaluation of the culprit in light of many other mitigating factors such as their age, their mental capacities, their frame of mind and perhaps a number of socio-economic factors too. In doing so our evaluation of the act differs from the evaluation of the actor. In sport, when there is a disciplinary hearing for an athlete who has committed a violent act, the athlete might put forward their exemplary disciplinary record as evidence of previous good character as mitigation. There is of course the opposite view. Some will argue that our moral judgements ought to focus solely on the action. It might be argued that no mitigation is deserved (in any circumstances) and a plea for clemency won't be accepted in any situation (see Jones and Fleming 2007 for an analysis of these issues in relation to racism in sport). As far as alcohol consumption is concerned, I believe that an individual's drinking patterns are not simply a result of basic "choice". Again this is a controversial claim which cuts across a number of theoretical debates in both ethics and psychology. My argumentation strategy was as follows:

Step 3. Binge drinking is part of sport

I tried to argue that far from being "deviant" behaviour, excessive alcohol consumption, particularly in terms of "binges" at certain times in a season, is custom and practice in sport. Using a range of published material (academic books and journal articles, biographies, autobiographies and a range of print and other media sources) I argued that drinking was an important part of sporting culture. This is a descriptive or sociological claim and it's crucial to my argument that I can prove this. One way would be to gather primary data about "booze culture" in sport, but I used secondary sources including newspaper reports, biographies, autobiographies, anecdotal evidence from my own experiences and conversations I have had with people who are inside the culture (I aim to conduct empirical research in the future with [ex]professional sportsmen to get a clearer picture of the role of drinking in sport). So,

Claim 3: There *is* a booze culture in professional sport (empirical/factual claim).

Step 4. The power of context

The next stage was to argue that the *facts* about a booze tolerant culture have moral significance when it comes to evaluating the behaviour of drunken players. In order to do this I used two important theoretical concepts, namely *ethos* (Loland and McNamee, 2000) and *habitus* (Bourdieu, 1990). These concepts have been used by philosophers and sociologists of sport to explain how players learn about "being" a football or rugby player and the way in which the norms and expectations of a practice community are constructed, maintained and transmitted. Using the concepts of *ethos* and *habitus* I argued that the booze tolerant culture in professional sport "encourages" certain patterns of alcohol consumption (as emphasised in the following claim).

Claim 4: A booze tolerant culture (ethos or habitus) exercises a genuine conforming influence on individuals; sportsmen are initiated into problematic drinking patterns (empirical/factual claim).

Step 5. Moral significance of contextual influences

Finally, I used some classic social psychological arguments to show how difficult it is for human beings to resist external pressures and influences. Stanley Milgram's (1974) (in)famous experiments in the 1960s showed that given the right sort of external coercive forces, subjects acted very differently to what was expected of normal American citizens. The point is that although it is individuals that get drunk and cause trouble, it's important to consider the background and the culture in which these individuals are socialised and educated. Here I am not just making the psychological claim that our characters are shaped by our backgrounds, but a more controversial moral claim that our moral evaluations of individuals should be informed by these facts (as emphasised in the following claim).

Claim 5: When making moral judgements about the behaviours of individual sportsmen's drinking habits, the ethos and habitus *should* be taken into account (value judgement/moral claim).

Do young professional sportsmen have an obligation to be good role models and if so why?

To address this question I wanted to argue that there is a moral obligation to be good role models.

Step 6. Give an account of what is meant by the concept of a role model

First, this involved discussing the psychology of role modelling. In other words, explaining what function is played by influential persons (parents, teachers, and people in the public eye) in the development of children and young people. This required using theory (neo-Aristotelian virtue based accounts of moral development) and data (social and educational psychology) to back up the claim that professional footballers' actions and behaviour can and do have a "role modelling" impact. Central to Aristotle's theory of moral development is an exemplar who exemplifies moral excellences. Pupils acquire these excellences through a process of emulation and guided practice. Fleming et al. (2005) found that young rugby league players had role models and held them in esteem for a number of different reasons (as emphasised in the following claim).

Claim 6: Professional footballers' behaviour *does* have an influence on children and young people (empirical/factual claim).

Step 7. An account of the concept of emulation

I argued that emulation is the disposition to "copy" or to "model" one's own behaviour on the behaviour and character of others we admire or look up to. Given the high-profile status of professional football players and their important position in the public consciousness, they are the object of children and young people's emulation (as emphasised in the following claim).

Claim 7: Children and young people look up to professional sportsmen and *do* emulate them (empirical/factual claim).

Step 8. Is there a duty to be a good role model?

Even if we accept claims 1 and 2, it doesn't necessarily follow that professional sportsmen are obliged to be good role models. This required further philosophical argumentation using my chosen virtue theoretical approach. How and in what ways duties or obligations attach to individuals is a complex issue. I argued simply that, if you know your behaviour can influence children and young people in a bad way, you ought, as far as possible, to behave so that you have a positive influence rather than a negative one. I rejected (through careful argumentation) the counter-claim that professional players have not *chosen* to be role models and therefore are not obliged to be good examples. My argument was that with certain roles come rights and privileges, but they also come with certain obligations and responsibilities. A professional athlete is one such role which, like it or not, carries an obligation to set a good example (as emphasised in the following claim).

Claim 8: Like it or not, professional athletes *have a duty* to set a good example (value judgement/moral claim).

How good does a role model have to be?

This final question is a particularly complex one and has taxed the brains of most of the great moral philosophers over the centuries. The question touches on some of the basic moral philosophical issues such as "moral development", "moral excellence", "moral goodness" and "the nature of moral character". I took a stance on some of these key issues based on ideas and beliefs of a number of writers. In other words, I borrowed a perspective from philosophers who are wiser and more intelligent than me. This is a perfectly legitimate strategy in applied ethics (and in research in general, i.e., a psychologist might employ a tried and tested approach to researching mental toughness). I chose a theory (not at random, but based on its philosophical merit) and attempted to see how the theory could help me answer the question I was interested in. At the outset I mentioned I favoured a virtue theory approach and I attempted to establish two important ideas using the following steps, namely that there are a variety of ways to be good and that role models don't have to be moral saints.

Step 9. Different ways to be good

I argued that moral goodness is not reducible to "one" primary moral quality or virtue like justice. There are different ways in which people may be morally good. This is both a descriptive and a normative claim (i.e., people *have* different moral strengths and this is *justifiable*).

Claim 9: There are *varieties* of good character (value judgement/moral claim).

Step 10. Heroes and saints

Moral goodness can be exemplified in a variety of different ways and in a variety of different situations. A person can demonstrate their moral character through their dedication to their projects such as teaching, nursing, soldiering and importantly through their sport. Commitment, dedication, loyalty, integrity, fair play and generosity are virtues displayed by many professional athletes. To help make the argument that professional players can be role models I borrow a distinction from Blum (1994) between moral saints and moral heroes. A moral saint is someone who dedicates their life to doing well and helping others, for example Mother Teresa, Nelson Mandela and a host of other less well known individuals who live their lives at a level of moral excellence and consistency beyond the reach of most human beings. They clearly stand as excellent role models even though most people will have neither the ability nor the desire to match their sacrifices. A moral hero on the other hand exercises a narrower range of moral excellences. They may be morally excellent in a certain field, for example their job, or their family. A moral hero might be someone who demonstrates exemplary courage in the face of a situation or incident. They may show incredible courage or honesty, or loyalty despite the extreme difficulties they find themselves in, even though their character in general might have significant flaws. The example Blum uses to illustrate a moral hero is Oscar Schindler who risked his own life to save Jews from the gas chamber during the Second World War. Although Schindler was a womaniser and fraternised and bribed German soldiers and was motivated, at least in part, by money, he saved over a 1,000 Jews from death. This act alone, argues Blum, qualifies him as a moral hero and worthy of our admiration despite his other less saintly qualities (as emphasised in the following claim).

Claim 10: Role models *don't* have to be moral saints, they can demonstrate moral excellence in a narrower more restricted way (both in terms of range and duration), yet still be considered worthy of admiration and emulation (value judgement/moral claim).

Contribution to knowledge and practice

Above is an account of how I went about answering my four research questions. I have shown the steps in my argument and the claims that arise from the analysis and discussion in each step. The next and final stage of writing the article is to try and *discuss* the implications of the claims. Below I list the claims again and give a brief summary of what I argued were the important implications.

Claim 1: Alcohol *causes* a wide range of harms when used excessively.

Claim 2: The excessive consumption of alcohol and associated anti-social behaviour *are* examples of vice.

Claim 3: There *is* a booze culture in professional sport.

Claim 4: Booze tolerant culture (ethos or habitus) exercises a genuine conforming influence on individuals; sportsmen are initiated into problematic drinking patterns.

Claim 5: When making moral judgements about the behaviours of individual sportsmen's drinking habits, the ethos and habitus *should* be taken into account.

In relation to these claims I argued that it is important to change the problematic drinking and drink-related behaviours. This involves some form of moral education or intervention to help players act more responsibly around drink. Given the strong influence of the ethos of professional sport, it is important to recognise that there needs to be a change at the cultural level and not just the individual level. Changing the culture will have at least two positive outcomes. First, excessive drinking will become "abnormal" rather than "normal" and this change in the culture will have positive effects on individuals. There is a lot of talk in sport about how developing a "winning culture" and a "professional culture" has positive outcomes for individual and team performances. Developing a "safe and sensible drinking culture", I concluded, will have similar positive effects. Secondly, a "safe and sensible drinking culture" will help to identify early individuals who may have problems with controlling their alcohol consumption and their behaviour while drunk. If appropriate, these individuals can be helped with their behaviour (this last comment highlights an issue which I hope to research further in the near future).

Claim 6: Professional footballers' behaviour *does* have an influence on children and young people.

Claim 7: Children and young people look up to professional sportsmen and *do* emulate them.

Claim 8: Like it or not, professional athletes *have a duty* to set a good example.

Claim 9: There are *varieties* of good character.

Claim 10: Role models *don't* have to be moral saints, they can demonstrate moral excellence in a narrower more restricted way (both in terms of range and duration), yet still be considered worthy of admiration and emulation.

The key discussion arising from these claims was that given a professional football player is a role model, what kind of role model should they aspire to be. I argued that wherever possible they should try and lead good lives, but they are not expected to be moral saints (psychologically impossible and not morally necessary). They can, however, be moral heroes in a number of ways. I gave a few examples such as Tony Adams who has tackled addiction and set up a treatment centre to help other professional football players with addictive illnesses. Ryan Giggs is an excellent example of a player who has shown dedication and commitment to a particular way of life. He has enjoyed a very successful and long career thanks to his efforts, loyalty, dedication and hard work. Both Giggs and Adams are good role models in a certain way.

There are three important ways in which my arguments in the article could influence policy and practice. The first is to encourage professional clubs and institutions like the FA, RFU and WRU to recognise their responsibility in the problem. Of course these organisations condemn the behaviour of individual players who step out of line, yet at the same time organise or sanction excessive drinking at certain points in the season. Gavin Henson recalls how the Wales team in 2005 were obliged to attend a function organised by Brains brewery, the team's sponsors at the time, at one of their pubs in the centre of Cardiff. That afternoon of drinking came after the previous night of heavy drinking and Henson himself believes that this was ill advised. The standard image of players celebrating an important victory on the field of play by drinking champagne out of bottles supplied by the sponsors is a common practice that according to my argument is ill advised. It galvanises the wanton consumption of alcohol as the cornerstone of celebration and these images of champagne being sprayed, swigged from bottles and trophies become deeply embedded in the public consciousness as the pinnacle of sporting achievement. The England rugby team were criticised during the 2011 World Cup for allowing their players, not only to drink, but to get drunk publicly. The Welsh team seemed to avoid any public embarrassment in relation to alcohol, yet their coach was quick to insist that the team were not tee-total. The association between drinking and male team sports remains strong and in my paper I advocate a rethink of both the drinking "ideology" and the drinking "practice" of professional team sports. I believe that momentum is shifting towards a more responsible drinking culture, and I hope my article will contribute to that momentum.

The other potentially important contribution to practice from the article is to change attitudes towards sportsmen who seem to be "repeat" offenders. Mike Tindall, Mike Phillips, Gavin Henson and Danny Cipriani, for example, are rugby players who seem to get into trouble with drink repeatedly. If rules are broken, then punishment is of course essential as a deterrent for them and others, however, I believe there is a need to consider some sort of therapeutic intervention into the self-destructive behaviours of certain players. Given that excessive drinking and associated behaviour is "normal" among young men, there may be reluctance on behalf of both individuals and institutions to see (occasional) excessive drinking as a problem. It clearly is a problem for some and my paper tries to argue this point. Following his most recent high-profile incident, Mike Phillips apologised for his behaviour and claimed he was seeking help with the "pressures" of being an elite high-profile rugby player. My argument is that the relationship with alcohol might have a causal role in the behaviour rather than simply being a symptom of pressure or stress.

Reflection

A key strength of the paper is its uniqueness. It is the first article written in sports ethics about the ethics of excessive drinking and the role-modelling influence of drunken sports stars. Although there has been plenty of discussion among commentators and journalists, the paper marks the first concerted and philosophical attempt to tackle this important public issue. A second strength is the breadth of the article. The article covers a lot of ground combining the insights of moral philosophy, public health research, and moral psychology and touches on some therapeutic ideas, but there is a strong consistent moral theoretical thread in the paper. I see the paper as an opening position in an important sports ethics and public health debate and hope others will point to flaws and weaknesses in my arguments. It is by such scrutiny of authors' published ideas and arguments that progress is made in philosophy.

Since I wrote the article, Ryan Giggs has been exposed by the newspapers for his infidelity and his lack of consideration for his family. His conduct in relation to his relationships is by no means exemplary. It could be argued that this new information about Giggs undermines both his suitability as a role model and consequently my argument in the paper that professional football players can be good role models. I don't think my argument is defeated by Giggs' sex life, but I would need to revisit some key theoretical issues and arguments. A key element in defending my argument, however, is my discussion of emulation as a virtue. I have argued that moral exemplars play an important role in the development of character. Children and young people will emulate their heroes and idols. Emulation, however, can be shaped and influenced by teachers, parents, coaches and the media. In other words, we can guide children towards the appropriate features of their role models. At the risk of oversimplification, children can be encouraged to value Giggs' qualities as a player, but not his qualities as a husband. Although the breadth of the essay is a key strength, it could be seen as a weakness too. There are perhaps too many arguments and claims for one article, but I felt it was important to deal with the issue in its entirety. The issue would benefit further from a substantive and sustained analysis beyond the scope of the word limits for journals. The arguments could be further strengthened by empirical data and psycho-therapy theory. I intend to undertake some primary data collection with ex-professional footballers, draw further on psycho-therapy insights, and tackle some additional key philosophical ideas. One crucial distinction I intend to explore is the difference between mental illness and vice and the corollary distinction between therapy and character development. Given the breadth and complexity of these issues, I intend to write a monograph in which the ideas can be analysed in more details without the constraint of journal word limits.

In this chapter I have attempted to describe moral philosophical research in relation to character, ethos, role models and alcohol consumption. I have discussed how philosophers attempt to answer questions relating to value using careful philosophical analysis and argumentation. In some cases, the facts of the matter are important in answering these questions, but my goal was not to uncover these facts, but to argue about the moral significance of these facts. Describing precisely the philosophical method is notoriously difficult, but there are some resources that can help you to get an insight into what philosophers do. I hope, through this example, to have given an insight into the kind of research moral philosophers of sport do. It is important to remember that another moral philosopher, even one with similar theoretical convictions, might disagree with my conclusions. They might do this by disputing some of the facts I have used or pointing out that I have misinterpreted a particular philosophical position or pointing to errors of logic and showing where I have been inconsistent. The scrutiny and critique of our ideas is crucial to the development of knowledge and should be welcome. As Popper, a famous philosopher of science, argues, we learn more from data that falsifies theories than data which further verifies them.

> If you liked this chapter, you should read Chapter 5 where Martin Roderick describes a research process that focuses on the uncertainties surrounding the working lives of football professionals.

References

Blum, L.A (1994) *Moral Perception and Particularity*. Cambridge: Cambridge University Press.

Bourdieu, P. (1990) *The Logic of Practice*: Cambridge: Polity Press.

Fleming, S., Hardman, A., Jones. C., & Sheridan, H. (2005). Role models amongst elite young male rugby league players in Britain. *European Physical Education Review, 11,* 51–70.

Fraleigh, W. (1984) *Right Actions in Sport*. Champaign, IL: Human Kinetics.

Jones, C. & Fleming, S. (2007) "I'd rather wear a turban than a rose": the (in) appropriateness of terrace chanting amongst sport spectators. *Race, Ethnicity and Education, 10,* 401–414.

Loland, S. & McNamee, M.J. (2000) Fair play and the ethos of sport: an eclectic philosophical framework. *Journal of the Philosophy of Sport, 27,* 63–80.

MacIntyre, A. (1985) *After Virtue*. London: Duckworth.

Magee, B. (1982) *Popper*. London: Fontana Press.

McFee, G. (2004) *Sport, Rules and Values*. London: Routledge.

McNamee, M. (2008) *Sports, Virtues and Vices; morality plays*. London: Routledge.

McNamee, M., Olivier, S. & Wainwright, P. (2007) *Research Ethics in Exercise, Health and Sports Sciences*. London: Routledge.

Milgram, S. (1974). *Obedience to Authority*. New York: Harper and Row.

Moller, V. (2010) *The Ethics of Doping and Anti-Doping*. London: Routledge.

Pincoffs, E. (1986) *Quandries and Virtues; against reductivism in ethics*. Lawrence, KS: University Press of Kansas.

Tamburrini, C. (2000) What's wrong with doping, in T. Tanssjo and C. Tamburrini (eds) *Values in Sport*. London: Routledge, pp. 200–216.

2

EXERCISE AND HEALTH

Could exercise help breast cancer patients with how they feel?

Nanette Mutrie and Anna Campbell

Article reference

Mutrie, N. et al. (2007). Benefits of supervised group exercise programme for women being treated for early stage breast cancer: pragmatic randomised controlled trial. *British Medical Journal, 334*, 517–520.

Article summary

The objectives of this study were to determine the functional and psychological benefits of a 12-week supervised group exercise programme during treatment for early stage breast cancer, and to conduct a 6-month follow-up of the programme. The design was a pragmatic randomised controlled prospective open trial with additional qualitative methods to explore participant views. The study was set in three National Health Service oncology clinics in Scotland and community based exercise facilities. The participants were 203 women who entered the study, 177 of whom completed the 6-month follow-up. The intervention was a supervised 12-week group exercise programme in addition to usual care and this was compared with usual care. The main outcome measures were: Functional Assessment of Cancer Therapy (FACT) questionnaire, Beck depression inventory, positive and negative affect scale, body mass index, 7-day recall of physical activity, 12-minute walk test, and assessment of shoulder mobility. Mixed effects models with adjustment for baseline values, study site, treatment at baseline, and age gave intervention effect estimates (intervention minus control) at 12 weeks of 129 (95 per cent confidence interval 83 to 176) for metres walked in 12 minutes, 182 (75 to 289) for minutes of moderate intensity activity reported in a week, 2.6 (1.6 to 3.7) for shoulder mobility, 2.5 (1.0 to 3.9) for breast cancer specific subscale of quality of life, and 4.0 (1.8 to 6.3) for positive mood. No significant effect was seen for general quality of life (FACT-G), which was the primary outcome. At the 6-month follow-up, most of these effects were maintained and an intervention effect for breast cancer specific quality of life emerged. No adverse effects were noted. It was concluded that supervised group exercise provided functional and psychological benefit after a 12-week intervention and 6 months later. We recommended that clinicians should encourage activity for their patients and that policy makers should consider the inclusion of exercise opportunities in cancer rehabilitation services.

Related author publications

Campbell, A., Mutrie, N., White, F., McGuire, F., & Kearney, N. (2005). A pilot study of a supervised group exercise programme as a rehabilitation treatment for women with breast cancer receiving adjuvant treatment. *European Journal of Oncology Nursing, 9,* 56–63.

Emslie, C., Whyte, F., Campbell, A., Mutrie, N., Lee, L., Ritchie, D., & Kearney, N. (2007). 'I wouldn't have been interested in just sitting round a table talking about cancer'; exploring the experiences of women with breast cancer in a group exercise trial. *Health Education Research, 22,* 827–838.

Personal prologues

Nanette

I have always wanted to understand why everyone did not enjoy physical activity the way I did and therefore why some people – even when they were told that their health might depend on it – could not find the motivation to be physically active. This led me first towards physical education teaching, then into education and with the help of a Fulbright Scholarship to a PhD at the Pennsylvania State University, USA under the supervision of Professor Dorothy Harris. Dorothy had written a book entitled *Involvement in Sport – the somatopsychic rationale.* Of course I came to know that book pretty well! Dorothy wanted me to pursue a research topic that showed the somatopsychic principles in action – this means that our bodies in motion influence how we think and feel. (The opposite principle is psychosomatic and is more commonly understood as our mind influences our body.) After several PhD proposals were offered and rejected, I settled on the topic of depression and whether or not physical activity might alleviate the symptoms. This provided the structure for the rest of my career – how can we get people who really don't feel that good about physical activity or exercise or sport to become more active and what are the mental health benefits they might experience? When a colleague in the Health Board in Glasgow asked me if I thought that physical activity or exercise might help women with the fatigue they experienced during cancer therapy, the idea for the research project we are describing was born. It sits perfectly within the somatopsychic framework.

Anna

Until 2000, my research had concentrated on laboratory based work in the areas of biochemistry and immunology. My interest in clinical exercise developed in 1998 when, as a research topic for my MSc in Sport and Exercise Science, I studied the effects of exercise on clinical depression. Consequently, the opportunity arose to work with Professor Mutrie on a pilot study into the effects of exercise on breast cancer patients. This area was very under-researched at this time and was of particular interest to me as it utilised my interest in clinical medicine, cellular biology and physical activity.

We began working on this topic because Nanette was working with the local health board on the physical activity strategy and a health promotion officer working in the area of cancer asked the question 'Could exercise help breast cancer patients with how they feel?' At this stage (2000) there were only a small number of studies in this area – mostly quasi-experimental (meaning that these studies were not true experiments because they compared intact groups such as patients coming to one hospital with an exercise programme versus those going to another hospital with no exercise programme) or with small numbers. Most cancer patients at this time were told to rest during and after treatment – but there was no evidence to determine what the correct evidence was. One breast cancer clinical nurse specialist (Gaye Patterson) said that she always told her patients to rest during treatment for breast cancer but was unsure if this was the correct advice. I was completing an MSc at the time and we were given some money to employ me to begin to explore this question. Some further funding allowed a pilot study and data began to emerge.

The process we engaged in began modestly with a pilot study – but it was robustly designed and included elements of a randomised controlled trial. We obtained some very positive results but realised that the pilot study, with small numbers and lessons to learn about recruitment, was certainly not a complete picture. So we used the emerging guidance from the Medical Research Council about the design and evaluation of complex interventions to frame our plans to mount a 'fully defined intervention' (Campbell et al., 2000). This framework suggests pilot stages, qualitative work and preferred a randomised controlled trial (RCT) design to provide a comprehensive answer to the research question. Our proposal, guided by this framework was funded by Cancer Research UK.

The findings of the study described in this chapter added further knowledge on the benefits of exercise during breast cancer treatment as it was the largest RCT to date undertaken with women during breast cancer treatment and it was the first to look at the long-term benefits of the intervention. The implications of the study for informing applied practice was that it was a pragmatic intervention which could be implemented in the UK within a community/NHS referral system.

Moving from a research problem to a research question

At the time of the study, the literature suggested that for many women after a diagnosis of breast cancer, physical activity levels reduced significantly and remained low long after treatment was completed (Irwin et al., 2004). Although there was some evidence of an effect of exercise interventions on quality of life and fatigue levels with breast cancer survivors, many of the early studies were methodologically limited, using quasi-experimental, cross-sectional (meaning comparing groups of patients by their activity levels) or retrospective research designs.

Systematic reviews of the available literature have become a critical starting point for all researchers. A systematic review is more than a literature review and follows systematic procedures to obtain all possible references, determine the quality of the evidence, and make conclusions about the evidence that are free from bias. The Cochrane review process provides an excellent set of procedures for conducting a systematic review and the library of available reviews is also a good starting point for researchers (www.thecochranelibrary.com). A Cochrane review, which examined exercise interventions exclusively during treatment for breast cancer (Markes et al., 2006) found improvements in physical fitness and activities of daily life but no significant improvements in quality of life (QoL) or fatigue. The review stated that there were a number of shortcomings that needed to be addressed in future studies. In previous studies, the results were based on self-reported levels of exercise or on individually supervised exercise. More studies were needed with objective indicators of physical activity and interventions such as attendance at structured group classes, in order to study whether exercise in a group setting could influence QoL and functional changes and/or exercise motivation and adherence. Also many of the earlier intervention studies commenced months or even years after the end of treatment for breast cancer and did not include any long-term follow-up. This is a shortcoming because patients will normally be expected to improve over time anyway and if there is no follow-up of a short-term intervention we cannot say if exercise helps people more than is expected by normal recovery processes.

The original research problem was 'Can exercise help women with symptoms of fatigue during breast cancer treatment?' Based on the issues above, this evolved into a more complex question around quality of life and functional improvements that may result from a pragmatic community based group exercise intervention for women undergoing treatment for breast cancer. We set out to answer four research questions as follows:

1   Is exercise an effective intervention during cancer treatment to decrease fatigue levels and improve quality of life and physical functioning and mood?
2   Were there any sustained benefits of exercise at 6 months post-intervention?
3   What were the perceived benefits and difficulties surrounding exercise for this patient group?
4   What were the health service costs of providing the intervention?

In relation to these four research questions, we tested the hypotheses that 12 weeks of supervised group exercise, as an adjunct to usual care, would improve quality of life for women during treatment for early stage breast cancer and that benefits would be maintained for 6 months after the intervention.

Choice of method (matching the method to the research question)

We used an RCT design with compliance to the CONSORT statement. The CONSORT statement has been provided to guide how to conduct and report on randomised controlled trials and the following website is a must for anyone considering such a design: http://www.consort-statement.org/extensions/.

Part of the statement suggests that researchers follow a checklist of criteria that guide the quality of a trial and allow unbiased interpretation of results that flow from the trial. The checklist must be submitted with the manuscript when it is reviewed and authors must identify the page number of the manuscript in which each item is identified. The CONSORT checklist that we submitted with the article that was reviewed and published in the *BMJ* in 2007 can be seen in Appendix 1.

We chose an RCT design to provide a causal conclusion about the role of group exercise. We were operating within the Complex Evaluation Framework recommended by the Medical Research Council (Campbell et al., 2000). The framework suggested that when interventions are complex, that is there are many factors which could affect outcomes, a staged process should be followed. Early steps included pilot work and appropriate development of the intervention and later steps include a fully defined trial and this very often takes the form of an RCT. With sufficient participants to provide statistical power to detect the expected changes, and with random allocation to either intervention or control group, this design should allow causal inferences to be made about the observed differences (if any) between the groups. The final steps of the framework involve implementing the findings into practice. The framework has since been updated (Craig et al., 2008).

A further reasoning about the use of the RCT design is that when systematic reviews are conducted or guidelines produced from agencies such as the National Institute of Health and Clinical Excellence (http://www.nice.org.uk/), then reviewers are hoping to minimise bias in their conclusions and the RCT design is therefore most likely to be included as good evidence for or against particular interventions. The RCT design minimises biases of all kinds (by the researchers, by local circumstances, by individual differences of the participants) and is commonly considered to be the best design when the cause of an observed change is sought – for example in our case we wanted to make sure we could reasonably make conclusions about the effect of the exercise programme. When we were designing our intervention the most current systematic review suggested that more RCT trials of good quality were needed before clear conclusions could be made on the role of exercise during treatment for early stage breast cancer (Mcneely et al., 2006).

The main outcomes from the RCT were quantitative measures which we analysed statistically (see section 4, data collection) but we also used qualitative methods to find out the experiences of the women who took part in the trial. This mixed method approach is critical in psychology to help interpret the numbers provided by the quantitative methods and provide insights that are not available from quantitative methods. We used qualitative methods to gather in-depth information about how women with breast cancer perceived exercise and to explore their perceptions of the trial. We were particularly interested in exploring how respondents in the intervention group perceived the group intervention (i.e., exercising with women in a similar situation, as opposed to exercising alone). For this reason, we decided to replicate the group context by using focus groups (structured discussion groups) rather than individual interviews. Focus groups are commonly used in health research and are an excellent way to study both what people think and why they think as they do. The interaction between respondents ensures that priority is given to their language, concepts and frameworks for understanding the world, and minimises the chance that the researcher leads the discussion.

Data collection

Outcome measures

The primary outcome measure was change in Quality of Life (QoL) as measured by the Functional Assessment of Cancer Therapy – General (FACT-G) questionnaire (Cella et al., 1993). This core questionnaire is a compilation of general questions divided into four primary QoL domains: physical wellbeing, social/family wellbeing, emotional wellbeing and functional wellbeing. It is considered appropriate for use with patients with any form of cancer and this seemed more appropriate than other available quality of life questionnaires. Subscales have been developed addressing relevant disease, treatment or condition related issues. In this study we have used the breast cancer specific subscale which when added to the FACT-G score is described as FACT-B (Brady et al., 1997), likewise the fatigue subscale added to FACT-G results in FACT-F (Yellen et al., 1997), and the endocrine symptoms subscale when added to FACT-G gives the FACT-ES score (Fallowfield et al., 1999). Other secondary outcomes were BDI (Beck depression inventory) (Beck et al., 1996) which was chosen because of the known possibility that exercise can influence depression levels, PANAS (positive and negative affect scale) (Watson et al., 1988) which was chosen to allow changes in positive mood to be measured because other mood scales often measure only decreases in negative mood, BMI (body mass index) a standard measure of body composition and weight change because this is a possible side effect of treatment, SPAQ (Scottish Physical Activity Questionnaire)

(Lowther et al., 1999) a relatively easy 7-day recall of physical activity validated on a Scottish population, the 12-minute walk test (Mcgavin et al., 1976) chosen to allow a functional rest related to fitness without laboratory equipment, and a test of shoulder mobility because this is an aspect of function that may be limited following treatment (Halverstadt, 2000).

Participants

From January 2004 to January 2005, trained recruiters approached women during appointments at outpatient clinics for chemotherapy or radiotherapy at three NHS oncology centres in Scotland, UK and provided information about the study. Potential participants agreed to attend a pre-screening meeting. Exclusion criteria to the study were women with concurrent unstable cardiac, hypertensive or respiratory disease; cognitive dysfunction; or who participated in regular exercise. The data presentation section gives an insight into the advantages of using trained dedicated recruiters. It is important to have a robust recruiting strategy in place to ensure that you have the highest possibility of attaining the numbers of participants required for the statistical analysis of the intervention.

Ethical approval

All procedures were approved by the West Ethics Committee of Greater Glasgow Health Board (LREC Ref: 03/22(2)). One ethical issue we addressed was to ensure that all eligible patients fully understood what the study entailed before committing to participate. This was addressed by providing all necessary information about the study in layman's terms in a Patient Information Sheet and ensuring that all participants had read, understood and agreed to take part. Another ethical issue was guaranteeing that all data collected would remain confidential. This was managed by ensuring that all participants had an ID number. This meant that the researchers working on the statistical data had no personal details and those working on the administrative side had no study result data. All data was password protected and stored in a locked safe place. We also had to ensure that the participants were aware that this study did not affect or reduce their standard cancer care in any way and that they were free to leave the study at any time.

Procedure

After obtaining informed consent, participants completed questionnaires, had height and weight measured and performed the 12-minute walk and shoulder mobility tests. The women were then randomly allocated into one of two groups. The randomisation was stratified by hospital (Glasgow Royal Infirmary (GRI), Beatson Oncology Centre, Crosshouse Hospital) and therapy at baseline (chemotherapy, radiotherapy or combination), and used randomised permuted blocks of length 4 and 6 (i.e., for sequences of 4 or 6 women in each hospital–therapy combination, exactly half were allocated to each group). This process was sensible because we were recruiting on a rolling basis and wanted even numbers in intervention and control as we went along. Randomisation was performed by telephone to an Interactive Voice Response system implemented by the Robertson Centre for Biostatistics (RCB). All study data were entered and managed at the RCB in an anonymised format; patient contacts and other administrative data were held in a separate database by study researchers. The study was a randomised, prospective, open trial (meaning that the patients knew which area of the trial they were in and so did the researchers), with steps taken to blind the evaluations (e.g., questionnaires in sealed envelopes, 12-week and follow-up measures taken by researchers who had not taught that participant in classes). A letter was sent to GPs informing them of their patient's participation in the study.

Study groups

Those randomised to the usual care group were given a leaflet on staying active during cancer treatment. At the end of the follow-up period (9 months later) they were given a personalised exercise consultation to help them to become independent exercisers. Thus the control group were not denied any standard procedures and were given some information that could help them. This is a good ethical stance to take but even with this many women were upset that they did not receive the more active intervention. Those randomised to the exercise intervention were asked to attend two community based classes each week for 12 weeks and encouraged to do one additional exercise session at home each week. Fourteen exercise classes led by specifically trained exercise specialists took place in eight community exercise facilities that were all accessible by public transport. Classes were timetabled at various times in the day and the evening on weekdays and weekends.

The intervention

The exercise intervention consisted of a warm-up of 5–10 minutes, 20 minutes of exercise (e.g., walking, cycling, low level aerobics, muscle strengthening exercises, or circuits of specifically tailored exercises), and a cool-down and relaxation period. The exercise class lasted 45 minutes in total. Women were monitored throughout the class to ensure that they were exercising at a moderate intensity level. Each week, for six weeks, a specific theme was covered in group discussion after the exercise (e.g., the health benefits of exercise, enhancing self-efficacy, and setting goals) and supported with specifically constructed materials. These themes were guided by a model of behaviour change and were designed to promote independent exercise after the intervention (Marcus et al., 1994). The 6-week block was repeated on a rolling basis, allowing all participants to hear the same themes. At the end of the 12-week intervention, the women were helped to construct an individual exercise programme and invited to join a local general practice exercise referral scheme.

With the RCT there were a number of issues with recruitment that we tried to address. One of the key learning points from the pilot study (where we mostly recruited young educated women who had been very active prior to diagnosis) was that we needed to ensure that *all eligible women* were introduced to the study. This was accomplished by employing clinical trial recruiters at each recruitment site and all treatment points – surgery, chemotherapy and radiotherapy. The clinical recruiters attended two training sessions at which the following topics were discussed: pilot study results including the barriers to recruitment; the aims and objectives of the proposed study; definition of eligibility criteria; how and when to approach eligible women; explanation of RCT to eligible women using the patient information sheet; relaying information on recruitment to study investigators; recording reasons why women declined to take part. The recruiters were issued with notebooks and they kept all patient details in these books throughout the entire duration of the trial. They were also encouraged to note down any trial related problems or issues they wished to discuss with the team when they met every four weeks. The chief researcher was also able to keep the recruiters up to date with the study progression and gave them feedback on the women they had personally referred. All three recruiters attended the exercise classes at different points in the study and therefore had an insight into what the intervention involved.

Uptake to the study was slower than anticipated, particularly at certain times of the year, therefore we added a new recruitment site – another oncology unit in a hospital in the outskirts of Glasgow. Also we added posters to the waiting rooms of the recruitment sites with photographs of women taking part in the class to reassure potential participants that this intervention was safe, fun and for women of all ages and fitness levels. We also provided travel expenses for all participants.

Key message: Recruitment of large numbers to physical activity trials of any kind needs a planned strategy and should use varied routes to reach the target audience. Contingency plans need to be considered and planned (Foster et al., 2011).

Data analysis

With 91 subjects in each group, the study was designed to have 90 per cent power at a 5 per cent level of significance to detect an intervention effect of approximately 7.5 units on the change in FACT-G score after 12 weeks, assuming a standard deviation of this outcome of 15 units. This change represents a shift from requiring bed rest half the waking day to being fully ambulatory (being strong enough to walk) with symptoms (Brady et al., 1997).

The primary analysis, and the main analysis applied to each secondary outcome, was to test whether there were significant differences between the exercise and control groups in outcomes at the end of the 12-week intervention period and at 6 months post-intervention, adjusting for the stratification variables (study site and therapy at baseline), age and baseline value of the outcome.

At the study outset, using age as a stratification variable was considered, but rejected on the grounds that this would result in too few strata, and it was decided that age would be adjusted for in all analyses. Also, although the sample size calculation was based on an analysis of the differences between groups in the change over baseline value, it is standard statistical practise to analyse such data using regression models adjusting for baseline values giving greater power to detect differences between groups (Vickers & Altman, 2001).

For each outcome, a mixed effects linear regression model was fitted for the values of outcomes measured at both follow-up visits, with predictor variables for the stratification variables (as categorical variables), age (as a continuous variable), the baseline outcome variable measurement (as a continuous variable), and the visit-specific effects of the intervention; the likely correlation between outcomes measurements at the two follow-up visits were accounted for by the inclusion of a random participant effect.

Data presentation

The results of the main study follow. We have provided the results that we gave to the funding body (Cancer Research UK, CRUK) because they are fuller than the results that the limited word count for the *British Medical Journal* article allowed (for example, the *BMJ* cut the section on costs of the treatment from our original submission and we presented the findings in relation to the qualitative data in a separate article). The analyses were standard approaches used in intervention studies that provide details on the changes observed in each group while taking into account many of the confounding variables that could also explain the results observed. This is the regression analyses with adjustments made for such things as age and socio-economic status. Without such adjustments results may remain biased because one group has more of a variable that could influence the results – for example if there were more younger women in one group then this could lead to a biased finding and so age is accounted for in the analyses. What we report is therefore close to the effect of the exercise condition itself having taken into account in the analyses many of the possible confounding variables. We also chose to report the results as effect sizes in the graphs. With high numbers of participants it could be possible to reach statistical significance with an effect that has no clinical meaning. Our effects are often moderate to strong – often thought of as around 0.5 of a standard deviation – and therefore a substantial change that could have clinical impact.

We will also report on recruitment as this is an under-reported aspect of many trials and the process by which researchers achieve the desired numbers is not always transparent. The topic of how best to recruit participants requires further research.

Recruitment

Prior to commencement of recruitment, three dedicated clinical recruiters were trained to introduce the study to all eligible women being treated for early stage breast cancer and attending outpatient chemotherapy and radiotherapy clinics at three sites (Campbell et al., 2005). Women were invited to join the study around the time of their 2nd or 3rd chemotherapy cycles or during 2nd/3rd weeks of radiotherapy treatment. This ensured that treatments had been established with no particular problems noted. Eleven hundred and forty-four women were approached by the recruiters and 313 agreed to attend pre-screening. Reasons why women declined to participate were monitored in order to gain information on the barriers to recruitment to an exercise intervention during treatment and this information is being prepared for a separate manuscript. For details of the participant flow through the trial see Figure 2.1.

Participant characteristics

The use of dedicated recruiters was successful in that we achieved more than the statistically required number of participants into the trial. The women we recruited into this trial were on average aged just over 50 years, slightly overweight according to BMI, doing the same amount of activity as other sedentary populations and with baseline walk test levels similar to breast cancer patients during treatment in other studies (Mock et al., 2005). These characteristics are shown in Table 2.1.

Findings in relation to research questions

Four research questions were posed and the results relating to each question are now presented.

1. Is exercise an effective intervention during cancer treatment to decrease fatigue levels and improve quality of life and physical functioning and mood?

Table 2.2 summarises the outcome variables measured at the baseline, 12-week and 6-month post-intervention assessments, for the exercise and control groups separately. Also shown are the intervention effect estimates (adjusted for study site, therapy at baseline, age and baseline measurement), with 95 per cent confidence intervals (CIs) and associated p-values. Finally, the differences between the intervention groups in the changes from 12 weeks to 6 months are also reported. Figure 2.2 shows these effect estimates and CIs for all variables, standardised in the sense that all effect estimates are reported in units of one standard deviation of the outcome variable in question.

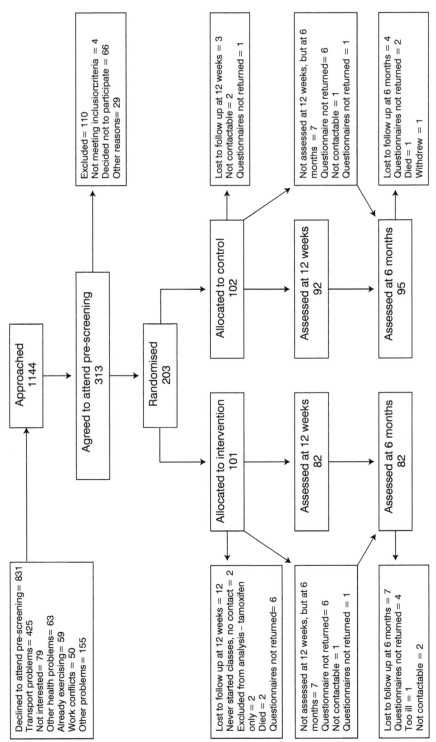

FIGURE 2.1 Participant flow through treatment

TABLE 2.1 Baseline characteristics; number of participants and mean (SD) for continuous variables or N/Total (%) for categorical variables measured at baseline, for all participants and by intervention group

		All Participants	Exercise Group	Control Group
N (maximum)		201	99	102
Age (years)		51.6 (9.5)	51.3 (10.3)	51.8 (8.7)
Treatment Plan	Chemotherapy	15/201 (7.5%)	8/99 (8.1%)	7/102 (6.9%)
	Radiotherapy	57/201 (28.4%)	28/99 (28.3%)	29/102 (28.4%)
	Combination	29/201 (64.2%)	63/99 (63.6%)	66/102 (64.7%)
Study Site	1	33/201 (16.4%)	17/99 (17.2%)	16/102 (15.7%)
	2	151/201 (75.1%)	74/99 (74.7%)	77/102 (75.5%)
	3	17/201 (8.5%)	8/99 (8.1%)	9/102 (8.8%)
Height (cm)		160.8 (6.1)	160.6 (5.9)	161.1 (6.3)
Weight (kg)		70.8 (14.6)	70.2 (12.5)	71.5 (16.4)
BMI (kg/m^2)		27.4 (5.6)	27.3 (5.2)	27.5 (6.0)
Days since diagnosis		162.0 (73.8)	162.2 (78.0)	161.9 (69.8)
Mastectomy	No	120/201 (59.7%)	60/99 (60.6%)	60/102 (58.8%)
	Yes	81/201 (40.3%)	39/99 (39.4%)	42/102 (41.2%)
Lumpectomy	No	82/201 (40.8%)	40/99 (40.4%)	42/102 (41.2%)
	Yes	119/201 (59.2%)	59/99 (59.6%)	60/102 (58.8%)
Reconstructive Surgery	No	178/201 (88.6%)	86/99 (86.9%)	92/102 (90.2%)
	Yes	23/201 (11.4%)	13/99 (13.1%)	10/102 (9.8%)
Current Employment Status	FT/PT	29/201 (14.4%)	16/99 (16.2%)	13/102 (12.7%)
	Sick	111/201 (55.2%)	49/99 (49.5%)	62/102 (60.8%)
	Housewife	26/201 (12.9%)	14/99 (14.1%)	12/102 (11.8%)
	Retired	35/201 (17.4%)	20/99 (20.2%)	15/102 (14.7%)
Occupation (prior to diagnosis)	Professional	48/171 (28.1%)	25/82 (30.5%)	23/89 (25.8%)
	Managerial	35/171 (20.5%)	18/82 (22.0%)	17/89 (19.1%)
	Clerical	55/171 (32.2%)	26/82 (31.7%)	29/89 (32.6%)
	Manual	33/171 (19.3%)	13/82 (15.9%)	20/89 (22.5%)

TABLE 2.2 Outcome variables and intervention effect estimates (95% confidence intervals) with p-values*

Outcome variable		Mean (SD)			Effect estimates (exercise–control)	
		Baseline	12 weeks	6 months	12 weeks	6 months
Maximum no:	Control	102	92	95	NA	NA
	Exercise	99	82	82		
FACT-G:	Control	73.3 (15.0)	77.3 (14.4)	77.1 (17.0)	1.0 (–2.7 to 4.7); p = 0.60	3.6 (0.0 to 7.3); p = 0.053
	Exercise	77.0 (12.4)	81.0 (16.8)	83.2 (12.8)		
FACT-GP:	Control	20.0 (5.7)	21.9 (5.1)	22.3 (5.3)	0.4 (–0.8 to 1.7); p = 0.50	0.7 (–0.5 to 2.0); p = 0.27
	Exercise	21.4 (4.8)	23.1 (4.9)	23.9 (4.3)		
FACT-GS:	Control	23.7 (4.8)	23.4 (5.0)	22.9 (5.5)	0.9 (–0.2 to 2.1); p = 0.10	1.4 (0.3 to 2.5); p = 0.014
	Exercise	23.6 (5.1)	24.2 (4.6)	23.9 (4.8)		
FACT-GE:	Control	18.3 (4.7)	18.9 (4.4)	18.6 (4.5)	0.7 (–0.3 to 1.7); p = 0.19	0.6 (–0.4 to 1.7); p = 0.23
	Exercise	19.0 (3.7)	20.1 (4.2)	19.7 (4.0)		
FACT-GF:	Control	11.3 (5.0)	13.1 (5.0)	13.6 (5.1)	0.4 (–0.8 to 1.6); p = 0.49	1.1 (–0.1 to 2.3); p = 0.067
	Exercise	12.9 (4.7)	14.6 (4.6)	15.8 (4.2)		
FACT-B subscale:	Control	21.3 (7.0)	22.4 (7.2)	24.2 (6.3)	2.5 (1.0 to 3.9); p = 0.0007	1.5 (0.1 to 2.9); p = 0.039
	Exercise	22.2 (6.7)	25.8 (6.0)	26.1 (5.6)		
FACT-F subscale:	Control	32.8 (12.7)	36.0 (12.1)	37.6 (11.8)	2.3 (–0.4 to 5.0); p = 0.091	1.9 (–0.7 to 4.6); p = 0.15
	Exercise	36.3 (11.7)	40.3 (10.4)	41.3 (9.7)		

Outcome variable		Mean (SD)			Effect estimates (exercise–control)	
		Baseline	12 weeks	6 months	12 weeks	6 months
FACT-ES subscale:	Control	39.9 (9.3)	40.3 (9.7)	39.7 (10.2)	1.1 (–1.2 to 3.4); p = 0.36	1.1 (–1.2 to 3.4); p = 0.35
	Exercise	40.6 (9.6)	41.6 (9.1)	41.0 (9.8)		
BDI score:	Control	13.0 (7.4)	11.5 (8.6)	10.8 (7.5)	–1.7 (–3.7 to 0.2); p = 0.083	–1.8 (–3.8 to 0.1); p = 0.064
	Exercise	11.8 (6.9)	8.6 (6.8)	8.4 (7.2)		
PANAS positive:	Control	28.0 (9.2)	29.3 (9.8)	29.2 (10.5)	4.0 (1.8 to 6.3); p = 0.0005	3.9 (1.6 to 6.1); p = 0.0008
	Exercise	27.7 (8.4)	33.4 (8.5)	33.0 (8.1)		
PANAS negative:	Control	19.1 (7.7)	17.7 (7.4)	17.4 (6.9)	–0.7 (–2.5 to 1.0); p = 0.41	–0.7 (–2.5 to 1.0); p = 0.39
	Exercise	17.3 (6.9)	15.6 (6.6)	15.7 (6.1)		
12-minute walk (m):	Control	975 (235)	984 (221)	1013 (190)	129 (83 to 176); p < 0.0001	105 (60 to 151); p < 0.0001
	Exercise	997 (211)	1135 (143)	1127 (166)		

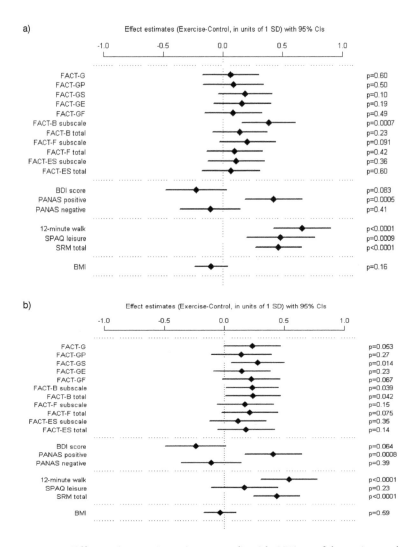

FIGURE 2.2 Effect estimates (exercise–control) with 95% confidence intervals and p-values for outcome variables at (a) the 12-week assessment, and (b) the 6-month follow-up assessment, expressed in units of one standard deviation (SD) of the outcome distributions, based on mixed effects models adjusting for baseline values, study site, therapy at baseline and age

At 12 weeks, the intervention group had significantly increased metres walked in 12 minutes (effect estimate +129 m, p < 0.0001), self-reported minutes in moderate intensity activity in the previous week [SPAQ] (+182 mins, p = 0.0009), shoulder mobility (+2.6 points, p < 0.0001), positive mood [PANAS positive] (+4 points, p = 0.0005) and perceived quality of life in relation to breast cancer specific symptoms [FACT-B subscale] (+2.5 points, p = 0.0007). There was weaker evidence of increases in perceived quality of life in relation to fatigue (+2.3 points, p = 0.091) and reduced depression [BDI score] (–1.7 points, p = 0.083). Our results therefore show that participation in the exercise programme resulted in improvements in both physical and psychological functioning. Nevertheless, we did not show improvements in the main study outcomes of general quality of life or fatigue as measured by FACT-G.

2. Were there any sustained benefits of exercise at 6 months post-intervention?

Table 2.2 shows that many of the observed intervention effects were maintained at the 6-month follow-up, with the original intervention group showing improvements on positive mood (+3.9 points, p = 0.0008), breast cancer specific QoL (+1.5 points, p = 0.039), metres walked in 12 minutes (+105 m, p < 0.0001) and shoulder mobility (+2.5 points, p < 0.0001). In addition, the exercise group showed improvements on the social component of the general QoL score [FACT-GS] (+1.4 points, p = 0.014) and the FACT-B total score [FACT-B subscale + FACT-G] (+4.9 points, p = 0.042), as well as non-significant trends towards improvements on the primary outcome [FACT-G] (+3.6 points, p = 0.053), the functional component of the FACT-G score [FACT-GF] (+1.1 points, p = 0.067), the FACT-F [fatigue] total score [FACT-F subscale + FACT-G] (+5.5 points, p = 0.075) and depression (–1.8 points, p = 0.064).

The increase in self-reported minutes of moderate intensity physical activity per week at the end of the intervention period was not found at 6 months post-intervention, and a tendency for the difference between the two groups to decrease between the end of the intervention and 6 months later (–118 m, p = 0.083), due mainly to a decrease in the activity levels of the exercise group between the end of the intervention period (mean 585 minutes) and the final assessment (mean 492 minutes). None of the other outcomes demonstrated any evidence that the intervention effects changed significantly between the end of the intervention period and the end of the study.

3. What were the perceived benefits and difficulties surrounding exercise for this patient group?

Table 2.3 shows how we selected respondents for the focus groups. Our qualitative data showed that women perceived a number of benefits from the exercise classes; these included a more positive mental state, better physical functioning, improved mobility in arms, sleeping better and being less tired, enhanced confidence and feeling more in control. Many respondents emphasised how much they enjoyed the social aspect of exercising with other women with breast cancer, and described being motivated by other participants, as well as by the instructor. Exercise was also perceived as a route to getting back to 'normal' life. In addition, some women felt that their enjoyment of the classes meant that they made more effort to prioritise exercise for themselves and spent more time

TABLE 2.3 Description of selection criteria for focus groups

Time point	Intervention group	Control group
	• Group 1: respondents from pilot RCT (mixture of intervention and control group)	
12 weeks	• Group 2: respondents who attended a high number of classes (70%+) • Group 3: respondents who attended a lower number of classes (< 70%)	
6 months	• Group 4: respondents who reported exercising regularly (more than 30 minutes exercise > 5 times a week) • Group 6: respondents who reported that they did not exercise regularly (< an hour a week)	• Group 5: respondents who reported exercising regularly (more than 30 minutes exercise > 5 times a week) • Group 7: respondents who reported that they did not exercise regularly (< an hour a week)

being physically active with friends and families. A range of quotes from women who provided these views are shown in Table 2.4.

Some of the perceived barriers to exercise were similar to those described by the general population (e.g., lack of motivation, practical barriers such as public transport, time and location of classes, and work and family commitments), while others were specific to this patient group. For example, some women described how their families were over-protective and worried that they were pushing themselves too hard by exercising. Others discussed how they sometimes missed classes because they were very tired from cancer treatment. In addition, women in the control group had negative experiences at standard exercise classes. Some were advised not to exercise during treatment. Others felt demoralised due to their lack of energy and loss of confidence, or felt that they were regarded as lazy because they could not work as hard as usual. In addition, it was difficult for women to attend standard classes because of barriers associated with body image (e.g. exercising with a wig on or getting changed in communal changing rooms after breast surgery). The exercise intervention helped to overcome many of these barriers.

4. What were the health service costs of providing the intervention?

The economic evaluation was exploratory only and did not have the resources to definitively answer the question posed. The NHS costs of the intervention are as follows: a group of 10 women will attend 24 classes, each lasting one hour, run by a fitness instructor (paid £30/hour) in a sports centre (room hire £50/hour).

TABLE 2.4 Quotations from respondents that illustrate some of the main themes in the focus group data

Perceived benefits of the exercise intervention

You felt better after it ... lifted. I just felt generally that my health had improved in that hour. Aye, I think I was on a high possibly! (Respondent 3, group 3, intervention arm)

I might have had to crawl down (to the class) but when I came out after it was over I felt totally different. I had so much more energy. (Respondent 1, group 6, intervention arm)

The important role of the specialist class and expert instructor

To go along to a class at your local sports centre in no way would measure up to what's offered by Anna (facilitator) ... it is tailored to your needs and you don't have to explain yourself. And that's really important, because you don't want to be explaining yourself all the time! You just want to be relaxed. (Respondent 1, group 2, intervention arm)

You lose a lot of physical confidence when you've had surgery. I was a bit wary of doing things and I didn't want to go to a normal gym ... You felt safe with Anna. It was quite a secure environment. (Respondent 4, group 1, intervention arm)

Examples of negative experiences at 'standard' exercise classes

I've joined a keep-fit (class) ... I thought it was a bit strenuous, but it was just after the chemo. I think maybe I started too early. (Respondent 2, group 5, control arm)

I tried going to exercise classes and found that I was being asked to do things that actually hurt ... when I said 'I'm sorry I can't do that', it was kind of like 'well why not?' and I was 'well because I've had a lump out of my breast and I've had a bit out of my arm and I can't lift that weight'. And there was a kind of annoyance ... so in the end you stop going. (Respondent 6, group 7, control arm)

The importance of the group context of the exercise intervention

It was a wee kind of light for me at the end of a big long tunnel. And I just think having contact with other women ... that was what really appealed to me. (Respondent 4, group 1, intervention arm)

I really looked forward to it ... you were meeting people that were the same as yourself. And you could get on with your exercise and have a laugh at the same time. (Respondent 1, group 6, intervention arm)

Gendered barriers to exercise: body image and family commitments

You can't hide in a swimsuit and even with the prosthesis, see when it was wet ... you still thought, it's not quite right you know? And I was just far too self-conscious, especially after it fell off (in the pool). I was mortified. (Respondent 5, group 5, control arm)

For such a long time I had been – through choice – bottom: three young children, a husband, a house. So therefore it was the first time I thought, 'no, (need to) get on with it (exercise)' ... I think I was typical ... had been very fit, got married, had children, became very unfit! (Respondent 5, group 4, intervention arm)

Administration is minimal and the NHS does not contribute to travel expenses. The total cost is £1,920, or £192 per woman.

Given that we have shown physical function and psychological gain in both the short and longer term it seems likely that the intervention would achieve the conventional standards of cost-effectiveness. This has been demonstrated without taking account of any future health service costs avoided as a result of women being more physically able and reporting better psychological wellbeing.

Contribution to knowledge

After 12 weeks of supervised exercise, the intervention group showed benefits in physical and psychological functioning in comparison with the control group. No adverse events were reported. The benefits to the intervention group reported at 12 weeks were maintained to the 6-month follow-up, with the exception of self-reported minutes of physical activity. The benefits to breast cancer specific quality of life (FACT-B) from the intervention emerged only at the 6-month follow-up, when most women were post-treatment. Similar results during breast cancer treatment have been reported, but the exercise intervention was either home based or an individualised gym programme and no follow-up data were reported (Segal et al., 2001). The study showed that *group exercise* during treatment provided short- and long-term physical and psychological benefits to breast cancer survivors. This was the first full scale randomised controlled trial in the UK of a group based exercise programme for breast cancer patients during treatment. It differed from previous studies which looked at the efficacy of exercise on specific outcomes by using prescribed specific individual exercise interventions (such as 30 minutes cardiovascular exercise on a treadmill working at a specific speed and % VO_2 max). This study was also one of the first RCTs to provide information on the long-term effects of the intervention – it showed that the positive effects were still present for most of the physical, functional and psychological outcomes 6 months later. Only the self-reported levels of physical activity had decreased at this time point but interestingly some outcomes had not changed significantly at the end of the intervention (e.g., fatigue, depression and quality of life were now nearing significance for a beneficial impact).

Impact on practice

Our study showed that a very simple group exercise intervention that provided physiological and psychological benefits to women undergoing treatment for breast cancer could be translated into a cheap and effective community based service. From these results, more clinicians working with breast cancer patients during adjuvant therapy are aware of the benefits of staying active and now encourage their patients to become or remain as physically active as possible. In addition, provision of group exercise classes as a cheap, safe and effective way of helping women cope with the side effects of cancer treatments are being provided by cancer charities such as Macmillan in community halls and leisure centres throughout the UK (e.g. http://www.activeabc.org).

Policy makers within the NHS are now trying to find ways to include opportunities for exercise in cancer services, perhaps using a similar model to the exercise component in cardiac rehabilitation. To ensure that health professionals can confidently refer their patients to safe and effective community based programmes, a Level 4 cancer exercise qualification recognised by Skills Active and the register of exercise professionals is now available for those fitness instructors who wish to work with cancer survivors to become more active (e.g. www.canrehab.co.uk).

Dissemination

The findings have been presented at National and International Cancer and Clinical Exercise Science conferences in the form of posters and presentations. The results have been presented to oncology teams and cancer steering groups (cancer leads in NHS trusts, surgeons, oncologists, radiologists, clinical nurse specialists and allied health professionals) throughout the UK to increase their knowledge and awareness of the evidence that exercise can provide benefits to their patients. It has been presented to the original participants of the study and to cancer survivors support groups contacted through charities such as Macmillan and Breast Cancer Care. There has been dissemination to the general public through public lectures at Dundee University, articles in the local and national press and publicity on the local and national news on radio and television. The research findings have been integrated into teaching modules for Clinical Exercise Science undergraduates and masters students.

Reflection

At the time (2007) we had conducted the largest RCT testing the hypothesis that exercise could improve quality of life for women undergoing treatment for early stage breast cancer. Our approach was unique in that we used community facilities, a group setting and included discussion each week on how to achieve long-term behaviour change.

A longer follow-up would have been beneficial but that was not possible within the funding provided by CRUK. That has been solved now with funding from Macmillan Cancer Support. We might have included both physiological and biochemical markers, to allow assessment of cardiovascular benefit or effects on immune function and inflammatory markers, but this would have exceeded funds available and would have produced an increased burden for the participants. It would have been ideal if we had been funded to pursue a more extensive economic evaluation. Ultimately costs will determine whether or not this approach could ever be adopted within the NHS.

We pursued various ways of funding a follow-up study before achieving success with Macmillan Cancer Support. We have now conducted a five-year follow-up of the women in the original trial (Mutrie et al., 2012). The five-year post-diagnosis time point is a critical clinical review point for all cancer patients. Women who were in the original trial were contacted at 18 and 60 months after intervention. Original measures were repeated and qualitative data on views of physical activity were collected. Of the 148 women from the original study who agreed to be contacted again, 114 attended for follow-up at 18 months and 87 at 60 months. Women in the original intervention group reported an average of 2 hours more leisure time physical activity and more positive moods at 60 months than women in the original control group. Irrespective of original group allocation, women who were more active consistently reported lower levels of depression and increased quality of life compared with those who were less active.

In this follow-up study we have shown that there are lasting benefits to an exercise intervention delivered during treatment to breast cancer survivors. Regular activity should be encouraged for women with early stage breast cancer as this can have lasting implications for physical and psychological functioning.

Since the publication of our results we continue to operate within the MRC Complex Evaluation Framework (Craig et al., 2008) by researching ways of implementing and evaluating the research findings in 'the real world' (i.e., development of exercise based cancer rehabilitation service within the NHS). Group exercise programmes for women with breast cancer undergoing treatment – based on the study intervention – are now running in Glasgow and Dundee in council community leisure centres. These are currently being evaluated for uptake, adherence, level of physical activity pre- and post-intervention and on follow-up. In parallel with this a number of different referral pathways and exercise services for cancer survivors are being evaluation by Macmillan.

If you liked this chapter, you should check out Chapters 8 and 12 as they also involve intervention designs.

References

Beck, J., Steer, R.A., & Brown, G.K. (1996) *Beck Depression Inventory manual* (2nd Edition). San Antoni, TX: Pyschological Association.

Brady, M., Cella, D., Mo, F., Bonomi, A., Tulsky, D., Lloyd, S., Deasy, S., Cobleigh, M., & Shiomoto, G. (1997) Reliability and Validity of the Functional Assessment of Cancer Therapy Breast Quality of Life Assessment. *Journal of Clinical Oncology*, 15, 974–998.

Campbell, A.M., Whyte, F. & Mutrie, N. (2005) Training of clinical recruiters to improve recruitment to an exercise intervention during breast cancer treatment. *Clinical Effectiveness in Nursing*, 9, 211–213.

Campbell, M., Fitzpatrick, R., Haines, A., Kinmonth, A.L., Sandercock, P., Spiegelhalter, D. & Tyrer, P. (2000) Framework for design and evaluation of complex interventions to improve health. *British Medical Journal*, 321, 694–696.

Cella, D.F., Tulsky, D.S., Gray, G., Sarafian, B., Linn, E., Bonomi, A., Silberman, M., Yellen, S.B., Winicour, P., Brannon, J., Eckberg, K., Lloyd, S., Purl, S., Blendowski, C., Goodman, M., Barnicle, M., Stewart, I., Mchale, M., Bonomi, P., Kaplan, E., Taylor, I.V.S., Thomas,

C.R., & Harris, J. (1993) The functional assessment of cancer therapy scale: development and validation of the general measure. *Journal of Clinical Oncology*, 11, 570–579.

Craig, P., Dieppe, P., Macintyre, S., Michie, S., Nazareth, I. & Petticrew, M. (2008) Developing and evaluating complex interventions: the new Medical Research Council guidance. *British Medical Journal*, 337, a1655.

Fallowfield, L., Leaity, S., Howell, A., Benson, S., & Cella, D. (1999) Assessment of quality of life in women undergoing hormonal therapy for breast cancer: validation of an endocrine symptom subscale for the FACT-B. *Breast Cancer Res Treat*, 55, 189–199.

Foster, C.E., Brennan, G., Matthews, A., McAdam, C., Fitzsimons, C., & Mutrie, N. (2011). Recruiting participants to walking intervention studies: A systematic review. *International Journal of Behavioral Nutrition and Physical Activity*, 8, 137.

Halverstadt, A.L.A. (2000) *Essential Exercises for Breast Cancer Survivors*, Boston, MA, Harvard Common Press.

Irwin, M., Mctiernan, A., Bernstein, L., Gilliland, F.D., Baumgartner, R., Baumgartner, K., & Ballard-Barbash, R. (2004) Physical activity levels among breast cancer survivors. *Medicine and Science in Sports and Exercise*, 36, 1484–1491.

Lowther, M., Mutrie, N., Loughlan, C., & Mcfarlane, C. (1999) Development of a Scottish physical activity questionnaire: a tool for use in physical activity interventions. *British Journal of Sports Medicine*, 33, 1–6.

Marcus, B., Eaton, C., Rossi, J.S. & Harlow, L. (1994) Self-efficacy, decision-making, and stages of change: an integrative model of physical exercise. *Journal of Applied Social Psychology*, 24, 489–508.

Markes, M., Brockow, T., & Resch, K.L .(2006) Exercise for women receiving adjuvant therapy for breast cancer. *Cochrane Database of Systematic Reviews*, Art No. CD005001 DOI: 10.1002/14651858. CD005001.pub2.

McGavin, C.R., Gupta, S.P. & Mchardy, G.J.R. (1976) Twelve-minute walking test for assessing disability in chronic bronchitis. *British Medical Journal*, 1, 822–823.

McNeely, M.L., Campbell, K.L., Rowe, B.H., Klassen, T.P., Mackey, J.R. & Courneya, K.S. (2006) Effects of exercise on breast cancer patients and survivors: a systematic review and meta-analysis. *CMAJ*, 175, 34–41.

Mock, V., Frangakis, C., Davidson, N.E., Ropka, M.E., Pickett, M., Poniatowski, B., Stewart, K.J., Cameron, L., Zawacki, K., Podewils, L.J., Cohen, G. & Mccorkle, R. (2005) Exercise manages fatigue during breast cancer treatment: A randomized controlled trial. *Psychooncology*, 14, 464–477.

Mutrie, N., Campbell, A., Barry, S., Hefferon, K., McConnachie, A., Ritchie, D., & Tovey, S. (2012). Five-year follow-up of participants in a randomised controlled trial showing benefits from exercise for breast cancer survivors during adjuvant treatment. Are there lasting effects? *Journal of Cancer Survivorship*, 1–11. doi: 10.1007/s11764-012-0233-y

Segal, R., Evans, W., Johnson, D., Smith, J., Colletta, S., Gayton, J., Woodard, S., Wells, G. & Reid, R. (2001) Structured exercise improves physical functioning in women with stages I and II breast cancer: results of a randomized controlled trial. *Journal of Clinical Oncology*, 19, 657–665.

Vickers, A., & Altman, D.G. (2001) Statistics notes: analysing controlled trials with baseline and follow up measurements. *British Medical Journal* 323, 1123–1124.

Watson, D., Clark, L.A., & Tellegen, A. (1988) Development and validation of brief measures of positive and negative effect: the PANAS scales. *Journal of Personality and Social Psychology*, 54, 1063–1070.

Yellen, S., Cella, D.F., Webster, K., Blendowski, C., & Kaplan, E. (1997) Measuring fatigue and other anemia-related symptoms with the Functional Assessment of Cancer Therapy (FACT) measurement system. *Journal of Pain and Symptom Management*, 13, 63–74.

Appendix 1

TABLE 2.5 CONSORT checklist of items submitted for review with the manuscript

PAPER SECTION and topic	*Item*	*Description*	*Reported on Page #*
TITLE & ABSTRACT	1	How participants were allocated to interventions (e.g., 'random allocation', 'randomised', or 'randomly assigned').	1 and 2
INTRODUCTION			
Background	2	Scientific background and explanation of rationale.	6
METHODS			
Participants	3	Eligibility criteria for participants and the settings and locations where the data were collected.	7
Interventions and web extra	4	Precise details of the interventions intended for each group and how and when they were actually administered.	8–9
Objectives	5	Specific objectives and hypotheses.	7
Outcomes	6	Clearly defined primary and secondary outcome measures and, when applicable, any methods used to enhance the quality of measurements (e.g., multiple observations, training of assessors).	8
Sample size	7	How sample size was determined and, when applicable, explanation of any interim analyses and stopping rules.	9
Randomisation – Sequence generation	8	Method used to generate the random allocation sequence, including details of any restrictions (e.g., blocking, stratification)	7
Randomisation – Allocation concealment	9	Method used to implement the random allocation sequence (e.g., numbered containers or central telephone), clarifying whether the sequence was concealed until interventions were assigned.	7
Randomisation – Implementation	10	Who generated the allocation sequence, who enrolled participants, and who assigned participants to their groups.	7
Blinding (masking)	11	Whether or not participants, those administering the interventions, and those assessing the outcomes were blinded to group assignment. When relevant, how the success of blinding was evaluated.	7
Statistical methods	12	Statistical methods used to compare groups for primary outcome(s); methods for additional analyses, such as subgroup analyses and adjusted analyses.	9 and 10

PAPER SECTION and topic	Item	Description	Reported on Page #
RESULTS			
Participant flow	13	Flow of participants through each stage (a diagram is strongly recommended). Specifically, for each group report the numbers of participants randomly assigned, receiving intended treatment, completing the study protocol, and analysed for the primary outcome. Describe protocol deviations from study as planned, together with reasons.	Figure 1
Recruitment	14	Dates defining the periods of recruitment and follow-up.	7
Baseline data	15	Baseline demographic and clinical characteristics of each group.	Table 2.1
Numbers analysed	16	Number of participants (denominator) in each group included in each analysis and whether the analysis was by 'intention-to-treat'. State the results in absolute numbers when feasible (e.g., 10/20, not 50%).	Tables and page 9
Outcomes and estimation	17	For each primary and secondary outcome, a summary of results for each group, and the estimated effect size and its precision (e.g., 95% confidence interval).	Table 2 and Figure 2
Ancillary analyses	18	Address multiplicity by reporting any other analyses performed, including subgroup analyses and adjusted analyses, indicating those pre-specified and those exploratory.	7
Adverse events	19	All important adverse events or side effects in each intervention group.	11
DISCUSSION			
Interpretation	20	Interpretation of the results, taking into account study hypotheses, sources of potential bias or imprecision and the dangers associated with multiplicity of analyses and outcomes.	11
Generalisability	21	Generalisability (external validity) of the trial findings.	12
Overall evidence	22	General interpretation of the results in the context of current evidence.	11

3

SPORTS MANAGEMENT

A forecast of the performance of China in the Beijing Olympic Games 2008 and the underlying performance management issues

Simon Shibli and Jerry Bingham

Article reference

Shibli, S., & Bingham, J. (2008). A forecast of the performance of China in the Beijing Olympic Games 2008 and the underlying performance management issues. *Managing Leisure, 13*, 272–292.

Article summary

This paper was concerned with making a forecast of the number of gold medals that China would win as host nation at the Beijing 2008 Olympic Games. Historical data revealed that China's achievement in the Olympic Games had shown considerable improvement by all commonly used performance measures in the period 1988–2004. However, China's success had been heavily dependent upon four key sports and the performance of its women athletes who significantly out-performed their male counterparts. A review of previous research revealed that reliance on population and gross domestic product as predictors of Olympic success under-estimated the performance in Athens 2004 of some nations taking a strategic approach to elite sport development. For these nations, regressing gold medals won over time produced more accurate predictions of actual gold medals won in 2004 than a multivariate regression based on macro-economic variables. Based on our analysis, we forecast that China would win forty-six gold medals in Beijing 2008. In making our forecast we sounded a note of caution that in some sports China has little room for improvement and in others with high number of medals available, notably athletics and swimming, there was no current evidence of China developing significant gold medal winning capability. However, China's ambitions were underpinned by: strong central government support; the extensive use of performance management principles; and, seemingly little concern for the issue of value for money.

Related author publications

De Bosscher, V., De Knop, P., van Bottenburg, M., Shibli, S., & Bingham, J. (2009) Explaining international sporting success: An international comparison of elite sport systems and policies in six nations. *Sport Management Review*, 12 (3), 113–136.

Shibli, S., Gratton, C. & Bingham, J. (2012) A forecast of the performance of Great Britain and Northern Ireland in the London 2012 Olympic Games, *Managing Leisure: An International Journal, 17*, 274–290.

Personal prologue

Simon

At the 1996 Atlanta Olympic Games, Great Britain and Northern Ireland (GBR) won just one gold medal and under the International Olympic Committee's (IOC) medals' table ranking rules was ranked 36th. For the UK, Atlanta 1996 was not the catalyst for a change of policy with respect to elite sport as some commentators have argued. The government had already decided that the UK needed a more coherent approach to the development and management of high performance sport if it was to achieve international success and was, at the time of the Games, in the very process of setting up UK Sport as the lead agency in this respect. Atlanta can instead be seen as an endorsement of all the arguments that had been made about the need for an organisation dedicated to high performance, and for greater public investment in this area. UK Sport was therefore established in 1997 and the rules concerning the distribution of National Lottery funds were relaxed to permit the use of these funds to help finance governing body-run World Class Performance Programmes and to provide elite athletes with financial contributions towards their living and training costs. In the Sydney Olympic Games 2000, GBR won 11 gold medals and was ranked 10th in the IOC medal table. This stunning turnaround around in fortune seemed to be an endorsement of the financial and policy support that had been invested in the UK's elite sport system. Nonetheless, despite GBR's improved performance in Sydney, five other European nations, namely Russia, Germany, Italy, France and perhaps surprisingly the Netherlands, performed better than the United Kingdom.

In 2002, UK Sport issued a research tender to investigate the elite sport development systems of those five nations that had performed better than GBR to identify if there was anything the UK could learn from them in order to make further improvements in the future. To differentiate our bid from other potential bidders, the Sport Industry Research Centre (SIRC) offered to look at performance in the Olympic Games in order to explore whether there was a link between elite sport policy and international sporting success. UK Sport liked this approach and SIRC was fortunate enough to win the contract which in turn led to the 2003 publication: *European sporting success: A study of the development of medal winning elites in five European countries.* The principal finding of this project was that the field of policy research in elite sport that enabled like-for-like comparisons on a transnational basis was limited and therefore represented a huge opportunity for some pioneering research.

Elite sport policy and performance has proved to be an area of personal research interest ever since for both Jerry and myself. Athens 2004 provided an opportunity to update the research, and the thinking behind it has also been applied to other major sports events such as the Commonwealth Games (see Shibli and Wilson 2004, 2006; and Ramchandani et al., 2010). In 2003 we became founder members of a European network called 'SPLISS', which is an acronym for 'Sport Policy factors Leading to International Sporting Success'. The SPLISS group conducted a pilot study benchmarking the policies and performance of six nations in elite sport and this was published in 2008 as a book entitled *The Global Sporting Arms Race* (De Bosscher et al., 2008).

The working relationship that Jerry and I have around elite sport originated by happenstance. I was lucky enough to be part of a team that won a contract that was out for tender, in a field in which I had limited experience, but which appealed to my positivist tendencies for dealing in incontrovertible facts. For me, measuring performance in elite sport relies on objective data such as medals won or ranking in a table and this provides an interesting contrast to other research that I do around monitoring and evaluation. In these projects data is often subjective, for example an interviewee's opinion, and can therefore be interpreted in different ways. In his role at UK Sport, Jerry's focus is on trying to make a difference to the performance of our (UK) athletes. As a custodian of public funding, it is incumbent on UK Sport, in conjunction with sports governing bodies, to set performance targets against which the effectiveness of its investments can be assessed. To support this task, Jerry and his colleagues need a range of data about the performance of UK athletes and their international competitors, helping them to understand trends and to make realistic assessments about what can be achieved in different sports. Jerry has also developed an index of medal-winning performances in 60 sports (the World Sporting Index) that seeks to evaluate the overall standing of nations in world sport and how that standing changes over time. What we both found interesting and valuable throughout the process was carrying out research that could be used to help improve the chances of our athletes being even more successful in international sport. It was a relatively new area of research which we just happened to be in on at the beginning. Feeling as though we were pioneers was a great motivation to extract as much as we possibly could from the data and to experiment with it endlessly.

Moving from a research problem to a research question

Whilst I do plenty of research on a contract or consultancy basis, occasionally it is something of a luxury to indulge myself in doing something out of sheer curiosity rather than any other reason. In other work that SIRC had done for UK Sport around the economic impact of major sports events, we started off by making estimates of the economic impact of events on the host location based on research conducted at the events. In essence, we survey athletes, officials, media representatives and spectators to identify their spending patterns and to quantify how much money an event brings in to the local economy. After doing six of these studies (UK Sport, 1998), we used the data and experience we had collected to produce and test an economic impact forecasting model. The purpose of the model is to make a pre-event estimate of the event's likely economic impact. Our model was first tested at the European Short Course Swimming Championships and we found that the forecast, based on secondary research (i.e. using existing data), was 82 per cent accurate relative to the actual economic impact found via primary research (i.e. research conducted specifically for the purpose). To me it was a logical extension of this type of thinking to use the data Jerry and I had on past performance, plus our knowledge on nations' elite sport policies, to see if we could forecast performance in the Olympic Games.

How nations perform in the Olympic Games has been fertile territory for researchers since the 1950s (for example: Jokl et al., 1956; Jokl, 1964; Shaw & Pooley, 1976; Colwell, 1982; Baimbridge 1998; Johnson & Ali, 2002). These researchers were primarily concerned with quantifying how many medals a nation would reasonably be expected to win given its resources such as population, wealth as measured by gross domestic product (i.e., the total value of goods and services produced by a nation), and other variables such as climate, religion and type of government. The technique used to compute expected or forecast medal counts is known as multiple regression, which aims to explain the relationship between the dependent variable (medals won) and a selection of independent variables such as population, wealth, degree of urbanisation (the proportion of people who live in towns and cities), political control, and dominant religion. Population and wealth alone has 'explained' more than 50 per cent of nations' success in the summer Olympic Games (De Bosscher, 2007) and the other significant variables in determining performance can be explained by past performance in the event and a host nation effect (Bernard and Busse, 2000, 2004). Where Bernard and Busse differed from other authors is that for both Sydney 2000 and Athens 2004 they published their forecasts in advance of the event and in so doing attracted considerable media attention.

Although our paper achieved global media coverage, this was not the rationale for writing it. In 2003 the UK government backed a bid by London to host the 2012 Olympic and Paralympic Games, and perhaps against many people's expectations, London saw off Paris to win the right to host the event.

Suddenly, the impact of host nation effect was no longer an academic exercise but an important piece of research that would be used in part to set targets for the future and to manage expectations based on the best evidence available. The Beijing Olympics provided an opportunity for Jerry and I to test our developing understanding of elite sport performance and we decided to use our techniques to forecast how China might be expected to perform in its host Olympics, not least with a view to using what we learnt from this research in the lead up to London 2012.

We knew from our statistical analysis of previous performance in the Olympic Games that since Seoul 1988 China had been on an unusual and near continuous improvement trend. Our analysis of the data had shown that it was very rare to see nations improve their performance in the Olympic Games over three or more editions of the event. We knew that, in policy terms, all the indications were that China was investing huge amounts of money into elite sport and was implementing the 'nine pillars'[1] of an elite sport development system as described by de Bosscher et al. (2006). We also knew that home advantage seemed to have a positive impact on the performance of the host nation (Nevill & Holder, 1999). Bringing these three pieces of knowledge together, we posed the question 'how will China perform in the Beijing 2008 Olympic Games?'

Choice of method (Matching the method to the research question)

The number of medals won by a nation in the Olympic Games is a quantitative measure and as positivists/realists it was inevitable that Jerry and I would employ primarily quantitative techniques to tackle the question. However, with our review of China's sport policy documentation, provided in our paper, outlining the nation's processes and ambitions, there was also a qualitative dimension to the research. We wanted to try a different approach to other researchers. It seemed to us that there were two approaches in common use: first, the multiple regression approach using macro-economic variables such as population and wealth; and, second, 'form based' forecasting using current rankings as championed by former head of the Italian Olympic Committee Luciano Barra. In our approach we wanted to bring together our analysis of China's historical performance, its stated objectives, and the impact of host nation effects.

As demonstrated in our paper, the problem with the multiple regression studies was that they seemed to underestimate the performance of nations known to be taking a strategic approach to elite sport development. We were of the view that if the nine pillars are in place, it is possible that nations can improve their sporting success at a greater rate than they can increase their population or wealth. Following Athens 2004 we had plotted Australia's performance in the Olympic Games against its population and it was clear to see that from the point of Australia's 'focusing event' in Montreal 1976, its performance (as measured

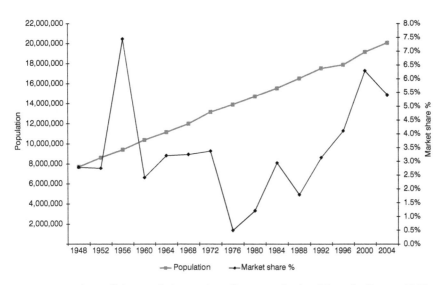

FIGURE 3.1   Australia's population and performance in the Olympic Games 1948–
2004

by market share,[2] see de Bosscher et al., 2008 op. cit.), grew at a greater rate than
its population, as shown in Figure 3.1.

Figure 3.1 illustrates that during the period 1976 to 2004 performance in the
Olympic Games improved more than tenfold (market share up from around
0.5 per cent to around 5.5 per cent), whereas population had not even doubled
(c. 14m to 20m). We took this evidence as an example of the impact that sport
policy factors can have on a nation's sporting success. China's performance in
Seoul 1988 was perceived by the Chinese authorities to be a humiliation after
the nation won five gold medals compared with 15 in its first Olympics in 1984.
In order to address its reversal in performance, or its 'focusing event', China
set about investing in its elite sport systems on an unprecedented scale. This
investment began to pay dividends quickly as demonstrated by China's medal-
winning success shown in Figure 3.2.

China's population and wealth were not growing at the same rate as medal-
winning success and we thus chose to focus on the impact of policy factors as
the principal drivers of success. For this reason we elected to conduct simple
linear regression using the variables of performance (as measured by market
share) and time.

We ruled out a form-based approach to forecasting because we wanted to
make our forecast from a 'whole system' perspective rather than getting pre-
occupied with event-specific and sport-specific analyses. By the term 'whole
system' we meant taking a top-down view over 28 sports and 41 disciplines
to forecast what China's elite sport system might be capable of achieving at an
aggregate level; rather than taking a bottom-up approach that tried to estimate
what each sport was capable of achieving on a piecemeal basis. Furthermore,

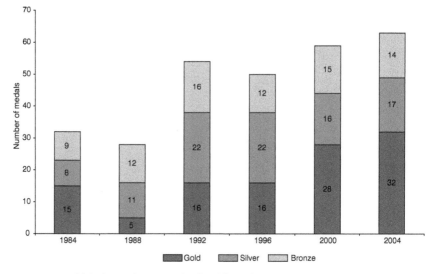

FIGURE 3.2 China's performance in the Olympic Games 1984–2004

we wanted to be able to make our forecast well in advance of Beijing 2008, with a view to using similar methods to make forecasts for London 2012. In our view the strength of our approach over the form-based approach is that we could have made our forecast for London 2012 immediately after Beijing 2008. By contrast the form-based approach is subject to revision every time a major championship is held in an Olympic sport.

In addition to regressing performance over time, we also needed to quantify the host nation effect and to add this to any forecast that would be derived under non-hosting circumstances. We knew from Figure 3.2 that China was on an upward trend anyway, but how much would home advantage add to its medal tally over and above what would be expected anyway? In short the method can be distilled down to two steps:

1   simple linear regression of performance over time, extrapolated to 2008; and
2   quantifying the host nation effect to add to the forecast from step 1.

Data collection

The data collection phase was remarkably easy as what we were doing was secondary analysis of existing data. This is a much under-rated research technique and avoids the cost of commissioning bespoke primary research. One of the advantages of this type of work is that there is no requirement for ethical approval of the research, as there are no human (or indeed animal) participants in the research. All we were doing was using data that was freely available in the public domain and re-analysing it for a new purpose. Furthermore, we did not require any specialist equipment other than computers, internet access and proprietary software such as Microsoft Office.

In this case, collecting the data was not difficult, knowing what to do with it posed the greatest cerebral challenge. For our 2003 research (see SIRC, 2003) into the development of medal-winning elites, SIRC had downloaded the results from every summer Olympic Games from the IOC website. From this basic raw material we reconstructed the data in Microsoft Excel so that from the final medal table we could analyse the data by gender, sport and discipline. So for example, if we wanted to have a look at the medal table for athletics in Barcelona 1992, the data was easily extracted. We spent a long time reconciling the data to ensure that the medals we had identified for specific nations in specific sports tallied with the overall total for that nation. There was no great 'technique' involved in this other than a good eye for detail and building in checks and balances to our workings to minimise errors. Where tables did not balance, we would go back to the source data and recheck it to identify the causes of any discrepancies. Typical issues we found were events in which there had been ties for first place and more than one gold medal had been awarded. Occurrences like this would put the medals' table out of line with the number of events contested and required near forensic investigation. Similarly, where medals had been awarded to one nation and had subsequently been reassigned following doping issues, there would be a discrepancy between the immediate post-event medals' table and any revised versions. Addressing these issues requires attention to detail and the discipline to reconcile data so that it is consistent with its original source. Via this process, Jerry and I already had in place the Olympic medals' tables from 1948 to 2004. China first competed in the Olympic Games in 1984 so what we actually needed was only a subset of the total data that had been compiled previously. It proved to be quite rewarding to take a medals' table apart and to recode it into around:

* 300 events;
* up to 28 sports;
* around 40 disciplines; and
* men's events, women's events as well as mixed or open events.

It was also rewarding to find that it all reconciled precisely to the raw data you started with in the first place. To do this successfully for each of the 15 summer Olympic Games that have taken place since 1948 was a great sense of achievement and provided the basis for recoding the data so that we could measure performance by descending order of gold medals won, total medals won, points won (where gold = 3, silver = 2 and bronze = 1), as well as by market share, whereby points won are expressed as a proportion of the total points available. A summary of the data collected for China is shown in Table 3.1. Having configured the data into the format we needed, we could analyse it in a way that best met our needs.

TABLE 3.1   China's performance in the Olympic Games 1984–2004

Year	Gold medals	Silver medals	Bronze medals	Total medals	Medal points[1]	Total points	Market share %[2]	Medals' table rank
1984	15	8	9	32	70	1359	5.2%	4
1988	5	11	12	28	49	1455	3.4%	11
1992	16	22	16	54	108	1592	6.8%	4
1996	16	22	12	50	104	1657	6.3%	4
2000	28	16	15	59	131	1829	7.2%	3
2004	32	17	14	63	144	1832	7.9%	2

1 Medal points: Gold = 3, Silver = 2, Bronze = 1, in 1984 ((15×3) + (8×2) + (9 ×1)) = 70.
2 Market share = ((Medal points / Total points) × 100) to give a standardised measure of performance.

Data analysis

We were lucky that Bernard and Busse had published forecasts for Athens 2004 because this gave us the opportunity to test our method against the established method of using macro-economic variables. We did this by running simple linear regressions (see Gratton & Jones, 2010) of performance over time to produce forecasts which could be compared with the Bernard and Busse data. Our first regression is shown in Figure 3.3 and shows the number of gold medals won by China during the period 1984 to 2000. Drawn between the various data points is the 'line of best fit' (a straight line that best represents the data on a scatter plot) and in the top right-hand corner of the graph you can see the equation for the line ($y = $) which quantifies the relationship between the dependent variable (gold medals won) and the independent variable (in this case, time). Also shown is the coefficient of determination (r^2), which explains how much the change in gold medals is 'explained' by time. By the word 'explained' we mean the power of the model to predict future outcomes – in theory the higher the r^2 score, the better the predictive power of a forecasting model. Please note that 'explained by' does not mean 'caused by'. Our argument was that the cause of China's increase in gold medals was more attributable to the effectiveness of its policies (the nine pillars) than to changes in macro-economic variables such as population and wealth. The strength of the relationship, or the correlation (r), between the two sets of data is the square root of the coefficient of determination (in this case the square root of 0.5147, or 0.72). According to Cohen and Holliday (1979) a correlation of 0.7–0.89 would be described as being a 'high correlation' or in other words, a strong relationship between the data.

Using the equation in Figure 3.3 to forecast China's performance in 2004 yielded a result of 27 gold medals, as shown below.

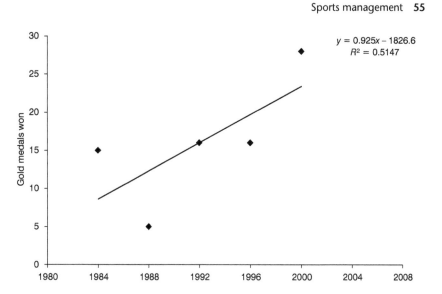

FIGURE 3.3   The relationship between gold medals won and time for China 1984–2000 (I)

$y = 0.925x - 1826.6$
if $x = 2004$, then $y = (0.925 \times 2004) - (1826.6)$
        $= 1853.7 - 1826.6$
        $= 27$ gold medals

This forecast of 27 gold medals was exactly the same as the forecast made by Bernard and Busse using their model based on population, wealth, past performance and host nation effect. Deep in the recesses of my memory I recalled doing a similar piece of work as a student at Loughborough University in the early 1980s. We had been asked to regress the winning time in the final of the Olympic Games 100m (athletics) over time in order to forecast what the winning time would be in 1984. The tutor asked us how we might improve our forecasts and nobody was able to offer an answer. He explained that in Mexico 1968 the Olympic Games were held at altitude, which led to some unusually strong performances in sprint and power events. In the 100m Jim Hines won gold in a new world record of 9.95 seconds and this record was not broken until 1983 – about the time I was doing my assignment! To counter the effect of this unusual data point, my lecturer suggested leaving out the Mexico data, which improved the quality of the forecasts thereafter. Using this thinking, I thought that 1984 was an atypical edition of the Olympic Games because it was boycotted by the Eastern bloc nations. The effect of this boycott was that the level of competition for medals was not as high as it might otherwise have been. As a result China probably did better than it would have done had there not been a boycott. This point seemed to make sense given that China won just five gold medals in 1988 when there was no boycott compared with 15 gold medals

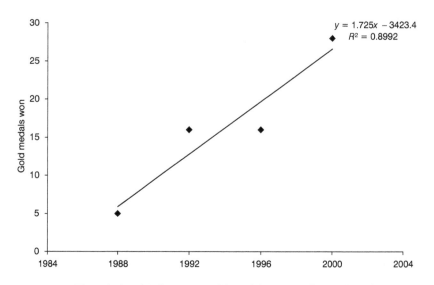

FIGURE 3.4   The relationship between gold medals won and time for China 1988–2000 (II)

four years earlier in Los Angeles. Running the regression without the 1984 data produced the graph shown in Figure 3.4.

Taking the equation for the line in Figure 3.4 we are able to rework our forecast as shown below.

$$y = 1.725x - 3423.4$$
if $x = 2004$, then $y = (1.725 \times 2004) - (3423.4)$
$$= 3456.9 - 3423.4$$
$$= 34 \text{ gold medals}$$

Our revised forecast of 34 gold medals was two more than China actually achieved in Athens 2004 and was more accurate than 27 gold medals as per our first attempt (Figure 3.3) and the Bernard and Busse forecast. Thus for China we felt that relying on past performance as a proxy for policy factors would produce a more accurate forecast than predominantly macro-economic variables. What we learnt as researchers from the exercise was the importance of using judgement (making the decision to exclude the 1984 data point) as well as science (linear regression). In the world in which we work, most problems tend to be solved by a combination of science and professional judgement.

Having derived what we considered to be a sound basis for forecasting China's 'business as usual' performance for 2008, we set about quantifying the likely impact of China's home advantage. The research we were familiar with, notably Bernard and Busse (2000, 2004), treated home advantage as a 'dummy variable'. A dummy variable is a measure whereby the value can be only 0 or 1. Of the 200 or so nations that take part in the Olympic Games, only one can be the host. The host nation would have a 'score of 1' allocated to it and all other nations would

TABLE 3.2   The performance of the host nation in the Olympic Games 1988–2004

Year / Host	Nation	Change in rank	Change in no of gold medals	Change in total medals
1988 Seoul	Korea	6	6	14
1992 Barcelona	Spain	19	12	18
1996 Atlanta	USA	1	7	–7
2000 Sydney	Australia	3	7	17
2004 Athens	Greece	2	2	3

be allocated '0'. We wanted to have a more in-depth look at the effect of home nation status on the hosts and to measure it in greater depth than just yes (1) or no (0). For the same reason as we discounted China's performance in 1984, so too we looked at the performance of host nations from 1988 onwards – as to us this represented the 'uncontaminated' modern era of the Olympic Games (there had been boycotts in 1976, 1980 and 1984). In Table 3.2 we present an analysis of how the hosts of the Olympic Games have performed since 1988. Three measures of performance have been chosen: first, the change in medal table position between two editions of the Olympic Games; second, the change in gold medals won; and, third, the change in total medals won.

Between 1988 and 2004 all host nations had improved their medal table ranking and their number of gold medals won. The only negative figure in the whole table is the USA losing seven medals overall in Atlanta 1996. There was no precedent as to how we might quantify the host nation effect and we made two judgement calls. First, we would focus on gold medals because it is primarily gold medals that determine a nation's place in the overall medals' table. Second, solely out of pragmatism we decided to take the average increase in gold medals won by the last five hosts and to apply this to China. The sum of the 'change in gold medals' column is 34, which averaged out across the last five nations gives a score of seven gold medals. We had therefore arrived at a formula for deriving a forecast of China's performance in 2008 as a result of regressing gold medals won over time from 1988 to 2004 and then extrapolating to 2008 using the equation of the line. To this figure we would add an additional seven gold medals for the home nation effect. To get to this point, we had done little more than secondary analysis of existing data, some experimenting with Excel, and the application of a limited amount of judgement.

Data presentation

Confident that our approach was reasonable as a result of testing it on the 2004 data, we set about including the 2004 data point with a view to extrapolating what might happen in 2008. Figure 3.5 shows our data, the equation of the line and the coefficient of determination (r^2).

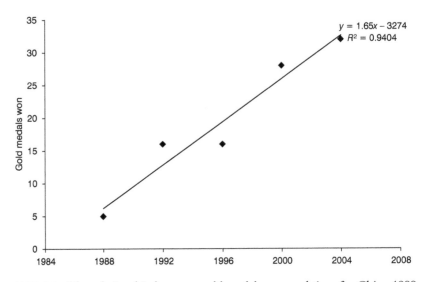

FIGURE 3.5 The relationship between gold medals won and time for China 1988–2004 (III)

It was immediately obvious that the strength of the relationship between the variables had increased and that there was a near perfect relationship (correlation = 0.97, being the square root of 0.9404) between the data. As before, if we substitute for x where x equals 2008, then the forecast from the linear regression can be determined as shown below:

$$y = 1.65x - 3274$$
if $x = 2008$, then $y = (1.65 \times 2008) - (3274)$
$$= 3313.3 - 3274$$
$$= 39 \text{ gold medals}$$

Thus, if China continued with its current rate of progress, it would have been reasonable to expect that it would win 39 gold medals, an increase of seven over 2004, if it was not the host nation in 2008. However, China was the host nation in 2008 and we needed to factor in the host nation effect. To illustrate the effect of being the host nation we experimented with our now commonly used 'flag' graphs whereby the flag of a nation was superimposed on the data point for the Games that that nation had hosted between 1988 and 2004. Although Table 3.2 contained all of the necessary data, it lacked visual appeal for both academic and practitioner audiences. Using a scatter plot graph and then overlaying it with host nation flags we created Figure 3.6.

In Figure 3.6 it is immediately clear that the last five host nations increased gold medals won and medal table ranking compared with their performance in the Olympic Games prior to being hosts. All of the nations are in the upper right quadrant of the graph and it is possible to grasp this point much more effectively than peering down the columns of a table.

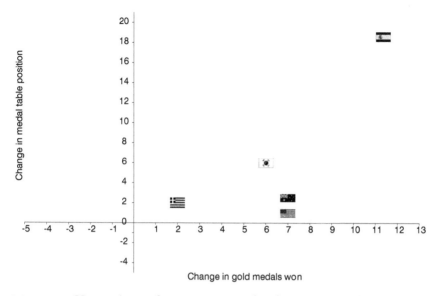

FIGURE 3.6   Host nation performance compared with Games immediately prior to hosting

With our forecast from the regression of 39 gold medals and our estimate of the host nation effect being worth a further seven gold medals, we settled on an overall forecast that China would win 46 gold medals. This seemed like a huge increase in performance because one thing that we knew from looking at previous performance in the Olympic Games is that improvement is very difficult. Figure 3.7 illustrates the nations which improved, and deteriorated, in terms of gold medals and market share achieved between Sydney 2000 and Athens 2004.

In Figure 3.7, Japan is identified as the most improved nation in Athens relative to Sydney, increasing its gold medals won by 11 and its market share by over 100 per cent. Japan had performed well from a relatively low base of only five gold medals in 2000. It was unprecedented for an already dominant nation such as China, which won 32 gold medals in 2004, to increase by a further 14 gold medals in the next Olympic Games. However, that was what the data was telling us and we decided to stick with the forecast. Meanwhile, Professor Bernard, now working on his own, had made a forecast that China would win 37 gold medals (Bernard, 2008) and Luciano Barra was quoted on the BBC as saying that China would win 38 gold medals (Williams, 2008).

So how did it all pan out in practice? The reality is that all of the forecasts fell short of what actually happened. China won 51 gold medals in Beijing 2008, increasing its tally from Athens 2004 by 19. Although our forecast was five short of China's final total, globally we believe it was the most accurate forecast made by researchers in this field. However, the point we were trying to make was not really about the accuracy of forecasts. What we were really saying

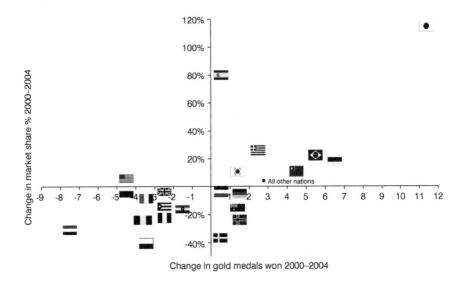

FIGURE 3.7 Change in performance analysis Sydney 2000 – Athens 2004

was that when nations take a strategic approach to elite sport, it is possible to achieve results that exceed the results that macro-economic models based on population and wealth would otherwise predict. In other words, there comes a point when proactive policy factors become more important than passive factors such as population and wealth. It would be unrealistic for governments to set about increasing their population and wealth for the sole purpose of trying to achieve success in elite sport. We had seen a pattern with Australia (see Figure 3.1) whereby sporting success was increasing at a much greater rate than population and that this could be attributed to policy factors. Our approach to forecasting how China would perform in 2008 was a way of applying this thinking to another nation which had taken an ambitious policy-based approach to achieving elite sport success.

Contribution to knowledge

In Box 3.1 we have included an extract from the discussion section of the paper to illustrate the contribution to knowledge. You should read this extract first and then the complementary narrative following it.

When advising students on how to discuss their findings relative to previous research, I encourage them to use the '3Cs' approach. What is meant by the 3Cs can be articulated as three questions. First, to what extent are your findings *consistent* with previous research? Second, to what extent do your findings *contradict* previous research? And, third, on the balance of evidence, what do your findings *contribute* to the overall body of knowledge?

BOX 3.1 Extract from the discussion

Although China has enjoyed improved performance in the Olympic Games and has increased the number of sports in which it has developed medal-winning capability, it does not necessarily follow that China's success is distributed evenly across the portfolio of sports and disciplines. Disaggregating China's overall performance by sport reveals that 39% of the 286 medals it won between 1984 and 2004 were won in three sports, namely: gymnastics, diving and weightlifting as shown in Table 3.3. Furthermore, 92% of China's gold medals in this period were won in its top nine sports which also account for 87% of all medals won. These findings suggest that historically China has pursued a policy of priority rather than diversity in its quest for Olympic success. According to Beech (2004) this prioritisation took the form of women's sport and 'little known sports that offer a profusion of Olympic medals' such as shooting. China's success can also be explained by principles of strategic planning such as environmental scanning and matching strengths to potential opportunities.

   Prioritisation as an approach is consistent with other nations adopting a strategic approach to elite sport, particularly in the early stages of programme development. For example, when the Australian Institute of Sport was established in the 1980s, it deliberately focused on just eight sports in order to build credibility for its approach. As soon as positive results were delivered, the scope of the provision was increased to include a broader portfolio of sports. In the United Kingdom, the National Audit Office conducted a review of UK Sport (the national agency for elite sport in the UK) and its support for elite athletes after the 2004 Olympic and Paralympic Games (National Audit Office 2005, op. cit.). It found that UK Sport prioritised its funding on four categories of sport, namely those:
- which can clearly demonstrate likely medal success in the current Olympic cycle;
- which have a track record of international success;
- in which there is an appropriate level of national governing body support for high performance programmes; and
- in which the investment is considered to represent value for money.

   The last of UK Sport's four categories, 'value for money', is noteworthy because it implies the need to operate within the bounds of a resource constraint. By contrast, in the case of China, success in the Beijing Olympic Games has been adopted formally as central government policy: 'whole country support for the elite sport system' (Hong et al. 2005, op. cit.).

continued...

Box 3.1 continued

China's desired outcome of Olympic sporting success appears to supersede value for money issues as indicated in the quotation below from Hong et al. (2005, op. cit.).

> This system [whole country support for the elite sport system] channelled all sports resources in the country into elite sport and effectively produced hundreds of thousands of young elite athletes in a short time in pursuit of ideological superiority and national status. Its main characteristics are centralized management and administration and guaranteed financial and human resources from the whole country to ensure it maximum support.

Whilst taking a prioritisation approach to elite sport development in the short term is an effective strategy, as it enables resources to be focused on those sports with the greatest potential, in the longer term continued improvement requires increased diversification for two reasons.

First, there are diminishing returns to scale when investing in sports in which a nation is already dominant. For example, in Athens 2004 China won six out of eight gold medals in diving. No matter how much more money is invested in diving, it is possible for China to win only two more gold medals in the discipline in 2008 than it did in 2004. Consequently, a point is reached where future growth lies in developing medal-winning capability in additional sports.

Second, having a broader portfolio of sports in which a nation has medal-winning capability insulates it from being over-reliant on a minority of sports to deliver a high volume of success.

Table 3.3 is consistent with Beech's analysis that China had historically prioritised women's sports and 'little known sports that offer a profusion of Olympic medals such as shooting'. China won its medals in a very different portfolio of sports compared with say the United States, which seems to prioritise sports that are dependent upon physical power such as athletics and swimming. By contrast the finding that China did not seem to be operating within the normal constraints of value for money was a contradictory position to the UK where the National Audit Office ensures that public funding of elite sport is subject to the same scrutiny as other areas of public policy. What we would like to think we contributed to the literature was the realisation that it is not possible for nations to improve their medal-winning success indefinitely by relying on dominating sports in which they have been traditionally strong. This is because there comes a point where future growth potential is either limited or impossible. Our view that China would need to diversify the range of sports in

TABLE 3.3   An analysis of China's medals won by sport 1984–2004

Sport / Discipline	Gold	Silver	Bronze	Medals	% of Total	Cumulative
Gymnastics	13	14	12	39	14%	14%
Diving	20	13	5	38	13%	27%
Weightlifting	16	10	8	34	12%	39%
Shooting	14	9	11	34	12%	51%
Table Tennis	16	11	6	33	12%	62%
Badminton	8	4	10	22	8%	70%
Swimming	6	12	3	21	7%	77%
Judo	5	2	7	14	5%	82%
Athletics	5	3	5	13	5%	87%

which it won medals to achieve growth was supported in Beijing 2008, when it won its first ever gold medals in rowing, sailing and boxing.

Impact on practice

Whilst we were to a certain extent indulging ourselves with this research and enjoying it for what it was, there is an immediate practical application for it. After Beijing 2008 we entered the London Olympiad and the sporting eyes of the world turned to the UK. One use of our research will be to evaluate the targets that are set for GBR in the run-up to London 2012. It is straightforward for anyone to replicate our methodology and to apply it to GBR in 2012 or indeed to Scotland in the Commonwealth Games in 2014.

Whatever basis others – politicians, press or sports organisations – use to establish expectations and targets, our approach enables a degree of objectivity to be used in setting realistic benchmarks. To illustrate the point, we used our method to forecast how many gold medals Canada would win as host nation in the 2010 winter Olympic Games held in Vancouver (Shibli, 2010).

Our forecast that Canada would win 10 gold medals proved to be four short of Canada's actual total, but was still comfortably more accurate than form-based measures favoured by the British Olympic Association and Luciano Barra. We were confident in our forecast because we knew that between Turin 2006 and Vancouver 2010, Canada had increased its investment in winter sports from £12m to £60m under its 'Own the Podium' programme. Clearly no nation makes a fivefold investment in elite sport to stand still. In the end, Canada achieved the most successful performance ever in the history of the winter Olympic Games. As was the case with Beijing in 2008, our forecast for Vancouver 2010 was short of what the hosts actually achieved, but nonetheless our method produced the most accurate gold medal forecasts that we are

TABLE 3.4 Forecasts versus actual for Canada at Vancouver 2010

Forecaster	Forecast Gold	Actual Gold	Variance
British Olympic Association	6	14	–8
Luciano Barra	6	14	–8
Shibli & Bingham	10	14	–4

aware of for both events (Table 3.4). As a result, we feel that from a research perspective we are gaining a greater understanding of the impact of host nation status on performance. This point is particularly relevant when nations use the staging of major sports to drive a step change in the effectiveness of their elite sport development systems.

Dissemination

We did not plan this paper from the outset as obvious material for a peer reviewed journal. I was fortunate enough to be asked to make a presentation at the 2007 National Olympic Academy (NOA) organised by the British Olympic Foundation. I had given a presentation at the NOA in 2005 and was delighted to be asked back. The audience is an interesting combination of academics, young researchers, current and former Olympians, as well as ordinary members of the public with an interest in the Olympic movement. In the year before an Olympic Games it seemed like the ideal sort of audience with which to try something different. In my first presentation to the NAO in 2005 I reviewed performance from the Olympic Games in Athens 2004. In my second, I decided to be a bit more adventurous and to look ahead to what might happen in Beijing 2008 and gave my presentation the title *Predicting the Performance of China in Beijing 2008*. The presentation seemed to be well received and afterwards I was approached by the editor of a journal who invited me to write it up for publication. This was very flattering and I agreed to do this at some point. As part of the process of working the material up into a journal article, we took the opportunity to present our thinking at an academic conference and our abstract was accepted for the 2007 European Association for Sport Management conference. Here we received some very useful feedback from members of the audience which helped to shape the final direction of the paper. The editor of the journal who invited me to write the presentation up into a paper subsequently rejected it. However, by taking on board some advice from colleagues at Sheffield Hallam University the angle of the paper was changed slightly so that it fitted the theme of a forthcoming special edition of *Managing Leisure: An International Journal* focusing on performance management. If we could get the paper published in that journal it would have been in print by July 2008 and would have been a genuine forecast in the sense that it was published before the event. This was sufficient motivation to make the necessary changes and to ensure inclusion in the journal.

What we learnt from this process is that getting a paper published is something of a journey. You start with an idea and experiment with the data in order to formulate an argument. Next you test your thinking on an audience and we were lucky to have the opportunity to present to both a practitioner audience and an academic audience. From this basis we had two reasons to go on and write a paper: first, the invitation from a journal editor; and, second, the feedback we had received from our audiences. The fact that we were rejected by one journal and accepted by another is all part of the learning process you go through when trying to get your research published. If nothing else, we had believed in our material and persevered with it enough to get it through the peer review process.

Reflection

Part of the research process is to look back on what you did and to pose yourself two questions. The first question is, 'to what extent does your research pass the "so what?" test'. What we mean by the 'so what?' test is the likelihood of your research being seen as adding to the overall body of knowledge and/or being genuinely useful. The second question is 'if I had to do this research all over again, how could I do it better?' In terms of the first question, we would like to think that we have provided an improved insight into the nature of home advantage. With the elite sport community now beginning to understand that the once almost mythical concept called 'home advantage' actually has a number of different dimensions, what we saw in the case of China was very strong evidence of the sort of policy factors that we had written about previously (de Bosscher et al. 2007, op. cit.) being implemented. Notable amongst these was a staggering level of investment and a nationwide focus on delivering success, seemingly regardless of cost. In terms of home advantage, we quantified what it had been worth to previous host nations, which was an alternative to treating host nation status simply as a dummy variable. We would also like to think that we made the concept of measuring performance in the Olympic Games interesting and accessible to people who might find multiple regression studies a bit too academic for their liking.

In terms of the second question, all research can be improved with the benefit of hindsight. In each Olympic Games the number of events contested, and hence the number of medals awarded, tends to change. In Seoul 1988 there were 237 events contested and in 2008 the total was 302. In order to derive a standardised measure of the home advantage effect it would have been technically correct to compute the increase in the *share* of gold medals won rather than the absolute number of gold medals won. Using this approach would probably have increased the home nation effect because the drivers of the average score of seven gold medals were Spain (1992), South Korea (1988) and the USA (1996) who all achieved their success on many fewer events than the hosts from 2000 onwards who have had at least 300 events in which to improve their performance. This learning point will be used to improve our approach for future forecasts. Bearing in mind the disappointment of being asked to write up our work for a journal and then having it rejected by that journal, we would take advice from colleagues earlier in the process. It is always a good idea to run draft material past people who are not as close to the research as you are, to get their feedback on your chain of thought and writing style. The two key lessons we take away are: first, the importance of your enthusiasm for your own research; and, second, the need for perseverance throughout the journey from idea to successfully published, peer-reviewed paper.

> If you liked this chapter, take a look at Chapter 10 in which Nic James describes part of a research process where he uses secondary data to develop position-specific performance indicators for rugby union.

Notes

1 The nine pillars of an elite sport development system are: 1. Financial support; 2. Well-structured and organised sport policies; 3. A mass participation base; 4. Talent identification and development systems; 5. Appropriate support during and after an athletic career; 6. Training facilities for elite athletes; 7. Coaching provision and coach development; 8. Exposure to national and international competition opportunities; 9. Use of scientific research and technological innovation.
2 Market share is a system that converts medals won into a points score (e.g. gold = 3, silver = 2 and bronze = 1). A nation's total points won is then divided by the total number of medal points awarded to compute the 'share' of points won. This system is useful because it takes into account all medals won; it makes a distinction between the value of medals; and most importantly it enables like-for-like comparisons to be made over time as typically the number of events contested and hence points awarded tends to change at every Olympics.

References

Baimbridge, M. (1998). Outcome uncertainty in sporting competition: the Olympic Games 1896–1996. *Applied Economics Letters, 5,* 161–164.

Beech, H. (2004) The price of gold, available at http://www.time.com/time/magazine/article/ 0,9171,678686-3,00.html.

Bernard, A. (2008). *Going for the gold: Who will win the 2008 Olympic Games in Beijing,* Tuck School of Business, New Hampshire, USA.

Bernard, A. & Busse, M. (2000). Who wins the Olympic Games: Economic development and medal totals, Yale School of Management Working Paper No. ES–03; Amos Tuck School of Business Working Paper No. 00-02.

Bernard, A. & Busse, M. (2004). Who wins the Olympic Games? Economic resources and medal totals. *Review of Economics and Statistics, 86,* 413–417.

Cohen, L. & Holliday, M. (1979). *Statistics for education and physical education.* Harper and Row, London.

Colwell, J. (1982). Quantity or quality: Non-linear relationships between extent of involvement and international sporting success. In A.O. Dunleavy, A.W. Miracle,

& C.R. Rees (Eds.), *Studies in the Sociology of Sport* (pp. 101–118). Fort Worth, TX: Christian University Press.

De Bosscher, V. (2007) Sport Policy factors Leading to International Sporting Success, Dissertation presented in partial fulfilment of the requirements for the degree of Doctor in Physical Education, Free University, Brussels.

De Bosscher, V., de Knop, P., van Bottenburg, M. & Shibli, S. (2006). A conceptual framework for analysing sports policy factors leading to international sporting success. *European Sports Management Quarterly, 6,* 185–215.

De Bosscher, V., Bingham, J., Shibli, S., Van Bottenburg, M. and De Knop, P. (2007) *Sports policy factors leading to international sporting success,* Oxford: Meyer & Meyer Sport.

De Bosscher, V., de Knop, P., van Bottenburg, M., Bingham, J. & Shibli, S. (2008). *The Global Sporting Arms Race: Sports Policy factors Leading to International Success.* Meyer & Meyer, Brussels.

Gratton, C. & Jones, I. (2010). *Research methods for sports studies,* Routledge, Oxon.

Hong, F., Ping, W., & Xiong, H. (2005) Beijing ambitions: An analysis of the Chinese elite sports system and its Olympic strategy for the 2008 Olympic Games. *The International Journal of the History of Sport, 22,* 510–529.

Johnson, K.N. & Ali, A. (2002). A tale of two seasons: participation and medal counts at the summer and winter Olympic Games. Retrieved February 15, 2003, from Wellesley college, MA website: www.wellesley.edu/economics/wkpapers/wellwp_0010.pdf.

Jokl, E. (1964). Health, wealth, and athletics. In E. Simin (Ed.), *International Research in Sport and Physical Education* (pp. 218–222). Springfield, IL: Thomas.

Jokl, E., Karvonen, M., Kihlberg, J., Koskela, A., & Noro, L. (1956). *Sports in the cultural pattern of the world.* Helsinki: Institute of Occupational Health.

National Audit Office (2005) *UK Sport: Supporting elite athletes, report by the Comptroller and Auditor General,* The Stationery Office, London.

Nevill, A.M. & Holder, R.L. (1999). Home advantage in sport: an overview of studies on the advantage of playing at home. *Sports Medicine, 28,* 221–236.

Ramchandani, G., Shibli, S. & Wilson D. (2010) *An Analysis of Scotland's Performance in the Commonwealth Games 1950–2010,* Edinburgh, sportscotland.

Shaw, S., & Pooley, J. (1976). National success at the Olympics: an explanation. In C. Lessard, J.P. Massicotte, & E. Leduc (Eds.), *Proceedings of the 6th international seminar: history of physical education and sport* (pp. 1–27). TroisRivieres, Quebec.

Shibli, S. (2010) How will Canada perform in the 2010 Winter Olympic Games? Unpublished working paper, Sport Industry Research Centre, Sheffield Hallam University, UK.

Shibli, S. & Wilson, D. (2004) *An Analysis of Scotland's Performance in the Commonwealth Games 1950–2002,* Research Report no. 95, Edinburgh, sportscotland.

Shibli, S. & Wilson, D. (2006) *An Analysis of Scotland's Performance in the Commonwealth Games 1950–2006,* Research Report no. 104, Edinburgh, sportscotland.

SIRC (Sport Industry Research Centre) (2003) *European Sporting Success: A Study of the Development of Medal Winning Elites in Five European Countries,* London, UK Sport.

UK Sport (1998). *Major events: The economics – measuring success,* UK Sport, London.

Williams, O. (2008). GB 'to meet' Olympic medal target, http://news.bbc.co.uk/sport1/hi/olympics/team_gb/7534962.stm.

4

EXERCISE PHYSIOLOGY

Prolonged exercise and cardiac function

Rob Shave

Article reference

Hart, E., Dawson, E., Rasmussen, P., George, K., Secher, N.H., Whyte, G., & Shave, R. (2006) β-Adrenergic receptor desensitization in man: insight into post-exercise attenuation of cardiac function. *Journal of Physiology, 577*, 717–725.

Article summary

The article presents data from a physiology study that adopted a mechanistic approach to understand the influence of prolonged elevations in catecholamines (adrenaline and noradrenaline) upon the heart's ability to function following prolonged endurance exercise. Previous studies demonstrated that ultra-endurance exercise resulted in a reduction in the heart's ability to contract (systole) and relax (diastole), however, very few studies had attempted to examine the mechanisms responsible for this change in heart function. This study used echocardiography to assess cardiac function and pharmacological intervention to assess the responsiveness of the β-adrenergic receptors pre- and post-completion of 4 hours rowing exercise. The findings demonstrate that in humans prolonged exposure to high levels of catecholamines following prolonged exercise results in desensitisation of the β-adrenergic receptors and that this is responsible, in part, for the acute reduction in cardiac function previously observed following prolonged exercise in ultra-endurance athletes.

Related author publications

Oxborough, D., Shave, R., Warburton, D., Williams, K., Oxborough, A., Charlesworth, S., Foulds, H., Hoffman, M.D., Birch, K., & George, K. (2011) Dilatation and dysfunction of the right ventricle immediately following ultra-endurance exercise: exploratory insights from conventional 2-dimensional and speckle tracking echocardiography. *Circulation: Cardiovascular Imaging*, 4, 253–263.

Shave, R., & Oxborough, D. (2012) Exercise-induced cardiac injury: evidence from novel imaging techniques and highly sensitive cardiac troponin assays. *Progress in Cardiovascular Disease*, 54, 407–415.

Personal prologue

The role of the cardiovascular system in athletic performance has been my academic passion since the first year of my undergraduate degree at the University of Wolverhampton. During my degree I was exposed to a number of physiological techniques involved with the assessment of cardiac structure and function (e.g., echo- and electro-cardiography) and whilst I did not possess the skills required to use these techniques during my undergraduate dissertation work, the ability to actually image and observe the heart working in real-time fascinated me. Following completion of my MSc in Human Performance at Frostburg State University in the USA I returned to Wolverhampton to study for my PhD under the supervision of Professors Greg Whyte and Keith George. During the initial stages of my PhD I gained the skills required to perform a basic cardiac ultrasound examination; this technique allowed me to complete a series of studies examining the influence of endurance and ultra-endurance exercise upon cardiac structure and function. These studies supported earlier work, and demonstrated that cardiac function is acutely impaired following prolonged exercise (> 4 hours) and that environmental factors such as temperature and altitude are likely to mediate the magnitude of response. These initial studies, examining the concept of "exercise-induced cardiac fatigue", completed as part of my PhD, set the bedrock for the next 10 years of my research career.

Following completion of my PhD I worked as an applied sport physiologist at the British Olympic Medical Centre (BOMC) for a little over two years. During this time I worked with numerous sports: assessing training status; monitoring acclimatisation; providing advice to coaches and athletes regarding training programmes; undertaking applied research; and most importantly, building relationships with coaches and athletes. Building meaningful relationships with colleagues and collaborators has been important over the course of my career to date. However as an applied physiologist establishing a good working relationship with both the athlete and the coach was essential; if my advice or ideas were to have any impact upon performance the athlete and coach had to trust me and believe in what I was saying. Whilst at the BOMC, as well as developing some of the softer skills that are not always part of a standard degree programme, I was also fortunate enough to observe and on occasions be involved with the Centre for Sports Cardiology that Professor Whyte had set up at Northwick Park. This experience further stimulated my interest in the effect of exercise upon the heart. Whilst I enjoyed working as an applied practitioner I was beginning to understand that my real passion was research and that I needed to find a position that allowed me to pursue my real interests. Fortunately, soon after I was appointed as a research lecturer at Brunel University where I received significant support (e.g., equipment, laboratory space and PhD studentships) allowing me to further develop my own independent research career.

Given that my PhD studies had raised more questions than they had answered, the area of exercise-induced cardiac fatigue seemed a logical area to continue studying, and more importantly the topic still held significant personal interest, which had been stimulated further by my time as an applied scientist. Although during my time at Brunel I was involved in a number of different areas of work, my primary research focus for 8 years was the impact of prolonged exercise on the heart. Working with highly talented and motivated PhD students, and part of a larger collaborative research team (e.g., Prof. Keith George, Dr David Oxborough, and Mr David Gaze), meant that I/we were able to undertake a large number of studies examining this area of research. Professionally, my major learning during this time was related to the importance of working as part of a team. This was something that had become obvious to me in my role as an applied practitioner, but was emphasised further in the research setting. In my experience, with the right individuals in place, the output (both quality and volume) of a team is always greater than the sum of its parts. This chapter describes the research process undertaken to complete a complex mechanistic study that was one part of a doctoral programme of research (by Dr Emma Hart) that I had helped to supervise. Emma's and indeed all of my PhD students' projects have required significant collaboration from a large team of individuals; without this varied input this study, and many others, would never have been completed.

Moving from a research problem to a research question

Whilst the concept of muscle fatigue is widely accepted within the literature, at the time of starting this study, the notion that the heart is also susceptible to fatigue was not widely accepted. Unlike skeletal musculature, following prolonged exercise the heart is unable to stop working and recover. Furthermore, cardiac muscle has been shown to be highly aerobic in nature, containing a high concentration of mitochondria, and is often referred to as fatigue resistant. Despite the widely held belief that the heart was "fatigue resistant", using echocardiography we had repeatedly shown that there was clear evidence for a change in the ability of the heart to contract and also relax following prolonged exercise such as marathon running (Shave et al., 2004; George et al., 2005; Middleton et al., 2006). Despite describing the phenomenon of exercise-induced cardiac fatigue (EICF) extensively, we and other groups had made little attempt to understand the mechanisms that might explain or underpin this occurrence.

In order to explore the potential mechanisms that may explain EICF we examined the physiological literature regarding endurance exercise. The physiologic milieu of prolonged exercise includes elevations in core temperature, increased acidity (lower pH), enhanced oxidative stress and increased mechanical stress on the heart subsequent to elevations in heart rate and blood pressure. All of these responses to exercise could theoretically damage the integrity of the cardiac muscle cell (cardiomyocyte) and ultimately result in an impaired cardiac function. Similarly, elevations in core temperature and hence skin blood flow, coupled with fluid loss associated with sweat production may result in a reduction in venous return. If venous return is reduced, preload on the left ventricle is also lower which due to the Frank–Starling mechanism will ultimately reduce stroke volume (see Klabunde, 2011). Furthermore, in order to meet the increased metabolic demand associated with prolonged exercise, cardiac output, and hence heart rate, needs to be persistently elevated. The enhanced chronotropic (heart rate) and inotropic (cardiac contractility) drive is associated with a sustained release of catecholamines (adrenaline and noradrenaline). Interestingly, in the clinical paradigm of heart failure persistent elevations in catecholamines, released in an attempt to improve cardiac function, paradoxically result in desensitisation of the receptors (β-adrenergic receptors) that they interact with to produce the positive inotropic effect. This desensitisation means that the catecholamines are not as effective in enhancing cardiac function. We postulated that the persistent elevation in catecholamines associated with prolonged exercise could also stimulate a desensitisation of the β-adrenergic receptors and hence explain the reduced cardiac function observed in previous prolonged exercise studies. Following an extensive review of the literature we therefore identified three potential mechanisms that may be responsible for EICF and were worthy of further study.

Emerging research questions

1   Does exercise-induced cardiac damage cause EICF?
2   Do alterations in cardiac preload subsequent to fluid loss through sweating and redistribution of blood explain post-exercise reductions in cardiac function?
3   Do prolonged elevations in catecholamines lead to desensitisation of β-adrenergic receptors and explain post-exercise reductions in cardiac function?

At that point in time there was no strong evidence that supported one specific mechanism over and above the others. Furthermore, we held the belief that it was wholly possible that EICF was multi-factoral in nature. Accordingly, the group decided to embark on a series of studies to explore each of the potential mechanisms in turn. Whilst this chapter focuses specifically on question 3 listed above, we have conducted a number of other studies that have examined the other two questions (Hart et al., 2007; Shave et al., 2005, 2007; Middleton et al., 2008). Emma Hart, a PhD student of mine between 2004–2007, took overall responsibility for the present study, and without her considerable effort the project would have failed from the outset.

Choice of method (Matching the method to the research question)

The technique of assessing cardiac structure and function using echocardiography was well established within our laboratory. It was, therefore, relatively simple and logical to choose this technique to examine the acute influence of prolonged exercise upon cardiac function. We were confident that we could once again demonstrate that cardiac function would be depressed if we chose an appropriately demanding exercise stimulus. Although we had conducted numerous studies demonstrating the change in left ventricular (LV) function subsequent to prolonged exercise, we had no experience in the examination of β-adrenergic sensitivity. It was this critical part of the study that posed significantly greater challenge during the planning stages. The two potential methods that can be used to examine β-adrenergic sensitivity are pharmacological manipulation, or Positron Emission Tomography (PET) scanning. PET scanning is an extremely expensive technique that involves the use of radioactive tracers, and as such was not going to be feasible in our chosen population (healthy endurance athletes). We therefore decided that pharmacological manipulation was the only realistic way in which we could assess β-adrenergic sensitivity pre- and post-completion of a bout of prolonged exercise. As we did not have this skill set within the research team we had to find appropriate collaborators who were experienced in the use of pharmacology to manipulate the cardiovascular system. Fortunately, a colleague (Dr Ellen Dawson) had recently taken a post-doctoral research post in Copenhagen, where they were expert in the invasive assessment of cardiovascular function including the use of pharmacological agents. Through initial discussion with, and via Dr Dawson, the team in Copenhagen led by Professor Niels Secher agreed to collaborate with us on the project. Through this multi-centre collaboration we were able to create a team with the various physiological assessment techniques to run the study.

Key message: Collaboration is often essential for high quality work to be produced. It is almost impossible for a single person to have all of the requisite skills to undertake large-scale projects. Therefore, wherever and whenever possible, it is worth building an effective group of collaborators that have complementary skills and knowledge. Furthermore, working on projects as part of a team is often a far more rewarding experience than working as a single scholar in isolation.

Data collection

Ethical considerations

As with any research study we had numerous ethical considerations related to this project. The major concerns were related to the use of invasive physiologic measures such as arterial and venous catheters and the use of pharmacological agents to manipulate cardiac function. Both the use of indwelling catheters and pharmacological agents have significant risk associated with them if used incorrectly. In line with this, the study was run in a hospital setting, with emergency facilities on hand should anything have gone wrong. Further, all invasive procedures and pharmaceutical administration were conducted by highly trained experienced clinicians.

The experiment

Following ethical approval and significant liaison between the two laboratories, Emma travelled to Copenhagen to complete the studies. Collaborative work between laboratories is always logistically challenging, however, if the other laboratory is in a different country the challenges are significantly increased. Central to our study was the assessment of cardiac function and the measurement of circulating catecholamines. These two aspects required the transportation of expensive, sensitive equipment from London to Copenhagen and also the transport of serum samples back to the UK. These types of logistics were only possible with a significant lead-in time and close communication between the two laboratories. Prior to Emma travelling to Denmark, the laboratory team in Copenhagen had recruited a number of high-level rowers to take part in the study. It would not have been possible for these participants to be recruited from the UK, and the personal contacts that existed between the laboratory in Copenhagen and the rowers made the study possible. The existing relationship with the rowers, and their willingness to take part influenced the mode of exercise that we decided to use. As the rowers were accustomed to taking part in laboratory studies using a rowing ergometer it was pragmatic for us to adopt rowing as the exercise stimulus for the study.

The experiment itself was complex in nature and involved a number of visits to the laboratory, accordingly there was a significant time commitment on behalf of the participants for which they received a nominal financial payment in recompense. A schematic of the study protocol is provided in Figure 4.1. Before volunteering to take part in the study all of the participants provided written informed consent. In order to assess the impact of prolonged exercise upon cardiac function a cardiac ultrasound assessment was completed prior to and immediately following completion of a four-hour bout of rowing. In addition, β-adrenergic sensitivity was examined prior to (the day preceding the exercise challenge) and following completion of the rowing bout. To do this participants were firstly infused with glycopyorolate to block the parasympathetic system (vagal control), then they were administered incremental doses of isoproterenol (a β-adrenergic agonist that acts in a similar fashion to adrenaline). Blocking the effects of the parasympathetic system meant that we were able to confirm whether any effect observed post-exercise was related to β-adrenergic sensitivity rather than simultaneous changes to vagal activity. Isoproterenol was

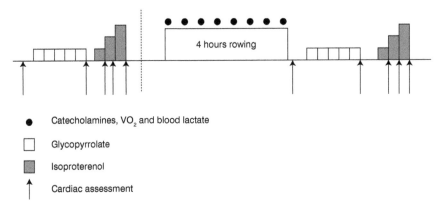

● Catecholamines, VO_2 and blood lactate

☐ Glycopyrrolate

▨ Isoproterenol

↑ Cardiac assessment

FIGURE 4.1   Schematic of protocol adopted

delivered incrementally so that the sensitivity (potentially small changes) of the β-adrenergic receptors could be identified. At the end of each incremental dose cardiac function was assessed using cardiac ultrasound. By comparing the cardiac response to incremental doses of isoproterenol before and after the rowing bout it was possible to examine whether the β-adrenergic sensitivity had changed in response to the prolonged exercise. Throughout the exercise challenge we also drew blood samples that were used to measure the circulating catecholamine concentration. Using these data we were able to examine the relationship between catecholamine release and the magnitude of change in cardiac function following completion of the exercise.

Data analysis

A number of different statistical analyses were conducted. Initially, we were interested in the effects of exercise upon cardiac function and so we needed to examine differences between the data we collected pre- and post-exercise. To do this we employed a simple one-way repeated measures ANOVA. In order to explore our primary hypothesis, we needed to examine differences in the response of the cardiovascular system to incremental doses of isoproterenol pre- to post-completion of the prolonged bout of rowing. To do this we used a two-way repeated measures ANOVA. Post-hoc analysis to identify the location of any specific differences pre- to post-exercise was conducted using pairwise comparisons and a Bonferroni correction. Finally, to examine relationships between catecholamine release and changes in cardiac function we used a Pearson's product-moment analysis. All statistical analyses were conducted using SPSS software (version 13; Illinois, USA) and a critical alpha level of 0.05 was set. Although SPSS is widely adopted for statistical analyses I do not favour the software for the generation of user-friendly figures. In line with this, figures for this study (and indeed the majority of my other projects) have been constructed using GraphPad Prism (http://www.graphpad.com/).

Data presentation

In line with popular convention, the results section for this study was presented in the same order as that presented in the methods section. In practice, this meant that information regarding the participants and their exercise responses were initially presented. This provided the background from which the key findings of the study could be interpreted. After outlining the exercise response using standard variables such as heart rate, blood lactate and oxygen consumption, the functional cardiac response to exercise was presented. This enabled us to describe the change in cardiac function following prolonged exercise. In essence these data were largely confirmatory of our previous studies showing an acute reduction in both systolic and diastolic function. The final data to be presented were the key, novel findings from the study, namely the influence of prolonged exercise upon the cardiovascular response to an incremental dose of isoproterenol (Figure 4.2). It is these data that relate to the key question and hypothesis of the study – *Do prolonged elevations in catecholamines lead to desensitisation of β-adrenergic receptors and explain post-exercise reductions in cardiac function?* And it is these data that demonstrate that desensitisation of β-adrenergic receptors likely explains the reduction in cardiac function following prolonged exercise.

The complex study that we had undertaken examined multiple variables over a number of different time points, and therefore generated a very large volume of data. In order to focus the results section onto the key variables we used figures for the most important/novel findings, whereas other supporting or background data were presented in tables or text. Figures tend to provide a very clear representation of the data, meaning that the reader can grasp the key findings very quickly, as opposed to searching through "data heavy" tables. Given the mechanistic insight provided by our data we chose to submit the paper to the *Journal of Physiology*. Accordingly, whilst preparing the manuscript we consulted and adhered to the specific guidelines set out by the Physiological Society. (http://jp.physoc.org/site/misc/author.xhtml#manguide).

Contribution to knowledge

Again, in line with popular convention the opening paragraph of the discussion highlighted the major findings of the study. Starting the discussion in this fashion enables the reader to quickly grasp what has been presented and what the key findings are. Once this has been stated it is possible to develop the full discussion of the results, commenting on how they pertain to previous findings and importantly what they mean within the overall context of the field.

> The findings of this study provide unique evidence of (1) reduced left ventricular systolic and diastolic function immediately following a 4 h bout of rowing, and (2) blunted post-exercise left ventricular chronotropic

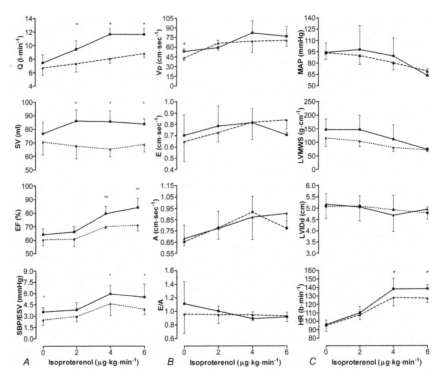

FIGURE 4.2   Left ventricular response to incremental isoproterenol infusion pre- and post-exercise. Inotropic (A), lusitropic (B) and chronotropic/loading (C) response to isoproterenol pre- (continuous line) and post-exercise (dashed line). Data are means +/− S.D. Different from pre-exercise *$p < 0.05$, **$p < 0.01$. Abbreviations: SBP/ESV, systolic blood pressure to end systolic volume ratio; EF, ejection fraction; Q, cardiac output; SV, stroke volume; E/A, ratio of early to late LV filling; E, peak velocity of early transmitral filling; A, peak velocity of late transmitral filling; Vp, flow propagation velocity of early transmitral filling; HR, heart rate; LVIDd, LV internal diameter in diastole; MAP, mean arterial pressure; LVMWS, LV meridional wall stress

and inotropic response to isoproterenol infusion following vagal blockade, with no significant alterations in diastolic function.

(Hart et al., 2006)

Whilst previous studies had shown a post-exercise reduction in cardiac function following prolonged exercise, none had examined rowing as the exercise modality. The first novel finding of our study was that similar to running and cycling, prolonged rowing resulted in an acute reduction in cardiac function. Importantly, however, it appears that rowing may provide a greater stimulus for exercise-induced cardiac fatigue as four hours of exercise led to reductions in *both* systolic and diastolic function. Previous studies of this duration, which examined running or cycling, had previously only shown impairments in diastolic function. It is possible that the afterload (blood pressure), which is considerably greater in rowing exercise, explains the difference between previous findings and the present data, however this hypothesis needs further investigation.

Although interesting, this finding related to the potentially more potent influence of prolonged rowing exercise upon cardiac function was secondary to the major findings – a reduced chronotropic and inotropic response to isoproterenol stimulation of β-adrenergic receptors following prolonged exercise.

> During isoproterenol infusion, there was a reduction in the inotropic response of the LV. Ejection fraction, stroke volume and, more importantly, cardiac output were reduced at all levels of isoproterenol infusion. Contractility, as assessed by the pressure/volume ratio, was also reduced post-exercise at the highest two doses of isoproterenol. This concurs with Welsh et al. (2005), who demonstrated a reduction in pressure/volume ratio during dobutamine infusion after a half-ironman triathlon. The elevation in circulating adrenaline at the end of exercise was related to the alteration in pre- to post-exercise ejection fraction, before glycopyrrolate infusion. Although this relationship does not prove cause and effect, it does support a role of increased circulating catecholamines in the genesis of altered LV systolic function following prolonged exercise.
>
> (Hart et al., 2006)

Although Welsh et al. (2005) had shown a reduction in inotropic state following prolonged exercise, their study had not controlled for potential changes in vagal tone which we achieved by using glycopyrolate as a parasympathetic blocker prior to isoproterenol infusion. Also, the correlational data between adrenaline and changes in contractility (estimated from the left ventricular ejection fraction) in our study strengthened the potential link between catecholamine exposure and reductions in cardiac function following endurance exercise. We therefore concluded that:

> Prolonged ergometer rowing resulted in a reduction in both LV systolic and diastolic function. Moreover, LV chronotropic and inotropic responses to isoproterenol were blunted as a result of prolonged exercise. Consequently, increases in cardiac output response to combined β1 and β2 stimulation were limited following exercise even when vagal tone was blocked. Thus, β-AR desensitization may explain attenuated LV systolic but not diastolic function following prolonged exercise.
>
> (Hart et al., 2006)

Since publication, these data have been included in a number of review papers that have explored the mechanisms responsible for exercise-induced cardiac fatigue (e.g., Shave and Oxborough, 2012) and it is now widely accepted that prolonged exposure to catecholamines secondary to prolonged exercise can result in an acute reduction in cardiac function in humans. Interestingly, a study examining the same phenomenon but using a rat model has recently not been able to corroborate our findings (Vitiello et al., 2011). Personally, this brings into question the use of animal models to investigate physiological phenomenon observed in humans. It is highly likely that the underpinning physiology in one species differs from that of others, and care needs to be taken when trying to extrapolate from one experimental animal to another.

Impact on practice

Similar to many fundamental mechanistic studies in physiology, it is not always clear how the findings from this study directly influence practice. Historically, the development of physiological understanding has provided the background, and often stimulus, for significant advances in many related disciplines such as medicine, zoology, ecology, dentistry etc. The importance of knowledge generation itself should not, therefore, be downplayed in any study. Notwithstanding, the results from the present study do have relevance to the applied sport practitioner. Understanding the direct influence of prolonged bouts of exercise training upon the heart in an acute setting is important when considering the prescription of exercise intensities. Athletes' training programmes are often predicated on the use of heart rate zones. Following periods of sustained endurance training it is possible that the athletes may notice an inability to raise their heart rate in the normal fashion in response to an exercise stimulus. Understanding that this *may* simply reflect a desensitisation of the β-adrenergic receptors due to prior bouts of prolonged training should reduce any undue concern. In time, these data may also be of use to practitioners who schedule prolonged bouts of exercise, whether for physiological training in the case of athletes, or in other non-sporting professions such as military or emergency personnel. Providing enough time for the acute desensitisation of the β-adrenergic receptors, and the associated reduction in cardiac function, to subside would seem prudent to maintain overall function and likely facilitate optimal adaptation. However, this requires further investigation.

Reflection

Having completed this study a number of years ago, and in the intervening years undertaking further investigation in the area, I feel as though I am now in a position to reflect appropriately on the study. Although at the time I knew that we were undertaking a complex mechanistic study I was somewhat unaware of the logistical difficulties or indeed the positive outcomes that would come from it. This was the first truly mechanistic study that I was involved in and one that I still gain reprint requests for. As alluded to earlier, collaboration was critical for the success of the study, however, working between two laboratories in different countries required significant planning and discussion. In this instance the work was only possible because of the drive and passion of the PhD student leading the project and the significant support from personnel in the laboratory in Copenhagen. Since this study, collaboration has remained central to much of the work that I undertake, however, I enter in to all collaborative studies cautiously and only once a good understanding has been established between all of the partners. It is important to discuss things such as ownership of data, authorship, financial expectations and time investment prior to the start of any projects. There were very few problems associated with the project presented within this chapter, and all of the collaborators worked effectively with each other for what I believe to be the best outcome of the study. However, this was more by luck than judgement and I have subsequently heard of many collaborative studies where people have felt disenfranchised, with their opinions overlooked or ignored. As with all aspects of research, appropriate planning and discussion up-front reduces the potential of problems or disagreements later. I now try to discuss everyone's expectations at the outset of all studies and to make sure that everyone is in agreement with their roles and responsibilities.

Completing this study has spurred me on to further mechanistic studies and made me realise that whilst I consider myself a "sport and exercise scientist" there is significant potential for crossover with other disciplines (e.g. physiology or medicine). I am now happy to consider conducting studies that I find interesting but that I do not necessarily have all of the requisite skills to conduct. If the question is interesting/important enough it is always possible to pull together an appropriate team to address the issue. This insight has led to many exciting projects that I would not have considered viable in the early stage of my career.

Since completion of this study, Emma finished her PhD, completed a prestigious post-doctoral project at the Mayo Clinic in the USA and has recently taken up a second post-doctoral position in Bristol. As Emma's supervisor, I believe that the skills and knowledge that she gained running this large collaborative study as part of her PhD placed her in an ideal position to take on her subsequent positions. Personally, since completion of this study I have been far more inclined to take on difficult/complex studies; whilst they can be logistically challenging the potential payback in terms of publication, interaction with collaborators and personal enjoyment is certainly worth the increased effort required.

If you liked this chapter, you should read Chapters 2, 8 and 12 as the authors describe research processes that focus on furthering knowledge in physiology, exercise and health.

References

George K, Oxborough D, Forster J, Whyte G, Shave R, Dawson E, Stephenson C, Dugdill L, Edwards B & Gaze D (2005). Mitral annular myocardial velocity assessment of segmental left ventricular diastolic function after prolonged exercise in humans. *Journal of Physiology*, 569, 305–13.

Hart, E., Dawson, E., Rasmussen, P., George, K., Secher, N. H., Whyte, G., & Shave, R. (2006) β-Adrenergic receptor desensitization in man: insight into post-exercise attenuation of cardiac function. *Journal of Physiology*, 577, 717–25.

Hart, E, Shave, R, Middleton, N, George, K, Whyte, G, & Oxborough, D (2007) Effect of preload augmentation on pulsed wave and tissue Doppler echocardiographic indices of diastolic function after a marathon. *Journal of the American Society of Echocardiography*, 20, 1393–9.

Klabunde RE (2011) *Cardiovascular physiology concepts* (2nd Edn). Lippincott Williams and Wilkins. Baltimore, MD.

Middleton N, Shave R, George K, Whyte G, Forster J, Oxborough D, Gaze D & Collinson P (2006). Novel application of flow propagation velocity and ischaemia modified albumin in analysis of post-exercise cardiac function. *Experimental Physiology*, 91, 511–19.

Middleton N, George K, Whyte G, Gaze D, Collinson P, & Shave R (2008) Cardiac troponin T release is stimulated by endurance exercise in healthy humans. *Journal of the American College of Cardiology*, 52, 1813–14.

Shave R, Dawson E, Whyte G, George K, Gaze D & Collinson P (2004). Altered cardiac function and minimal cardiac damage during prolonged exercise. *Medicine & Science in Sport & Exercise, 36*, 1098–103.

Shave RE, Whyte GP, George K, Gaze DC, & Collinson PO (2005) Prolonged exercise should be considered alongside typical symptoms of acute myocardial infarction when evaluating increases in cardiac troponin T. *Heart, 91*, 1219–20.

Shave R, George KP, Atkinson G et al. (2007) Exercise-induced cardiac troponin T release: A meta-analysis. *Medicine & Science in Sport & Exercise, 39*, 2099–106.

Shave R, & Oxborough D (2012) Exercise-induced cardiac injury: evidence from novel imaging techniques and highly sensitive cardiac troponin assays. *Progress in Cardiovascular Disease, 54*, 407–15.

Vitiello D, Boissiere J, Doucende G, Gayrard S, Polge A, Faure P, Goux A, Tanguy S, Obert P, Reboul C, & Nottin S (2011) β-Adrenergic receptors desensitization is not involved in exercise-induced cardiac fatigue: NADPH oxidase-induced oxidative stress as a new trigger. *Journal of Applied Physiology, 111*, 1242–8.

Welsh, RC, Warburton, DE, Humen, DP, Taylor, DA, McGovarck, J & Haykosky, MJ (2005). Prolonged strenuous exercise alters cardiovascular response to dobutamine stimulation in male athletes. *Journal of Physiology*, 569, 325–330.

5

SOCIOLOGY IN SPORT

A very precarious profession: uncertainty in the working lives of professional footballers

Martin J. Roderick

Article reference

Roderick, M.J. (2006). A very precarious profession: uncertainty in the working lives of professional footballers, *Work Employment and Society*, 20(2): 245–266.

Article summary

Based on semi-structured interviews with 47 present and former professional footballers, this article explores the uncertainty that is a central feature of the professional footballer's workplace experiences, contributing to sociological understanding of insecurities stemming from the social relations of this type of work. The professional football industry has always been marked by a competitive labour market, and players quickly grasp the limited tenure of contracts, the constant surplus of talented labour, and their vulnerability to injury and ageing. To deal with the feelings of insecurity that arise from these working conditions, players develop networks of a) friends to whom they can turn if they perceive their status to be under threat, and b) dramaturgical selves (Collinson, 2003) in order to maintain stable, masculine workplace identities. Addressing feelings of uncertainty is an ever-present dimension of their working lives.

Related author publications

Roderick, M.J. (2006). Adding insult to injury: workplace injury in English professional football. *Sociology of Health and Illness*, 28 (1): 76–97.
Roderick, M.J. (2012). An unpaid labor of love: professional footballers, family life and the problem of job relocation. *Journal of Sport and Social Issues*, 36 (3): 316–337.

Introduction

The object of my sociological research concerns an analysis of the careers of professional footballers in England. In 1997, a developed research proposal was accepted by Leicester University's Sociology department for part-time doctoral study, and empirical fieldwork with players commenced in 1998 and continued initially for a period of two years; qualitative semi-structured interviews were undertaken with 47 footballers. For the purposes of writing the article published in the sociology journal, *Work, Employment and Society* (*WES*), the focus of this chapter, the specific conceptual intention was confined to comprehending players' experiences of, and the meanings they attached to, periods of time in their careers when existential uncertainties tied to their futures as professionals were manifest. In interview, for many players such vulnerable passages threatened their workplace status as 'footballers'; and, accordingly, questions surrounding issues of identity, and how occupational identities are (re)constructed, underpinned this research.

Professional football is among the most popular and recognised sports globally. A great deal has been written about footballers by biographers, journalists and the players themselves. Even so, it is hard to think of a professional sporting practice in the UK that has been so mythologised yet so little researched by social scientists. With few exceptions, contemporary studies of the professional game are dominated by 'quasi-insiders' who focus on the public and commercial sides of the sport at the top levels. In this research I have tried in contrast to approach this occupation through its least well-known and least exposed sides. Thus, the central aims of the chapter are threefold:

1   to consider the ways in which I set about undertaking research on footballers' careers and explaining how players-as-employees offer sociologically interesting working lives;
2   to discuss the problematic journey I experienced of publishing a sport-specific research article in a mainstream sociological journal;
3   to help debunk myths surrounding the work of professional football.

Football as a sociological 'problem'

The question of how professional footballers deal with the highs and lows of their careers is not one frequently addressed among supporters of the game or, even, among football commentators. This is not because there is a lack of interest in players as 'real' people as such, or as an outcome of a narrow self-interest in club performances and match results. In undertaking the research upon which this chapter is based, and in pursuing an opportunity to publish an article in *WES*, a mainstream sociological journal of longstanding repute, it became increasingly evident that a set of ideological assumptions exist related to professional sport that dominates the hearts and minds of both committed followers of this sport and casual onlookers. These dominant ideas are discernible in a variety of ways, but are underlined by the basic idea that, in some ill-defined sense, football is a special, glamorous profession; in short, football is a labour of love, and footballers have a calling to play (Harding, 2003). This calling however involves more than the acquisition of exemplary technical, kinaesthetic ability. Obviously, football is something that a player's 'body' can do, but being a professional footballer is also embodied – occupational experience is constructed through the active body (McGillivray et al., 2005).

Many football writers have argued resolutely that the work of professional football may appear highly attractive to young hopefuls in relation to a number of dimensions of job satisfaction, including the opportunity to feel self-actualized at work, to live an idiosyncratic way of life, to feel a strong sense of community, and to publicly establish their character, ability and strength among a broader population of fans (Green, 2009; Cashmore and Parker, 2003; Szymanski and Kuypers, 1999). Yet in submitting my article, and in responding to reviewers' comments, the fashion in which these dominant ideological assumptions were disclosed proved challenging to address. For instance, two reviewers rejected my original submission outright, claiming that sociological research on the careers of footballers was not a topic about which the journal should be publishing. Their assumption in brief suggested that football was bound up with 'privilege'. The reviewers believed that this journal's readership was not a natural audience for social research of this kind and, in responding to Becker's (1967) classic methodological question, 'whose side are we on?', they posited a view in which, in any hierarchy of credibility, understanding the work of footballers was inescapably elitist and beyond the serious business of employment and labour processes. If *WES* should declare that it was on anyone's 'side', or to have political biases in establishing social research priorities, then for these reviewers it was highly questionable whether this academic journal, with its admirable history of defending the working rights of 'ordinary' (often working-class) employees and life's 'underdogs' (Halford and Strangleman, 2009), should be giving space to individuals who are presented stereotypically in the media as 'spoilt' millionaires who waste vast sums gambling, drinking, taking drugs and abusing women (Ortiz, 2006). In part, my subsequent re-construction of this article incorporated an implicit attempt to respond to (ill-informed) sceptics who questioned why, as sociologists, should we care about footballers-cum-celebrities who earn extortionately high rates of pay and who indulge themselves in life's luxury trappings.

This was a research dissemination problem of some significance that signalled an issue for which I have necessarily had to cultivate responses over the course of developing my research agenda: in short, I meet people regularly who, even though they watch matches avidly and consume football gossip endlessly, regurgitate unreflectively mythical representations of footballers and their work. As a backdrop to comprehending the journey I embarked on in relation to this publication specifically, and what I consider prejudiced ways of thinking about sport-as-work, it was necessary to weigh up the extent to which I had to convince reviewers, including the journal's (sympathetic) editor, that the focus of this article – the workplace uncertainties experienced by employees in this 'precarious' profession – in fact constituted a legitimate sociological problem. Specifically devoted to issues bound up with the sociology of work, a formerly dominant sub-discipline of this academic field, *WES* had never published any research on sport or exercise, and so my attempts represented a first and something of a publishing risk.

Developing a personal research agenda

Following the initial rejection, I was urged by the journal editor to rework and resubmit the article. Buoyed by very positive comments from Reviewer 3, I set about reconstituting the research for *WES* readers. I was encouraged to embed the analytically-rich qualitative data about which I was writing in terms more familiar to sociologists of work and careers – for example I restructured the arguments in terms of working conditions, forms of workplace control and labour processes – and also to align more closely the theoretical analysis I was presenting to studies located in *WES* and adjacent, mostly mainstream sociology journals. This was not a problematic rewrite from my perspective and it proved a useful exercise, not only because it led ultimately to a more focused research article, but perhaps more importantly because it highlighted the types of assumptions I was making about this profession – one about which I was claiming 'tenuous' expert knowledge – and the ways I was taking for granted conditions of work with which I had formally been familiar. This article was born out of data collected for my doctoral thesis, which examined sociologically the careers of professional footballers. Even so, in discussing with players in interview their career pathways, fateful turning-points and workplace contingencies in a fashion reminiscent of classic *interactionist* studies of occupational careers (Rose, 1962), issues emerged that offered valuable conceptual insight, not only in terms of the culture of work in this professional sport specifically but also in more general sociological terms.

My interest in this research had been initially stimulated by my experiences as a young professional – and semi-professional – footballer in the 1980s and 90s. During this time, like many of my team mates, I had considered – and sometimes enjoyed – the status of this 'profession', how my performances were being unavoidably scrutinised and judged by others, and my observable demeanour among colleagues, friends, and family. Yet, in spite of my (distinctly 'un-academic') personal reflections, I could never have imaged that, in time, these would form the basis of a sociological research project that would lead to a second career in academia. My departure from the professional game of course signalled personal rejection and a public recognition that I had failed to achieve the ambitions upon which I had formerly set my sights. It would be true to say that, throughout my subsequent postgraduate training as a sociologist at

Leicester University, the way I thought about this sports-work became subject to a much deeper level of scrutiny that led me to contemplate issues broadly concerned with 'self-identity': what type of person I had been as a footballer, how had I treated others during this time, who I was now – as researcher – and what type of person did I see myself becoming? Conceptually speaking, all these identity-based questions refocused my attention on the ways in which I had presented myself in my everyday life that, from my perspective, had unfolded in unpredictable ways; in hindsight my disengagement from the professional game constituted a classic example of involuntary exit (Swain, 1991). While I had considered this exodus at the time in idiosyncratic terms, it was, in fact, much like most other early transitions from this sport; at 21 years of age I had to reconcile the fact I would never make it to the 'big time'.

For research purposes, my individual recollections of life as a young professional provided first-hand evidence of the nature of the discussions I had regularly engaged in with age group team mates, and concurrently offered a starting point for the research process. This early period in my doctoral research was experienced as an obligatory opportunity to explore the meaning of particular episodes, and it drew my sociological attention to the cumulative effects of these experiences and the significance of face-to-face (and small-scale) focused interactions on perceptions of player identity in a more general sense. For instance, while life in the club at a specific point in time may be positive and self-affirming, this does not mean that players are blind to, or unaffected by, the kinds of situations (and reactions) which trigger a crisis of confidence for team mates. As young players we measured our progress collectively within the club (e.g., were we getting into the right teams, performing competently, demonstrating a good attitude to our work, and receiving encouraging reviews) and regularly considered who would be offered new terms – in short, we contemplated who would 'make it'. The felt disappointment of watching friends depart the club each year having been released; of being ridiculed or undermined by senior professionals in training; of returning to work on Monday morning following a poor performance on Saturday, were among the episodes that I came to explore with interviewees and which underscored the daily, inescapable worries experienced by players-as-workers.

My former experiences offered a great platform from which this qualitative research could advance, yet it concurrently provided inexorable methodological traps of which I had constantly to be mindful. In composing the research article for *WES*, I would necessarily need to address briefly the advantages an 'insider' status can afford qualitative researchers, whilst always being aware of how this former involvement may impact on my interpretive clarity. This of course relates to a classic methodological dilemma for social scientists: the question of subjectivity (Denzin, 1989). In other words, all academics undertaking interpretive research must consider carefully their own (subjective) position in the process of knowledge acquisition. Qualitative research of this kind is never unbiased, impersonal, or value-free, a situation which may raise concerns about the credibility and authenticity of a *social* scientific investigation in which behavioural regularities are discerned and data are given meaning (Silverman, 2001).

The issue of access and sampling dilemmas

The article prepared for *WES* involved interviews with 47 male professional footballers. Of these players, 34 were, at the time of interview, contracted to clubs in one of the four professional football leagues in England. Ten retired professional footballers were also interviewed. The ages of the 37 current players ranged from 18 to 35 years. All ten former players were over 35 years. All the players interviewed played for English professional football clubs. Certain demographic information was offered by the players during the course of their interview, in particular their ages. The players included this information unprompted for, I concluded, it was meaningful for them in terms of understanding the circumstances in which they were bound. Building a sample from personal acquaintances and contacts, I recognised however that I was unable to explore social class or minority group effects adequately. In other words, it was not my intention to 'force' interviewees to make reference to their ethnicity, gender, and social class, but to let them integrate such structural features in the course of retelling their stories.

The players who comprised the sample were not selected in accordance with a considered research design. The players interviewed were or had been professional footballers and, as such, all their career experiences were valid for analytical purposes. The majority of interviewees came via personal contacts (a point which is discussed later). Contact with some of the players had been made using information obtained from a former deputy chief executive of the Professional Footballers' Association who acted as gatekeeper. His recommendations were vital in a small number of cases. A number of players were sent letters speculatively; most of course did not respond. However, a very small number of players did reply. All players who were sent letters were asked whether they would be willing to be interviewed on a range of issues related to their playing careers.

Following the initial contacts, the sample was subsequently constructed largely on a 'snowball' basis. The players who were interviewed first were asked to recommend others who they thought may be prepared also to discuss their playing and career experiences. All the players who responded positively were interviewed, for there are problems attaining access to professional footballers in order to organise face-to-face research engagements. Footballers, on a local or national level, are public figures who acquire varying degrees of celebrity. They do not readily grant permission for 'unknown' academics to interview them for extended periods (Parker, 1998). Attempting to be selective with an occupational group who do not consent to extended interviews unhesitatingly would have constituted an error in judgement. At the outset of each interview the players were given an assurance of anonymity and that ethical procedures relating to their testimony would be adhered to strictly; each player received an audio copy of their interview plus a written transcript to check and edit, plus guarantees relating to the time their oral evidence would be retained and its safe keeping. Part of the 'access' problem involves a residual fear for players that they may be viewed either as openly criticising their team mates or team management, or more simply stigmatised as complainers. The players were asked questions to which their replies would almost certainly involve former and present playing colleagues. It was important to reassure them that their comments, however conveyed in interview, would not be traceable to them in publication. If they had not received these ethical assurances they may not have responded to questions so candidly.

The only self-imposed sample-construction criterion was to interview players who represented a range of playing experiences. A great deal of information is available about professional footballers, including information relating to playing statistics and career histories. There are many (auto)biographies of players also in which their thoughts and feelings are expressed 'openly'. However, between the extremes of outstanding success and miserable failure lie many middle courses. Most players who write up their memoirs tend to be those who, on balance, would be positioned closer to the 'outstanding success' extreme. For this study it was important to interview players who had experienced a variety of career trajectories, as I wanted to address the question of how players managed uncertain periods in time connected with contingencies such as injury and labour migration. Thus, in collecting research data, a number of different 'types' of players were interviewed. For example, some of the players were well-known international players; others had played for one club solely and had never personally experienced labour mobility, although all had been subject to managerial succession; the bulk of players however were 'journeymen'. A number of these players had played their careers to date in Divisions Two and Three, some had played for only Premiership and Division One clubs, while others had experienced first-team football in all four professional football leagues.[1] The interviews, which lasted between 45 and 90 minutes, generated a large amount of data that could be sociologically analysed. Even so, the sample was not randomly recruited, and this cannot be considered, in a positivist sense, to constitute a group that is statistically representative of a broader population of footballers. While this sample may fall foul of specific methodological standards, it is important to reiterate the point that, while footballers are often interviewed by journalists about their views on team performances and affairs, it is rare for players, like famous actors and other people who achieve celebrity, to agree to interviews in which they respond to questions so freely.

Undertaking in-depth semi-structured interviews was my only reliable option. The opportunity to have engaged in ethnographic fieldwork – a method that would be an alternative source of rich data – was all but nonexistent owing to access concerns. It would be unlikely that a sociologist could gain such unfettered admittance to the inner sanctums of training grounds.

The experience of doing research

My aim in developing the interview schedule was to encourage players to talk about specific career contingencies, and to enable them to 'furnish' their stories in various ways: ways appropriate to their perceptions of their workplace circumstances. Of most importance for me was to lead players in interview to offer detailed accounts of their personal journeys through various 'passages of vulnerability' – for instance, injury, managerial succession and labour mobility. I wanted to prompt players to explain how they came to define their situations, but also to understand how significant others reacted to them during these uncertain episodes. I wanted them to offer thick descriptions of the networks of relationships in which they were embedded. This was important because, as previous research demonstrates, issues of interdependence underpin social life: in spite of the unmistakable social structures which enable and constrain the employment activities of the players involved in this study, their narratives must – can only – be comprehended as enacted by real individuals in the ongoing flux of daily life (Lawler, 2008).

The first questions composed were generated from my own experience and from the vast sociological literature on careers (Blair, 2001; Collinson, 2003; Sennett, 1998), some of which focused on other highly contingent occupations in the entertainment industry (Turner and Wainwright, 2003; Wacquant, 1998; Wulff, 2001). Crucially, the nature and formulation of the questions posed was stimulated by the theoretical approach I adopted in this research: symbolic interactionism. At the start of the research process, my sociological curiosity had unwittingly become focused on more biographical issues, in part as an outcome of reading what I thought were brilliant interactionist studies of work and careers (Rose, 1962). While mostly focused on marginal or 'dirty' forms of employment, these studies offered some enlightenment in terms of the possible ways for me to approach the footballers in my study, some of whom I had observed struggle – like me – to make it their career. From an early point in the research process therefore I had been drawn to symbolic interactionism, a broad theoretical approach in which social life is closely interwoven with the analysis of the meaning of human action which individuals actively construct and interpret. For interactionists, the minutiae of social interaction in everyday life are significant in part because it is at the level of human interaction and interpersonal relationships that the fabrication of one's sense of self-identity evolves (Atkinson and Housley, 2003). My specific focus concerned the question of how the players' identities were sustained and managed as they encountered, time after time, unavoidable threats to the stability of their identities in the organisation of football club life. I wanted to comprehend players' perceptions of key 'symbolic' interactions within changing rooms on a daily basis and pre- and post-matches; meaningful encounters between managers and players on both a team and individual basis, for instance when players are left out for forthcoming matches; and strategic negotiations among managers, physiotherapists and players about whether an 'unfit' player should start a game. The analysis in the article developed for *WES* emphasised explicitly the issue of uncertainty as socially produced through the meanings associated with certain conditions of work and workplace relations.

Interactionism informed all stages of the research process, and it was essential for *WES* readers that I identified the conceptual reference points and sensitising ideas I employed in undertaking fieldwork and data analysis. There are additionally two other noteworthy *temporal* issues: firstly in terms of the age of players at the time of interview and the length of their career achieved to date, and secondly with respect to my attempt to characterise interviewee orientations to their careers and how these are affected by fateful events in their lives. In other words, it was significant for this research (and hence the article) to be aware of the workplace attitudes players bring to their job and how these change over the course of their playing careers. For instance, an evident *in vivo* theme emerged, captured perfectly by an inexperienced, lower league player in the following way: 'At the end of the day, you know, everyone is in it for themselves. And quite often players would shit on each other if it came to it.' This unambiguous pattern of ruthless individualism marked many player narratives and in a variety of ways – an idea which offers a more complex appreciation of what teamwork means to players and how they define and manage the dynamics of workplace relationships. But while the quote is illustrative of many statements in interview, it says however very little about how such frames of mind are acquired or how players continue to exist in this occupation with such an acute appreciation of their own self-alienation. Thus the success of the fieldwork was in part dependent on my capacity to ask questions of all interviewees that enabled them to feel sufficiently secure to articulate responses, some of which may be counter-intuitive in terms of dominant ideas associated with this profession, but that offer a more reality-congruent player perspective. Although I made novice errors from time-to-time – selecting in advance a supposedly private place to conduct the interview, which turned out to be anything but – I worked hard to put each interviewee at ease, trying to ask intelligent and apt questions and reacting with understanding to their responses.

The usefulness of pursuing interviews in a semi-structured fashion ensured that players felt able to construct their stories in their own terms and in ways that related to how they came to define the focused encounters and daily dramas in which they were bound. Even so, putting questions to a young player commencing his career was a qualitatively different research experience in comparison to engaging with a player facing retirement, whose range of relevant experiences was much broader and whose orientation to work was of a distinctly more cynical kind. Still, formulating questions targeted at specific workplace contingencies – injury and labour mobility – led me swiftly to recognise one of the more illuminating aspects of this research process.

I had made the decision that the first player interviews were going to focus specifically on player experiences of playing in pain and when injured. There was no scientific rationale for this starting point, other than I had several personal experiences of playing hurt, and felt comfortable in my appreciation of academic literature in this area, which extended to the nature of relationships among patients, physiotherapists and doctors, and the use of pain management drugs. In responding to my questions, though, the players naturally tied and situated their accounts to other contexts, contingencies, and relationships both within and beyond the football club. It was all but impossible for players to discuss their experience of injury without reference to what it meant to them in terms of, for example, losing their place in the team and giving an opportunity to another player, their age and the possibility of securing future contracts, whether they were prepared to be injected and risk further injury – and what it would mean for them if they refused – and the extent to which they felt a burden to significant others when rehabilitating and regaining match fitness. In fact, the range of meanings related to their experience of pain and chronic injury was extensive and rarely discussed in isolation of the network of interdependent relationships in which they were tied.

In the initial stages of each interview, players were asked to identify and subsequently talk me through a significant injury for them, one which they felt impacted on the stage at which they had reached in their career thus far. While a basic framework of questions was constructed, it became quickly evident that their ordering, and their relevance to the interviewee in question, was subject to the way that each player storied the events which unfolded for them. So, for example, some players recounted events related to the circumstances surrounding a broken bone or a dislocation; injuries which were instantly evident to critical onlookers. Other players talked initially about their attempts to conceal their discomfort from significant audiences and how they sought treatment privately. Eventually all the players had to admit to their employers they were in pain, which in most (but not all) cases led them to miss games. I encouraged interviewees during my questioning and probing to talk me through the injury process in order to discover the role of all the people with whom the player discussed their injury, and what their inputs amounted to:

- Who knew about their injury? Who did they tell first and why?
- Was surgery required and with whom did they discuss the timing of surgery? How were surgery-related decisions reached?
- Who decided whether they were 'fit for selection'? Did the injury break down?
- What was it like to miss matches and to watch the team play?
- What contact did they have with other players and how were they treated by them?
- Had they ever agreed to be injected? What negotiations preceded this medical action and with whom?

Not all questions on my interview schedule were relevant for all players, and so I had to be flexible and listen carefully to their testimony. As a relatively inexperienced researcher however it was clear from listening back to recordings that at times I had failed to ask appropriate questions at the most fitting moments. Even so, over time my confidence grew and I became better able to react to the relatively unique fashion with which each interviewee presented events surrounding their injuries and fitness to play.

By encouraging a more biographical response, players came to define their situations emotively, with recourse to the micro-politics playing out within the closed confines of the club (Potrac and Jones, 2009), and at other times in simple economic terms. All the questions formulated had a specific focus; I learnt quickly however that by permitting interviewees to articulate their stories without constraint and offering my questions as starting points, players could develop their responses in ways that were meaningful for them. This data collection approach proved worthy not only in relation to the detail and richness of the player narratives acquired, but also in terms of the kind of rapport I felt 'we' developed as an integral element of our research encounter.

Data collection

The circumstances in which the interviews were undertaken changed from one meeting to the next. To a large degree the players dictated the location, and I accepted their choices willingly and at their convenience. I attempted where possible to identify a specific site to undertake the interview within the confines of their chosen venue in order to reduce potential distractions. I was happier if I could persuade the interviewees to meet somewhere other than the football club or training ground. The more isolated the context – particularly from the surroundings of the football club – the greater the opportunity for me to gain the interviewee's full attention. I wanted to reduce the possibility that he or I would be disturbed by the presence of others, particularly colleagues or team management.

My former 'insider' status was valuable in terms of initially building an affinity with the interviewees. While my introductory admission to them that I had been a professional footballer clearly did not make me one of them, it did make me feel as though they would be less likely to see me as someone who knew nothing about the conditions of their work. I thought it might also lend greater legitimacy to my line of questioning. It is impossible to say with any certainty whether developing this initial bond – if, indeed, this is what I achieved – was helpful, as I presented myself in this fashion consistently. In the case of some of the players I was attempting to build a trusting relationship with people who were 'famous' both locally and nationally. I had obtained some knowledge of the interviewees prior to our sociological encounter. For instance, some of them were currently in, or had been involved with, international football squads, or had experienced football at the highest club levels. It was possible to read about their views concerning (mostly) football matches in which they had been involved, and some players had even spoken about career contingencies such as injury, ageing and labour mobility. Aspects of their career biographies were familiar and, thus, certain preconceived ideas about particular players had inevitably been formed prior to our meeting. Media-led interviews are relatively common occurrences for professional footballers. During these interviews they are generally reluctant to evaluate team mates or coaches overtly. However I did not want to recreate an interview similar in kind to those conducted by journalists. I wanted to understand their thoughts on their daily activities within the clubs and, in particular, about momentous and fateful moments during their careers. And in relation to these turning-points, I wanted to understand whether and how their relationships with significant others might be transformed. I was always aware however that they might view me as someone who could betray them.

Although the publicly-available information on all the interviewees did help in identifying areas for dialogue and formulating some specific questions prior to interview, I wanted to acquire more detailed and wide-ranging accounts than were commonly available from *media* sources. Additionally, among the central differences between the interviews that I conducted and those directed by journalists relates to time. The sociological interviews requested by me were considerably longer than 'normal' interviews with journalists. I accepted immediately the offers from players who were prepared to be interviewed for it is unusual to be in a position to learn intimate details about the *private* lives and thoughts of *public* figures about which a great deal is written. Insofar as I could conclude, all the players appeared openly to recount descriptions of events and express their thoughts and feelings about their experiences of both a positive and negative kind in a manner that conveyed a high level of trust.

The problem of involvement and detachment

During the process of fieldwork and data analysis I gave constant thought to the sensitising issue of the level of my former 'involvement' in this industry, and of the dynamic conceptual interplay between involvement and detachment (Elias, 1956). During each interview I was aware that, at times, I could recollect as a player experiencing certain emotions that were similar in kind (and context) to those recalled by the interviewees. During each interview I attempted to 'take the role' of the player, to view their circumstances from their perspective. Even so, although I could empathise with them when they describe unsettling career episodes, I do not recall feeling uneasy about probing passages of time which were privately (and often silently) endured. I was aware, as a researcher, that I was emotionally involved – how could I not be? – for I reacted to their commentary, yet while such involvement did not appear to paralyse my responses, it is necessary as a sociologist to recognise explicitly that my former familiarity with this occupational culture affected the research process in various ways.

The responses of some players concerned matters that were relatively new to me and at other times they recounted moments and events about which I had some experience and possessed a value stance. 'Insider' knowledge inevitably influenced the questions formulated for the interview schedule prior to the interviews; the patterns of behaviour I expected to identify; the 'meanings' players attributed to occurrences in their daily working lives; and the manner in which players interpreted fateful moments and turning-points in their careers. This list is not exhaustive however it is important sociologically to acknowledge the frames of reference that I brought to bear upon the research process. It became clear that comprehending my involvement in this familiar field of activity would generate levels of alternative, although for me no less relevant, types of data. For instance, in acknowledging the daily routines for injured players, evidence I treated at first in a largely straightforward and unreflective manner, I came to realise illuminated numerous issues related to the control of discreditable identities and asymmetrical employment relations.

Such research procedural issues were significant as I found it difficult to be neutral towards the interviewees. I liked those I interviewed and was humbled by the degree to which most seemed prepared to discuss bleaker moments in which they felt isolated from their colleagues, were distanced from their families, or considered themselves a burden physically and emotionally. I found real interest in what they had to say because I could, in part, contrast their experiences to my own (Finch, 1993). I considered continuously the balance of power between the interviewee and myself. Players are used to people in general, but particularly football supporters, treating them as though they are somehow 'special'. When I first began to interview players I too approached them with due deference. Thus, I was aware that in the context of the interview, at least initially, power differentials were skewed in their favour. I thought it was necessary to appear to be on their side when they described club micro-politics and expressed perceived moments of injustice. However, as someone who had experienced to some extent passages of vulnerability in relation to fateful moments in my own career, I came to wonder whether it was the case that my capacity for clear sociological thinking may have been clouded by my own feelings of relief of not having instrumentally pursued a career as a professional player and of establishing an alternative livelihood.

In the light of my playing experiences, I was conscious when representing their careers that I did not knowingly portray the interviewees as victims. It was clear to me that I developed sympathy for a number of them, particularly those journeymen who seemed so open when discussing their lives. My experiences of qualitative fieldwork led me to view all interviews as social encounters, and not solely as passive means of gathering research data (Burgess, 1984). One cannot neglect the fact that interviewees are people with 'meaningful' social lives and treat them simply as sources of data; as such an approach would certainly have consequences for the types or richness of data generated. I concluded that it was not enough to state that I was striving to be objective, and that it was extremely hard to have a clear understanding of whether I was achieving an appropriate balance between 'involvement' and 'detachment'. How could I, or anyone, ever be sure? It certainly seemed easier to foster analytic distance and to be neutral organising and reflecting upon interview scripts some time after the interview was conducted. It was a more difficult task to achieve an objective frame of mind in the grip of a strategic research encounter with an interviewee. It is tough to hold an assured comprehension of one's level of involvement, and I did not want to state that I had achieved a level of objectivity based on nothing more than a self-assessment of my sociological insight. I became resigned ultimately to the realisation that the degree to which I had been successful in terms of understanding the careers of professional footballers would be judged, in the fullness of time, by readers of the research.

Data analysis

Undertaking semi-structured interviews enabled me to tease out complex views and explore with respondents their wider networks of workplace relationships. In the course of interviewing, observing the interviewees, and reflecting upon their responses, sociological patterns of behaviour were identified from the outset and (re)examined during later interviews. As the fieldwork and data analysis progressed concurrently, potential enduring themes and categories of meaning slowly became apparent. Even so, I recognised that identification of themes alone fell short and offered only a naive empiricist account – in which there is no obvious engagement with theory – and so I considered these data continuously in the light of the interactionist theoretical approach adopted. Denzin (1989) suggests that the 'empirical' and 'rational' dimensions of sociology should be constantly and consciously interwoven and so, throughout the fieldwork, I reflected on each interview, and whether I needed to develop additional questions. For example, as I transcribed and read through the interview transcripts, over and over, I reconsidered questions and player responses robustly in relation to orienting concepts identified in the literature including 'career', 'identity', 'self-image', 'networks of interdependency', and 'control'. I considered whether the turning points discussed had similar meanings for players, and if they interpreted fateful moments in comparable terms. Examining 'work' from an interactionist perspective enabled an investigation of the opportunities, dangers, sanctions and rewards that characterise the living world of this occupational setting (Atkinson and Housley, 2003).

Throughout the fieldwork, and then as I (re)read the transcripts throughout the course of the data analysis, I wrestled with the identification of patterns of behaviour and the types and formulations of 'meaning' among players within playing squads. Certain themes emerged, were cross-examined thoroughly with my research supervisor – who independently considered the interview transcripts – and reached what might be termed a saturation point;

a good example of which is the notion of *career uncertainty*. My theoretical concern therefore turned to how players coped with and adapted to career uncertainties pragmatically and to the problem of the presentation of self-identity in their everyday working lives; propositions which are central to the interactionist strand of the sociology of work. In presenting the analysis for publication, my theoretically-informed interpretation of the player narratives was substantiated by the inclusion of testimony that is representative of *my interpretation* of the data set upon which this sociological analysis rests. As is customary in sociological research, I organised these data and interpreted them such that readers could comprehend the specific explanations of the broader behavioural patterns identified; in other words, I arranged the empirical evidence and accompanying explanations such that I could build up for readers a picture of what was going on in this profession. It must never be forgotten though that this analysis remains my reading of the culture of work in this industry.

In the article, I wanted to offer *WES* readers an explanation of daily life, social interaction and the production of self-identity in this occupational context. To help my endeavour I employed the famous theatrical metaphor developed by Goffman (1959), looking at what is most habitual in the ways that players perform and stage manage impressions to critical audiences within the work setting. Goffman argued that 'performances' involve individuals – in this instance football players – in continually monitoring the impressions they give off to, and make upon, others. Public identity is thus performed for an audience – coaches, team mates, club supporters – and, Goffman suggests, the private self knows that such performances are essential to identity and to the maintenance of respect and trust in routine workplace interaction. At times, distance is generated when separation exists between role (requirements) and the preservation of self-identity, and this may happen as an outcome of contingent events. For example, it was clear that missing games as a result of de-selection or injury caused major existential worries, and the following section of data exemplifies perfectly the necessity for players to develop a dramaturgical self (Collinson, 2003). When asked to comment on how he felt having to watch rather than play in games when injured, this young player responded in a manner typical of all interviewees:

Player:	Oh I don't like watching matches. I hate it. You get it stuck in your mind that someone's in your place, doing better than you, and you're not going to get back in the team.
Interviewer:	Does that lead to a conflict of interests?
Player:	It does sometimes, yes. I think it does with every player. I don't think other players would admit it, but it certainly does, yes. I mean, I don't think you blatantly want your team to lose, but you wouldn't mind them scraping a 1–0, and not playing very well and your man [the replacement] having a nightmare.

This exchange is significant in the light of an assumed sense of team ethic – portrayed by common clichés such as 'there's no I in team' – yet the player offers a more individualised take on this all but unavoidable occurrence in this occupation. In suggesting that he did not think other players would 'admit' to such self-seeking thoughts, which are clearly out of step with social conventions assumed of team workers, the player exposed a silenced but familiar way of thinking for all players who are unproductive on match days. Thus, I wanted to draw out for readers the intimate connections between the construction of self and contexts of interaction by examining the face or facade that players seek to achieve in the stylisation of their conduct with employers and work colleagues. I wanted also to offer *WES* readers an appreciation of the grim sense of the psychological costs of impression management in a workplace culture in which a premium is put on appearance.

Reflection

I worked hard to prepare for each interview but, without question, with each interview I felt I became more capable and adaptable in my approach to fieldwork. I realised quickly that there is only so much information one player could offer at one point in time – particularly when being asked to reflect on periods in their life history – and all interviewees constructed their biographies in different ways, with alternative emphases. Not all players were equally eloquent and for some I needed to find alternative ways to address the issue at hand. My ability to be flexible in approach – and to 'think on my feet' – certainly developed over this period in time.

I often despair as I read about seemingly irresponsible big-time players in the national press who fail to recognise the significance of their status as role models, yet all the players I interviewed harboured rather more 'ordinary' concerns, in spite of their apparent material comforts. Throughout the course of undertaking my research I listened carefully to numerous players, many of whom were wealthy individuals but who were struggling in ways that are rarely exposed publically and which are more-or-less silenced within the confines of the club. The following two examples are indicative of this point:

1   I interviewed one Premier League club captain at his home: a large, beautiful house. We were discussing his playing career and in particular a bad knee injury which had threatened his future when we were interrupted momentarily by his young son and daughter. At that point the mood of the interview changed abruptly and he went on to explain *at length* how desperate he had become with his inability to help them with their primary school homework. He believed he was failing them and, to use his term, he felt 'hopeless'. He said that to most onlookers he must appear to have everything, yet for him there were some simple fundamentals of life which were beyond his reach and were a cause of great disquiet.

2   I arrived at the home of one experienced player and was greeted by his wife. She explained that he was running late and that I would have to wait for him to return. Looking a little embarrassed she apologised for the 'state' [tidiness] of the house – there were removal boxes everywhere – and went on to explain that they had moved five times in two seasons as a result of his continual movement between clubs. She said that she had been very unsettled and stressed, and was increasingly resentful of her husband's job. She had been unable to find work, and their children were tired of losing friends. Neither the player, his wife nor their children were happy with their lack of stability, which was a cause of terrible unease; even so, the player needed to earn money and football was the only thing he knew.

Both examples point to routine concerns encountered by many players (and family members) who must cope with such upheavals with little support from clubs, agents, or other industry personnel. I realised throughout this research that, however prosperous players may be in the short term, in this occupation they are infantilised to varying extents, and many become socially incapacitated within the tight control structures of clubs. Personally ill-equipped to deal with (within-career) transitional life events, which were often-times played out in the public eye, in interview players became exercised also in relation to concerns associated with family life, which rarely make headlines. Following the completion of my PhD, I have continued to undertake research on the careers of professional athletes, specifically in relation to issues of welfare.

This research exposed examples of multiple workplace uncertainties; the narratives of players made clear that in all corners of their clubs it was impossible to evade the occupational contingencies which may threaten their futures. In professional football there are inherent forms of failure that are ineluctable; contexts that players attempt to avoid, but cannot. Feelings of paranoia were ubiquitous among the interviewees and many feared the prospect of job loss, chronic injury and their own biological ageing. All understood however that encountering success and misfortune were regular features of this form of labour. On reflection, my methodological concerns did not, I hope, unbalance my examination of this profession or my sociological explanation of what was going on. I always recognised however that there were many empirical and theoretical issues remaining which I did not address sufficiently well in either my doctoral thesis or in subsequently publishing peer-reviewed articles. For example, I was struck unexpectedly by my increasing fascination with the players' home lives, their partners and children, and the unceasing depths to which the structure and form of players' daily lives intruded on significant others – whether or not they were happy with this imposition. I was also disturbed by the levels of conscious self-alienation expressed by the players, which I inferred was an outcome of the cumulative effects of the ups and downs of their lives by a sport and its inhabitants which controlled their conduct heartlessly; at first for them it was all about appearances and opportunity, but in time, their souls corrupted by disappointment, the players spoke of a lack of enjoyment, of making ends meet and of feeling 'used'. Most unsettling from an academic perspective therefore is the prevailing attitude – manifest by a palpable lack of compassion – with which such stories of disillusionment are dealt with in particular by journalists and commentators. Perhaps only now, with increasing numbers of players disclosing clinical forms of depression, even among the very wealthy and apparently successful, we should be re-addressing this misguided orthodoxy through research and recognising that, as students of sport, we must once again challenge the dominant idea of the 'beautiful game'.

If you liked this chapter, you should read Chapter 1 where Carwyn Jones describes a philosophical research approach to addressing whether sport provides good role models when it comes to alcohol-related behaviour.

Notes

1 A concern experienced whilst undertaking the research was attempting to make clear when quoting from the player transcripts the changes to the titles of the football leagues and divisions. The descriptors employed related to the division in which each interviewee was playing at the time of the incident to which he was referring, or it related to the highest status position achieved by him by division.

1963–1992	1992–2004	2004–2005
Football League Division One	The FA Premier League The Premiership	The FA Premier League The Premiership
Football League Division Two	Football League Division One (i)	Football League The Championship
Football League Division Three	Football League Division Two (i)	Football League League One
Football League Division Four	Football League Division Three (i)	Football League League Two

References

Atkinson, P. and Housley, W. (2003) *Interactionism: An essay in sociological amnesia*. Sage: London.

Becker, H.S. (1967). Whose side are we on? *Social Problems, 14(3)*: 239–247.

Blair, H. (2001). You're only as good as your last job: the labour process and labour market in the British film industry. *Work, Employment and Society, 15(1)*: 149–169.

Burgess, R.G. (1984). *In the field: An introduction to field research*. Abingdon, UK: Routledge.

Cashmore, E. and Parker, A. (2003). One David Beckham? Celebrity, masculinity and the Soccerati. *Sociology of Sport Journal, 20*: 214–232.

Collinson, D.L. (2003). Identities and insecurities: Selves at work. *Organization, 10(3)*: 527–547.

Denzin, N. (1989). *The research act: A theoretical introduction to sociological methods.* Englewood Cliffs, NJ: Prentice Hall.

Elias, N. (1956). Problems of involvement and detachment. *British Journal of Sociology, 7(3)*: 226–252.

Finch, J. (1993). 'It's great to have someone to talk to': Ethics and politics of interviewing women. In M. Hammersley (ed.), *Social Research: Philosophy, Politics and Practice.* London: Sage. pp. 166–180.

Goffman, E. (1959). *The presentation of self in everyday life.* New York: Doubleday Anchor Books.

Green, C. (2009). *Every Boy's Dream: England's football future on the line.* London: A&C Black.

Halford, S. and Strangleman, T. (2009). In search of the sociology of work: Past, present and future. *Sociology, 43(5)*, 811–828.

Harding, J. (2003). *Living to play: From soccer slaves to socceratti – a social history of the professionals.* London: Robson Books.

Lawler, S. (2008). *Identity: Sociological Perspectives.* Cambridge: Polity Press.

McGillivray, D., Fearn, R. and McIntosh, A. (2005). Caught up in and by the beautiful game: A case of Scottish professional footballers. *Journal of Sport and Social Issues, 29(1)*: 102–23.

Ortiz, S.M. (2006). Using power: an exploration of control work in the sport marriage. *Sociological Perspectives, 49(4)*: 527–557.

Parker, A. (1998). Staying on-side on the inside: problems and dilemmas in ethnography. *Sociology Review, 7(3)*: 10–13.

Potrac, P. and Jones, R. (2009). Micro-political workings in semi-professional football coaching. *Sociology of Sport Journal, 26*, 557–577.

Rose, A.M., (1962) (Ed.), *Human behaviour and social processes: An interactionist approach.* Henley: Routledge.

Sennett, R. (1998). *The corrosion of character: The personal consequences of work in the new capitalism.* New York: W.W. Norton.

Silverman, D. (2001). *Interpreting qualitative data: Methods for analysing talk, text and interaction.* London: Sage.

Swain, D. (1991). Withdrawal from sport and Schlossberg's model of transitions. *Sociology of Sport Journal, 8*, 152–160.

Szymanski, S. and Kuypers, T. (1999). *Winners and losers: The business strategy of football.* London: Viking.

Turner, B.S. and Wainwright, S.P. (2003). Corps de ballet: the case of the injured ballet dancer. *Sociology of Health and Illness, 25(4)*: 269–288.

Wacquant, L. (1998). A fleshpeddler at work: Power, pain, and profit in the prizefighting economy. *Theory and Society, 27(1)*: 1–42.

Wulff, H. (2001). *Ballet across borders: Careers and culture in the world of dancers.* Oxford: Berg.

6

SPORTS BIOMECHANICS

A biomechanical modelling approach to understanding the physical demands of impact landings

Marianne J.R. Gittoes

Article reference

Gittoes, M.J.R. & Kerwin, D.G. (2009). Interactive effects of mass proportions and coupling properties on external loading in simulated forefoot impact landings. *Journal of Applied Biomechanics, 25 (3)*, 238–246.

Article summary

The article presents a biomechanical research approach used to develop understanding of the influence of a sports performer's mass profile, which includes measures of the relative proportion of soft and hard (rigid) tissues in the body, on the mechanical demands experienced in potentially injurious impact landings. Epidemiological research regarding injury rates of landings frequently performed in sport is used to inform and develop the study rationale. A contemporary simulation modelling approach, which facilitates manipulation of individual elements of a performer's mass profile, is developed and applied within the study. Findings relating to the contribution of individual mass profile characteristics (e.g., thigh mass proportions) to external impact loading are appraised to inform the inherent mechanisms that may predispose a performer to lower limb injury in a commonly executed sports manoeuvre.

Related author publications

Gittoes, M.J.R., Kerwin, D.G. & Brewin, M.A. (2009). Sensitivity of loading to the timing of joint kinematic strategies in simulated forefoot impact landings. *Journal of Applied Biomechanics, 25*, 229–237.

Gittoes, M.J.R., Brewin, M.A., & Kerwin, D.G. (2006). Soft tissue contributions to impact forces using a four-segment wobbling mass model of forefoot-heel landings. *Human Movement Science, 25,* 775–787.

Personal prologue

Injury prevention and performance enhancement are the primary objectives of any sports performer. As a performer and academic, I consider the merger of science and applied experience essential for understanding and potentially influencing the successful address of these objectives. From a personal perspective, the objectivity associated with quantitative analyses in particular, has been a key attractor of the biomechanics discipline area that I have subsequently followed within my own career and research interests. The ability to identify and monitor explicit changes in injury potential and performance due to the systematic procedures involved in quantitative research, supported my interest in using biomechanics theory to inform applied practice in sport and exercise.

My initial interest in the biomechanics of impacts emerged following my BSc degree in Physical Education and Sport Science (Loughborough University, 2000). At the time, female participation in sport and exercise was rapidly increasing with a consequential alarming rise in injury prevalence. Since the maintenance of physical activity is crucial both for the development of competitive performance and in ensuring the pursuit of a healthy lifestyle, an understanding of mechanisms that may assist injury prevention emerged as an important and potentially rewarding research area to examine. I subsequently began to investigate injury rates in physically active and competitive female performers and identified a high prevalence in demanding activities involving rapid impacts with the ground (e.g., football cutting movements, landing from a jump in basketball). The chance to pursue a PhD with Professor Kerwin (a leading authority in sports biomechanics) at the University of Bath provided an invaluable opportunity for me to examine the specific research problem, and to therefore contribute to the development of injury prevention strategies in sport and exercise.

Gaining an understanding of injury mechanisms from a biomechanical perspective has been inherently challenging due to the existence of multiple potential risk factors or mechanisms (e.g., a performer's technique, experience, conditioning, and anatomical profiles). Similar to many sports biomechanists, I began to address the research problem using a traditional experimental approach, which focused on the collection of field or laboratory data. However, following a review of the relevant literature and a further acknowledgement of the difficulty in testing injury mechanisms using non-invasive measurement techniques, it emerged that in order to gain a further insight into the research problem an alternative approach should be considered. My research over the past 10 years has subsequently focused on developing a mechanical knowledge of potentially injurious impacts using a less conventional biomechanical modelling approach. The chapter describes the research process undertaken to examine the specific influence of innate and regulatory mass profiles of female performers on the subsequent loads experienced in challenging and potentially injurious impacts.

Moving from a research problem to a research question

Injury trend data from epidemiology studies suggested female performers involved in impact sports were predisposed to injury. Compared with males participating in the same sports, females had been found to be 4–5 times more likely to sustain a knee injury in impact movements (Hewett, 2000). The initial review of literature I had conducted in 2000 demonstrated that the causes of women sports injuries had been a topic of vigorous speculation, particularly in the late 1990s. Several mechanisms including a performer's lower leg alignment (Arendt, 1996) and use of an improper landing technique (Boden, Griffin, & Garrett Jr., 2000) had been highlighted as primary mechanisms influencing the loads (i.e., forces acting on the body) experienced by females. However, problems in identifying and gaining an understanding of how each mechanism individually influenced or contributed to loading and injury predisposition were emerging from the research.

The ability of a performer to modify their landing technique had frequently been discussed as being influential in the success with which loading on the body may be attenuated (McNitt-Gray, 1991). Biomechanical studies of impacts had subsequently attempted to obtain empirical evidence of the influence of regulatory (modifiable) landing techniques on the predisposition of performers to high loading conditions, and a subsequent increased injury risk. A prevalence of studies examining gender differences in landing techniques emerged in the literature, and suggested a tendency for females to use diverse lower body techniques to perform simple landings when compared with males. For example, a study conducted by Decker et al. (2003) had reported that females may partly be at a greater risk of knee injury compared with males because of the use of a 7° more extended joint during first contact with the ground. However, due to difficulties in isolating and controlling independent joint motions (e.g., the amount of knee flexion in field or laboratory studies), limited consensus on the effects of gender-specific landing techniques had been achieved.

Following a focus on gender-based comparisons, and an innate injury predisposition in impact landings, contemporary theories relating to internal (within the body) mechanisms were becoming more prominent in the literature. Body mass (magnitude) and mass proportion (relative amount of soft and rigid tissue masses in the body) were introduced as possible contributors to the external loads (e.g., ground contact force), experienced during running impacts (Liu & Nigg, 2000). Higher ground contact forces were evident with increased rigidity in the lower body and greater magnitudes of either movable soft tissue (wobbling mass) or rigid mass. Wobbling mass had typically been defined as the combined movable skin, adipose tissue and muscle of the body, whereas bone has been considered to be rigid mass.

Diverse mass and mass proportions within the body (innate mass profile) potentially explained a predisposition to high external ground contact forces during running. However, limited insight existed into the influence of innate wobbling and rigid mass profiles on the loads experienced in more dynamic landings, which are traditionally associated with traumatic injuries in sport. Further examination of the effects of a performer's innate mass profile was subsequently warranted in order to assist the long-term development of landing techniques and injury prevention strategies.

While injury prevention strategies may be developed to accommodate an individual's own mass and mass proportion profile, there are obvious limitations in the extent to which these could be manipulated for an individual performer (i.e., the size and shape of an individual is partially defined by their genetics). A regulatory mechanism associated with the mass profiles of the body was however emerging within the research area. That is, individuals potentially possessed the ability to regulate how soft tissue vibrates by altering the coupling (the way in which masses are linked or joined together) between soft and rigid masses (Wakeling, Von Tscharner, Nigg & Stergiou, 2001). The mass coupling profiles had been considered a partial response of conscious or involuntary muscle activity (muscle tuning) and had been found to assist the reduction of ground contact forces in running (Nigg & Liu, 1999). Muscle tuning was therefore emerging as an important regulatory mechanism that may be used to attenuate the external loads experienced in impacts.

Investigations of mechanisms influencing the loads experienced in impacts had typically been approached using laboratory data collections and direct intervention requiring control over the mechanism of interest. However, due to clear problems in controlling and manipulating the innate and regulatory mass profiles of a performer, insight into the effect of the respective mechanisms on loading in impact landings had been inhibited. It was clear that an alternative research approach was necessitated in order to gain a better understanding of the research area.

The critique of the *epidemiological* and *empirical research* literature had highlighted a number of important research questions. The progression of the emerging questions further supported the need to consider an intervention design in the selected research approach.

Emerging research questions

1   Are female performers of dynamic impact landings predisposed to high loading on the body because of their innate mass profile?
2   What are the mass and mass proportion profiles of female performers who experience high loads in dynamic landings?

3   Are performers able to alleviate the loads imposed by their innate mass profiles using sensitive, regulatory strategies (e.g., muscle tuning, landing technique changes)?
4   What strategies can be used to alleviate the high loads incurred by an individual's innate mass profile?

Following an appraisal of the key questions emerging from the review of literature, and as exemplified in the first stage of the research process I employed, a clearly-defined aim was developed for my study:

Research aim

*   To develop understanding of how a performer's mass profile contributes to the external loads incurred in potentially injurious impact landings using a biomechanical research approach.

In order to ensure a maintained address of the overall research aim, I developed an explicit research question and several underpinning objectives, which could be achieved within the time-frame of the specific study:

Research question

How do innate and regulatory wobbling and rigid mass profiles contribute to the ground contact forces experienced by female performers in potentially injurious impact landings?

Study objectives

1   To develop and apply a biomechanical research approach, which would allow specific examination of the innate and regulatory mass profiles to external loading in potentially injurious impact landings;
2   To appropriately control and modify a performer's wobbling and rigid mass, mass proportion and mass coupling profile using a 'true' experimental design whilst maintaining ecological validity;
3   To quantitatively examine the independent (separate manipulation of the innate and regulatory factors) and combined (simultaneous manipulation of the innate and regulatory factors) mass profile effects on the ground contact forces experienced during impact landings.

Choice of method (Matching the method to the research question)

The method of scientific inquiry is one of the most demanding in terms of the systematic and rigorous techniques employed. Biomechanical studies have traditionally employed *field or laboratory data collections* to maintain external and ecological validity, and to systematically control or modify variables of interest, respectively. For example, Zhang et al. (2000) manipulated the step-off landing height in a laboratory study examining ankle, knee and hip joint contributions to energy dissipation in landing.

In order to appropriately address the research question, it had become clear that an intervention design that allowed the mass profile of the human performer to be modified was necessary. However, traditional field or laboratory studies could not be used to facilitate the intervention (i.e., manipulation of the performer's mass profile) and to achieve the internal validity (i.e., independent control of variables such as the amount of thigh mass) required. An alternative *biomechanical modelling research approach* was considered, which due to the use of a 'modelled' rather than an 'actual' living human performer, would allow control and isolated manipulation of the mechanisms of interest. For example, the 'modelled' performer's mass proportions of the lower body could be readily changed without invasive or unrealistic intervention. While the biomechanical modelling approach initially offered a logical solution to the problem of mechanism control that is commonly associated with more traditional scientific approaches, a potential lack of realism to the living performer was a justifiable concern.

In a review of the future of biomechanics research, Yeadon and Challis (1994) had advocated the use of an integrated theoretical-experimental approach (see Figure 6.1), suggesting that experimental (field or laboratory) data may be used to 'ensure that the model has sufficient accuracy and to provide realistic input data on which to base simulation (experimentation) analyses'.

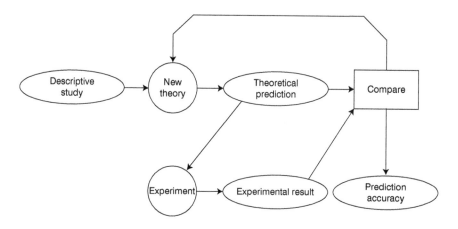

FIGURE 6.1   The theoretical-experimental approach to scientific research (adapted from Yeadon & Challis, 1994)

Nigg (1999) had further described a series of steps common for the development of biomechanical models comprising:

1   Definition of research question(s)
2   Definition of the system of interest
3   Review of existing knowledge
4   Selection of procedure (model) to be applied
5   Simplifications and assumptions
6   Mathematical formulation
7   Mathematical solution (using appropriate input data)
8   Evaluation of the model
9   Discussion, interpretation and application of results
10 Conclusions.

While Nigg's approach highlighted the necessity to evaluate the model to maintain validity, the importance of using field or laboratory data from the system of interest (frequently the human body) in the model development and evaluation was not recognised. I developed and used an adapted theoretical-experimental approach to integrate the external validity associated with a traditional field or laboratory approach with the internal validity provided by the theoretical approach. The adapted version, which incorporated a more comprehensive address of how field (or laboratory) data could be integrated into the theoretical prediction stage defined by Yeadon and Challis (1994), is represented by Stage 2 and Stage 3 of the research process I employed (see Figure 6.2).

Field data collection

The collection of field data in Stage 2 was necessary to alleviate the potential lack of realism that had been linked to a purely theoretical approach. To allow for a potential sensitivity in the research outcome to different performers' mass profiles and landing techniques, multiple single-subject studies were employed. The field data were required to personalise the model (developed in Stage 3) to each human performer (Individual Customisation) being investigated and the individual landing performances being executed (Movement Customisation).

Unlike previous theoretical studies of landing, which have typically examined dynamic movements performed by males, female-specific field data were obtained for this investigation. The focus on female performers ensured an explicit address of the research problem, which had highlighted high relative injury rates compared with males. A negative aspect of the single-subject/performer approach was that only two performers could be investigated due to the time required to develop and apply the model (i.e., approximately 3 years). As highlighted by Bates, James and Dufek (2004), the single-subject design provided an explicit advantage in allowing the effects of a number of treatment

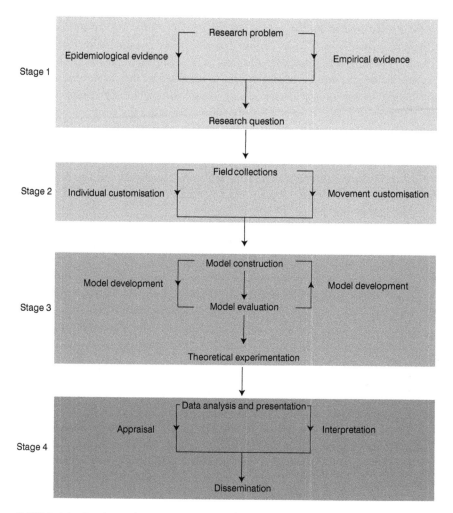

FIGURE 6.2 A schematic representation of the process undertaken to address the research problem

conditions to be effectively evaluated, which was pertinent to the respective research problem.

The primary concerns I had in collecting the field data for Stage 2 of the process were centred on ensuring data could be obtained ethically, non-invasively and accurately using laboratory measurement systems. The submission of, and subsequent local approval of, a written ethical application ensured the planned protocol was valid and safe, and that the measurement techniques were risk free and non-invasive in nature. Prior to the submission of the ethical application, a risk assessment was conducted by a specialist laboratory technician to ensure the data collection area was hazard-free and the measurement equipment was reliable and safe to use on human performers. Enabling studies (small experiments or pilot tests used to inform a larger study or data collection) conducted over several months allowed the development and application of methods required to obtain accurate and ecologically valid field data. While enabling studies may not provide innovative and original advances in knowledge, they are a fundamental component of rigorous scientific inquiry and ensure the distinct objectives of the research aim can be systematically addressed using the proposed research approach. The following enabling studies were conducted prior to the final field collections in Stage 2 of the research process:

- *Enabling Study 1*. Establishment of a safe and ecologically valid protocol that detailed the landing manoeuvre, and height and surface conditions for the field collections (Stage 2: Field Collections);
- *Enabling Study 2*. Development and evaluation of a method (Gittoes & Kerwin, 2006) to determine each performer's size and shape profiles for the model (Stage 2: Individual Customisation);
- *Enabling Study 3*. Development of a method to estimate the elastic properties (e.g., tendon stiffness) of performers (Stage 2: Individual Customisation);
- *Enabling Study 4*. Determination of the accuracy of defining landing techniques using motion analysis markers placed on joint centres (e.g., ankle, knee joints) (Stage 2: Movement Customisation)

Model construction

Since a model requires a simplified representation of the system or object being investigated, the model construction (Stage 3) required a number of *assumptions* to be made about the complexity of the human body. The degree to which the mechanical properties of the human body are known and the level of understanding required to answer the research questions were the primary factors used to decide on the model complexity.

A key objective of the construction process was to create a model that was complex enough to appropriately represent the human body but simple enough to allow the actual performer to be represented using 'real' data within the study timeframe. While I initially considered the inclusion of individual muscles in the model to reflect the joint force production contributions in the landing movements, King and Yeadon (2004) had highlighted that it can be difficult to obtain subject/performer-specific muscle parameters (e.g., strength characteristics, muscle stiffness). In order to inform the following decisions about the features of the model, a thorough appraisal of the field data and previous research in the area was undertaken:

1   *Complexity of human body segmentation:* The human body is made up of multiple segments such as the foot and thigh that contribute to the creation and control of movement. The model had to be capable of replicating the phasic joint-by-joint landing technique used by performers (McNittGray,

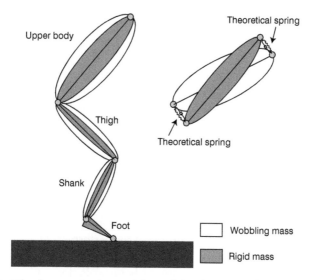

FIGURE 6.3 The human body model used in the research approach (adapted from Gittoes & Kerwin, 2009). The individual wobbling and rigid masses, and the theoretical springs used to control the wobbling mass motion are illustrated

1991). The foot, shank, thigh and upper body were considered primary segments contributing to the technique employed in landing and were therefore integrated into the constructed model (see Figure 6.3).

2   *Complexity of movement/technique represented:* Epidemiological research, which investigates health and illness distributions in a population, had indicated a high prevalence of injury in traditionally performed forefoot-first ground contact landings (e.g., as executed in gymnastic dismounting). The final field collections (Stage 2), further supported a preference for forefoot-first techniques in the 'real' landing performances. The model therefore integrated a separate foot segment, and heel and forefoot ground contact forces. The foot construction features were a new and innovative development since other models of impact landings (Gruber et al., 1998; Pain & Challis, 2002) had typically ignored the foot's leverage (the mechanical advantage gained from using the foot) and were therefore restricted to examination of less traditionally performed heel-first landings.

3   *Complexity of segment mass division:* The simplification of the human body to rigid, rod-like segments has been common in models traditionally used to investigate dynamic movements. Empirical information from high-speed filming of impacts had however clearly illustrated that the soft tissues of the human body 'start to wobble in a complex damped manner' (Gruber et al., 1998). Soft tissue motion analyses I obtained in the final field collections further provided quantitative evidence that wobbling masses (i.e., muscles, skin and fat) move differently to rigid masses (i.e., bones) in dynamic impacts. The shank, thigh and upper body segments were consequently

divided into separate wobbling and rigid masses in order to ensure a full understanding of how the respective mass characteristics may influence the ground contact forces experienced.

4   *Complexity of wobbling mass movement:* A consideration of the type and amount of wobbling mass motion allowed was needed to accommodate the diverse mass motions in the body. It was clear from the field data that soft tissue moves in a complex manner (i.e., it vibrates, moves from side to side, and up and down). The permitted wobbling mass motion therefore had to be simplified to prevent extensive development time and over complication.

Simple theoretical spring systems (see Figure 6.3), which had been used previously in human body models (Gruber et al., 1998; Pain & Challis, 2001) were selected to control the wobbling mass motion and represented the mass coupling (stiffness and damping) profile of the performer. The springs' stiffness dictated the 'bounciness' of the wobbling mass motion and the springs' damping helped to gradually reduce the amount of 'bounce'. Performer-specific estimates for the mass coupling stiffness and damping properties were derived from skin marker movement analyses of the final field collections. The determination of the mass, mass proportion and coupling profiles of each performer was a particularly challenging aspect of the research due to the difficulty in obtaining appropriate 'real' values and the innovative integration of these features in a model used to investigate human landings.

Model evaluation and development

Following the model construction, Stage 3 of the research process was centred on the evaluation and development of the human body model. The evaluation provides an indication of the level of confidence that can be given to a model. As highlighted by Yeadon and King (2002), little credence should be given to the published results and conclusions without such an evaluation. In biomechanical research, a successful evaluation should ideally comprise a *quantitative comparison* of the theoretical and 'real' motion. Since the model I had constructed was being used to examine ground contact forces, the evaluation compared the theoretical ground contact forces of a landing performance with the corresponding 'real' force plate measurements obtained in the final field collections. Key features of the ground contact forces such as the maximum force experienced were specifically compared and selected due to an established link to a high injury potential.

The model evaluation demonstrated a reasonable level of agreement between the theoretical and measured ground contact forces (e.g., less than a 10 per cent difference in the maximum vertical ground contact force). Based on the level of success indicated by the evaluation, I undertook an arduous development process to improve the model assumptions I had initially made. Critical appraisal of my initial attempt at the model was necessary to allow the research to progress. I had originally restricted the wobbling mass motion along the length of ('up and down') and perpendicular to ('side to side') the rigid mass. Following a further appraisal of the empirical literature and final field data, I later modified the location of the theoretical springs (see Figure 6.3) to allow the wobbling mass to additionally rotate, thereby increasing the complexity with which soft tissue motion was represented in the model. The modified model was re-evaluated by a repeated, quantitative assessment of the level of agreement achieved between the theoretical and measured ground contact forces. The model developments were considered successful due to the subsequent improvement in the model accuracy, which was indicated by a lower percentage difference between the theoretical and measured ground contact forces.

Further developments and evaluations of the original model were achieved over a six-month period. The *evaluation–development–evaluation cycle* was a particularly challenging and time-consuming aspect of the research approach that was complicated by the difficulty in deciding when the model became 'accurate enough'. However, the use of a quantitative comparison (e.g., determination of the percentage difference measure between the theoretical and measured data) in the evaluation was a clear benefit of the approach since I was able to ascertain a level of *objectivity* based on numerical outcomes to inform the repeated developments.

Theoretical experimentation

Final evaluations indicated the human body model successfully replicated 'real' landing performances (i.e., similar loading measures were obtained with comparable landing techniques) and could therefore be used to conduct theoretical experiments to address the research question. A true experiment requires a change in the value of one variable (independent) to be made and the distinct effects on another variable (dependent) to be ascertained. True experiments are idealised in scientific research to allow an insight into causality (the identification of factors that have a direct influence on the measures of interest) but are typically precluded in field or laboratory studies due to difficulties in imposing control over the independent variable(s). For example, when examining the influence of the knee motion (independent variable) on sprint running velocity (dependent variable), absolute control over the knee action is required without a simultaneous modification in the co-joining ankle and hip motions. The ability to perform 'true' theoretical experiments (simulations) using the biomechanical modelling approach offered a distinct advantage over more traditional research approaches since a precise method of looking for evidence of causality between variables/mechanisms of interest (i.e., wobbling mass profiles and impact forces) could be achieved.

The theoretical experiments conducted in my research incurred a series of mass, mass proportion and coupling property manipulations for each performer. The level of manipulation had to be representative of natural variation (e.g., mass proportion differences between individuals), or modifications that could realistically be implemented (e.g., changes in mass coupling stiffness). The design process therefore required an examination of previously reported research and empirical studies to ensure independent variable changes within a realistic set of boundaries and a subsequent successful address of the research question. For example, the boundaries imposed for the mass coupling changes were selected to ensure that the amount of movement in the theoretical wobbling masses was realistic for humans. The following experiments were subsequently performed:

- *Experiment 1*: Independent manipulation (changes of ±5 per cent) of the 'real' wobbling and rigid mass proportions of the segments and whole body while maintaining the 'real' total mass of each segment (8 experiments for each performer).
  Purpose: To further understanding of the influence of a female performer's innate mass profile on the external loads experienced in potentially injurious landings.
- *Experiment 2*: Independent manipulation of the mass coupling stiffness and damping of each segment (±5 per cent of the 'real' values) while maintaining the 'real' mass proportions.
  Purpose: To gain insight into the influence of regulatory mass profile adaptations to the external loads experienced in potentially injurious landings.
- *Experiment 3*: Simultaneous manipulation of the mass coupling stiffness and damping of each segment (±5 per cent of the 'real' values) while maintaining the 'real' mass proportions.
  Purpose: To examine the sensitivity of the external loads experienced in potentially injurious landings to the multiple factors contributing to mass profile adaptations.
- *Experiment 4*: Simultaneous modifications to the 'real' mass proportions (5 per cent of the 'real' values), and mass coupling stiffness and damping properties (5 per cent of the 'real' values) of each segment and the whole body.
  Purpose: To gain an understanding of whether a female performer may adapt their mass coupling profile to influence the external loads incurred by their innate mass profile.

A direct relationship between injury potential and the ground contact forces experienced in impacts has proved difficult to establish (Nigg, Cole & Brüggemann, 1995). Measurement of the magnitude, rate, frequency and direction of the ground contact forces has, however, provided valuable insight into the loads experienced by the lower body in landing (McNitt-Gray, 1991) and the resulting potential risk of traumatic and chronic injury. Due to the dominance of vertical motion in impact landings, and the typical predisposition to traumatic injuries, the maximum ground contact force experienced in a vertical direction was selected as the primary dependent variable examined in the theoretical experiments.

Data analysis

As a consequence of a low sample size (typically one individual) and the subsequent difficulty in extrapolating the findings to a wider population, the successful application of a *performer-specific research approach* may be undermined by the existence of low external validity (Williams & Wragg, 2004). However, following experiences in using more traditional group analyses, I was aware of the possibility of masking the contributions of the mechanisms under investigation as a result of 'averaging' data for a group or sample. That is, grouping the key dependent measures (e.g., maximum ground contact force) in the study may have hindered the extent to which important factors contributing to individual loading predisposition could be ascertained. As a biomechanist specialising in understanding injury potential, I preferred a performer-specific analysis of the data generated in the theoretical experiments since the influence of the important mechanical contributors (i.e., rigid mass proportions and mass coupling properties) could be readily identified by the presence or absence of common responses (i.e., consistent increases or decreases in the ground contact forces) for several individuals. Furthermore, injury diagnoses performed by clinicians are typically specific to individuals and so I selected an analysis approach that would allow insight into the performer-specific mechanical contributors to injury predisposition.

Traditional inferential statistical analyses were discarded in my data analyses due to the reliance on large sample sizes that reflect a general population. Descriptive statistics were more appropriately employed in the model evaluation process since summaries of large data sets (i.e., continuous ground contact time profiles) using typical mean or average measures were required. Descriptive statistics were however negated for the main study analysis due to the potential masking of performer-specific responses in the discrete measure under investigation. *Direct quantitative comparisons, which included measurement of the absolute and percentage (relative) difference between discrete measures* of the theoretical ground contact forces incurred before and after each experimental manipulation, were alternatively made.

Data presentation

The selected mode of presentation was reflective of the distinct analysis approaches employed to address the individual research objectives of the study. Continuous time profiles of the theoretical and 'real' ground contact forces in a vertical (GFz) and horizontal (GFy) direction were presented for the impact landings (see Figure 6.4a). Although not directly informing the research question, the presented data were required to *address Study Objective 1* and to consequently indicate the model's success (accuracy) in replicating the impact forces for the duration of the movement, and not only the discrete measure of interest. In order to successfully *address Study Objective 3* and the overall research question, the presented results were focused on the performer-specific changes (e.g., Figure 6.4b) in the discrete measures (maximum vertical ground contact force: GFz_{max}) incurred in the theoretical experiments.

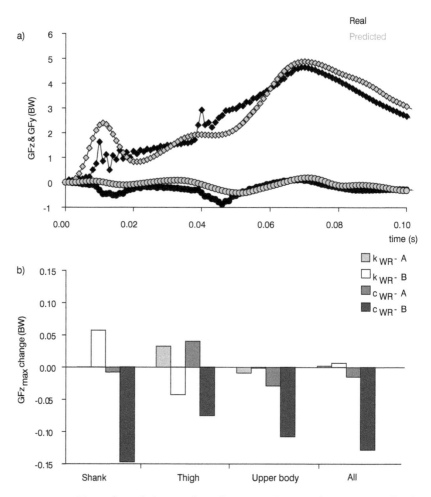

FIGURE 6.4 Examples of the modes of presentation used to present the key quantitative results. a) Time profiles used to present continuous quantitative data for the model evaluation. The profile illustrates the GFz (diamonds) and GFy (circles) ground contact force profiles for the 'real' and theoretical landing movements respectively. b) A bar chart representing discrete measures of the ground contact force changes produced with mass coupling stiffness (KWR) and damping (CWR) modifications (experiment 2) for individual performers (A & B) (adapted from Gittoes & Kerwin, 2009)

Interpretation and appraisal of findings

The appropriate interpretation and appraisal of data is perhaps one of the most challenging aspects of research and must reflect the primary research approach used. The interpretation of data using a case study approach is, for example, distinguished by the use of personal opinion. In contrast, the performer-specific approach I employed required an *interpretation of the data findings based on fact* (i.e., mechanical theory). The use of theoretical principles and fact, rather than opinion, ensured a maintained biomechanical perspective to my research and a simultaneous adherence to the requirements of a scientific research approach. As a consequence of the multiple data sets generated in the theoretical experiments I found it useful to develop a set of guidelines to adhere to when interpreting the data findings:

1   *Identify distinct performer responses:* Idiosyncratic responses could inform the development of customised injury prevention interventions;
2   *Identify similarities in performer responses:* Although using a performer-specific design, consideration of common responses in the performers may indicate important mechanical contributors to injury potential;
3   *Consider trivial and substantial changes:* A negligible change in the dependent measure may be as informative as a prominent change when identifying important contributors to the external loads experienced by the performers;
4   *Consider separate and interactive mechanism outcomes:* A quantitative comparison of the relative differences (e.g., percentage differences) in the discrete measure incurred in the single and combined factor experiments could indicate the most prominent contributing mechanisms;
5   *Maintain consideration of the wider research and practical implications:* The key findings should be appraised in relation to the original research aim (i.e., to develop insight into the contribution of a performer's mass profile to external loading in impact landings) using supporting literature and theoretical principles. Caution should be taken in suggesting explicit practical implementation of the findings based on the causal links established.

The primary findings were subsequently discussed using a logical appraisal comprising: the identification of the key finding (key finding); support using previous research (research support); explanation based on theory (theoretical explanation) and consideration of the implications (implication). The process undertaken to appraise the findings was exemplified in the following discussion points:

1   The ground contact force experienced by the performers was especially sensitive to their innate mass proportions (*key finding*). Liu and Nigg (2000) had previously suggested that ground contact force peaks in simulated running impacts were significantly heightened due to increased rigidity in the lower extremity (*research support*). Individuals may be susceptible to high and potentially injurious loading on the body in forefoot-first impact landings and less dynamic heel-first running impacts due to their innate mass profile (*implication*).
2   Mass coupling changes were typically not beneficial in attenuating the substantially higher maximum ground contact force generated with larger

rigid mass proportions (*key finding*). Pain and Challis (2004) similarly found that the forces experienced during a heel impact were sensitive to bone mass while the mass coupling stiffness produced a smaller effect (*research support*). A performer's predisposition to high loads in impact landings may not successfully be overridden by regulatory changes to mass coupling profiles through muscle tuning (*implication*).

3   Performer-specific responses were evident with mass coupling changes incurred independently or when combined with mass proportion changes (*key finding*). The finding confirmed the suggestion of Nigg and Liu (1999) that if the concept of muscle tuning is correct, a subject-specific response to loading should be expected (*research support*). Muscle force levels had been linked (Boyer & Nigg, 2006) to mass coupling stiffness while the visco-elastic nature of biological tissues had been linked to mass coupling damping responses. The performer-specific responses may therefore be partially explained by individual variations in muscle strength and structure, as well as the muscle activity generated (*theoretical explanation*).

Dissemination

While the study findings had enhanced understanding of the research problem, I was aware that research only truly makes an impact when communicated to the relevant people and communities. The initial dissemination of the research approach and subsequent findings to colleagues and peers was therefore an integral and carefully planned element of Stage 4 of the research process. While the communication of research is continuous throughout an academic career, I originally selected two traditional dissemination pathways:

1   *Abstract presentation* at national and international research conferences The conference abstract presentation provided an opportunity to receive feedback on preliminary findings, which later informed the development of a full research paper. Example: Gittoes, M.J.R., Kerwin, D.G. & Brewin, M.A. (2007). The influence of mass proportions and coupling stiffness on loading in a simulated forefoot-heel landing. In *Proceedings of the XXVth International Symposium on Biomechanics in Sport*, Ouro Preto, Brazil, 341–344.

2   Publication of a *full research article* in a peer reviewed journal The publication of a full article in the *Journal of Applied Biomechanics* allowed the research to be more formally communicated to a wider audience (e.g., sport, exercise, clinical and medical biomechanists) than achieved with the abstract presentation alone. Example: Gittoes, M.J.R. & Kerwin, D.G. (2009). Interactive effects of mass proportions and coupling properties on external loading in simulated forefoot impact landings. *Journal of Applied Biomechanics, 25 (3)*, 238–246.

Contribution to knowledge

Through a successful address of the research aim, the study made clear contributions to applied knowledge. Research studies in the area had previously focused on using field or laboratory approaches to gain insight into the physical demands of potentially injurious landings (e.g., Decker et al., 2003). The knowledge gained had subsequently been restricted by the descriptive level of questioning ('what?') that could be achieved. The less conventional research approach I employed also allowed a descriptive address of the research problem by demonstrating that a performer's innate and regulatory mass profile contributed to the ground contact forces experienced in potentially injurious landings. However, the theoretical approach further ensured a more comprehensive contribution to knowledge by allowing the scope of questioning to be extended to examining cause and effect ('how?') questions. The ability to isolate the effects caused by each mechanism allowed an explicit link between the wobbling mass profiles and discrete impact force measures to be ascertained, and an effective address of Study Objective 2. Furthermore, comparisons of the separate and interacting quantitative effects incurred by the mechanisms allowed the 'most influential' mechanism (mass proportion profile) to be distinguished and a successful address of Study Objective 3. The wobbling mass coupling properties (muscle tuning responses) were found to have less influence on the impact loading than the proportion of rigid mass in the body. A primary contribution of the study was subsequently evident in the suggestion that muscle activation (tuning) changes may not successfully overcome an individual's innate predisposition to high impact loading.

Impact on practice

A contribution to research practice was explicitly made by the study through the successful address of Study Objective 1, which was centred on identifying and developing a suitable biomechanical research approach to answer the research question. The constructed human body model represented the first formulation of a 'wobbling mass' model used to investigate impact landings that incorporated a foot segment. Previous models had typically been restricted to investigation of less commonly performed heel-only impacts (e.g., Gruber et al., 1998). Traditional models may continue to enhance insight into the chronic loads associated with running and potential for overuse injuries due to the tendency for performers to initially impact the ground with the heel. However, the appraisal of recent epidemiological and empirical literature had indicated that investigation of more dynamic impacts was warranted and required a unique consideration of the mechanics associated with more commonly incurred traumatic injuries. The innovative inclusion of the leverage of the foot in my constructed model ensured future investigation of dynamic landings (forefoot-only or forefoot-heel) eliciting particularly challenging loading conditions could successfully be achieved. When combined with a performer-specific analysis, the application of the constructed model provided insight into an individual performer's predisposition to high impact loading, and possible injury in dynamic landings. From an applied practice perspective, the study highlighted the benefits of considering individual responses in developing customised training and injury programmes for sport and exercise.

Reflection

In order to inform my future research, an appraisal of the research process undertaken in this study was important. On reflection, my readiness to consider a research approach that I was less familiar with was invaluable in allowing the study to make a notable and timely contribution to knowledge in the research area. While the need to develop a 'novel' set of research skills and a 'new' way of thinking was particularly challenging in the early stages of the research process, I have since been able to use the acquired skills and experiences to consider a wider scope of opportunities in terms of research questioning.

For future development, I continue to be aware of the need to review the way in which the human body is modelled to address the more complex research problems that will inevitably evolve in sport and exercise. For example, I accept that the simplistic approach used to represent soft tissue in my model restricts investigation of the individual effects of different masses (e.g., muscles and fat in the body). At the same time, I continue to recognise the need for simplicity and maintenance of ecological validity in the biomechanical modelling approach such that over-complication may lead to difficulties in obtaining 'real' data in the individual customisation process (Stage 2). Achieving an appropriate balance between simplicity and complexity was evidently crucial in determining the success of the approach used.

From an applied perspective, research should ideally have a meaningful impact on the wider community. The investigation of only two performers within this study was realistic within the time-frame of the study and successfully achieved the objectives of a performer-specific approach. The application of findings to the wider community was undoubtedly restricted by the respective approach. However, with an increasing emphasis on customised training programmes, gait re-training and individual injury prevention strategies, I continue to believe the biomechanical modelling approach has a distinct and valuable contribution to make in applied sport and exercise practice.

On final reflection, my experiences as a researcher have taught me that one of the most important outcomes of a research study is the natural evolvement of new research questions. While I will continue to consider the strengths of the theoretical approach when addressing future questions, I remain open-minded about investigating alternative approaches and solutions.

If you liked this chapter, you should check out Chapter 10 where Nic James describes a research process focused on developing a reliable framework for measuring performance in rugby, and Chapters 8 and 12 that use figures to represent research findings.

References

Arendt, E.A. (1996). Common musculo-skeletal injuries in women. *The Physician and Sports Medicine, 24,* 39–50.

Bates, B.T., James, C.R., & Dufek, J.S. (2004). Single subject analysis. In N. Stergiou (Ed.) *Innovative analyses of human movement.* Champaign, IL: Human Kinetics. p. 15.

Boden, B.P., Griffin, L.Y., & Garrett Jr, W.E. (2000). Etiology and prevention of noncontact ACL injury. *The Physician and Sports Medicine, 28,* 53–60.

Boyer, K.A., & Nigg, B.M. (2006). Soft tissue vibrations within one soft tissue compartment. *Journal of Biomechanics, 39,* 645–651.

Decker, M.J., Torry, M.R., Wyland, D.J., Sterett, W.I., & Steadman, J.R. (2003). Gender differences in lower extremity kinematics, kinetics and energy absorption during landings. *Clinical Biomechanics, 18,* 662–669.

Gittoes, M.J.R., & Kerwin, D.G. (2006). Component inertia modeling of segmental wobbling and rigid masses. *Journal of Applied Biomechanics, 22,* 148–154.

Gittoes, M.J.R., & Kerwin, D.G. (2009). Interactive effects of mass proportions and coupling properties on external loading in simulated forefoot impact landings. *Journal of Applied Biomechanics, 25,* 238–246.

Gittoes, M.J.R., Kerwin, D.G., & Brewin, M.A. (2007). The influence of mass proportions and coupling stiffness on loading in a simulated forefoot-heel landing. In *Proceedings of the XXVth International Symposium on Biomechanics in Sport,* Ouro Preto, Brazil, 341–344.

Gruber, K., Ruder, H., Denoth, J., & Schneider, K. (1998). A comparative study of impact dynamics: Wobbling mass model versus rigid body models. *Journal of Biomechanics, 31,* 439–444.

Hewett, T.E. (2000). Neuromuscular and hormonal factors associated with knee injuries in female athletes. *Sports Medicine, 29,* 313–327.

King, M.A., & Yeadon, M.R. (2004). Maximising somersault rotation in tumbling. *Journal of Biomechanics, 37,* 471–477

Liu, W., & Nigg, B.M. (2000). A mechanical model to determine the influence of masses and mass distribution on the impact force during running. *Journal of Biomechanics, 33,* 219–224.

McNitt-Gray, J.L. (1991). Kinematics and impulse characteristics of drop landings from three heights. *International Journal of Sport Biomechanics, 7,* 201–224.

Nigg, B.M. (1999). A nearly possible story. In B.M. Nigg & W. Herzog (Eds) *Biomechanics of the musculo-skeletal system.* 2nd edition. New York: Wiley.

Nigg, B.M., & Liu, W. (1999). The effect of muscle stiffness and damping on simulated impact force peaks during running. *Journal of Biomechanics, 32,* 849–856.

Nigg, B.M., Cole, G.K., & Brüggemann, G.P. (1995). Impact forces during heel toe running. *Journal of Applied Biomechanics, 11,* 407–432.

Pain, M.T.G., & Challis, J.H. (2001). The role of the heel pad and shank soft tissue during impacts: A further resolution of a paradox. *Journal of Biomechanics, 34,* 1061–1066.

Pain, M.T.G., & Challis, J.H. (2002). Soft tissue motion during impacts: their potential contributions to energy dissipation. *Journal of Applied Biomechanics, 18,* 231–242.

Pain, M.T.G., & Challis, J.H. (2004). Wobbling mass influence on impact ground reaction forces: A simulation model sensitivity analysis. *Journal of Applied Biomechanics*, *20*, 309–316.

Wakeling, J.M., Von Tscharner, V., Nigg, B.M., & Stergiou, P. (2001). Muscle activity in the leg is tuned in response to ground reaction forces. *Journal of Applied Physiology*, *91*, 1307–1325.

Williams, C., & Wragg, C. (2004). *Data analysis and research for sport and exercise science*. Abingdon, Oxon: Routledge.

Yeadon, M.R., & Challis, J.H. (1994). The future of performance-related sports biomechanics research. *Journal of Sport Sciences*, *12*, 3–32.

Yeadon, M.R. & King, M.A. (2002). Evaluation of a torque-driven simulation model of tumbling. *Journal of Applied Biomechanics*, *18*, 195–206.

Zhang, S., Bates, B., & Dufek, J. (2000). Contributions of lower extremity joints to energy dissipation during landings. *Medicine and Science in Sports and Exercise*, *32*, 812–819.

Further reading

Bates, B.T., James, C.R., & Dufek, J.S. (2004). Single subject analysis. In N. Stergiou (Ed.) *Innovative analyses of human movement*. Champaign, IL: Human Kinetics.

Whittlesey, S.N., & Hamill, J. (2004) Computer simulation modelling of human movement. In G. Robertson, G. Caldwell , J. Hamill, G. Kamen, & S. Whittlesey, *Research Methods in Biomechanics*. Champaign, IL: Human Kinetics.

Yeadon, M.R., & King, M.A. (2008). Computer simulation modelling in sport. In C.J. Payton & R.M. Bartlett (Eds) *Biomechanical analyses of movement in sport and exercise*. London: Routledge.

7

SPORTS COACHING

Reflecting on reflection: exploring the practice of sports coaching graduates

Zoe Knowles

Article reference

Knowles, Z., Tyler, G., Gilbourne, D. & Eubank, M. (2006). Reflecting on reflection: Exploring the practice of sports coaching graduates. *Reflective Practice, 17,* 163–179.

Article summary

The purpose of the study was to explore how six coaching science graduates from Knowles et al.'s (2001) study deployed reflective processes within their sports coaching practice outside the confines of a supported reflective based curriculum. A reflective interview guide was used based on Gibbs' model and staged reflective practice. Twenty-one raw data themes related to defining models of reflection, barriers of reflection, issues regarding written techniques and reflection with others. Results suggest the in-built reflective rigour present in the undergraduate programme was at variance with the post-graduation reality of sports coach employment. This differentiation was discussed with reference to the short-term contracts typical of sports coaching employment and a lack of professional accountability with recommendations made for future sports coach education programmes.

Related author publications

Knowles, Z., Borrie, A. & Telfer, H. (2005). Towards the reflective sports coach: Issues of context, education and application. *Ergonomics, 48,* 1711–1720.

Knowles, Z., Gilbourne, D., Borrie, A. & Nevill, A. (2001) Developing the reflective sports coach: a study exploring the processes of reflective practice within a higher education coaching programme. *Reflective Practice, 2,* 186–201.

Personal prologue

I became interested in the psychology of sports coaching and pedagogy through my undergraduate studies and also my own experience as a coach to national age group champions in women's artistic gymnastics. My coaching knowledge and developing expertise was not attributed to that taught on coaching courses per se but had emerged from tackling challenges with my own gymnasts, working through coaching problems in practice and from the experience of observing and working with others. This led me towards research exploring how this learning process actually occurred through considering the underlying associated 'theories'. As a start-point I focused on action research and allied methodologies as a stimulus for sport coaching based organisational change for my MSc dissertation. Action research was a popular means of researching practically derived knowledge in nursing and teaching with the *Journal of Advanced Nursing* offering many research studies often in the same issue. At around the same time I assisted on an independent review for the NCF (now SportsCoach UK) High Performance Coaching (CPD) program in 1999, which, amongst several recommendations, had called for a taught mechanism by which coaches could learn from and explore practice. Reflective practice was a prominent feature in the training of the 'educare' (derived from education and/or caring based professions) professions, such as teaching and nursing, and it was from here that I began to explore the potential to 'borrow' elements of practice from that well established in the training of professions to that of the sports coach. My PhD data collection took me into these allied fields shadowing and interviewing policy makers, educators and trainee practitioners to explore their experiences of reflective practice and recommendations. From this, a programme was designed and delivered to BSc (Hons) Coaching Science Students (see Knowles et al., 2001 for a review). This chapter describes a qualitative research project conducted three years after the graduation of those who undertook this 2001 programme. Participants were employed from part time to full time and in coaching roles ranging from community schemes to national development programmes. The study aim was to explore what reflective strategies graduates of this course used and were deemed effective to facilitate reflection on coaching practice in their 'real world' setting. From these identified strategies, recommendations were to be made to create a more effective reflection based learning programme. This chapter describes the process for gaining participants, instrument design, data collection, analysis and representation, and discussion of key findings.

Key message: Sometimes look and think outside of sport for ideas, research and examples of good practice. These can then be adapted to suit sports contexts.

Moving from a research problem to a research question

Evaluation of sports coaching effectiveness is almost exclusively focused on competitive performance outcomes. One consequence of this is that sports coaches are rarely judged on the quality of their *own* practice, such that the understanding and improvement of this element of practice is often ignored. At the time of the project, sports coaching science literature had begun to explore how sports coaches *think* rather than what sports coaches *do* (see e.g., Abraham & Collins, 1998; Côté et al., 1995; Knowles et al., 2005) and this led to a need to understand how coaches *learn*. A number of research articles suggested that effective elite sports coaching is based on the appropriate use of experiential or craft knowledge as well as theoretical or 'professional' knowledge (Salmela, 1995; Knowles et al., 2001, 2006). Despite this, the development of craft knowledge was not highlighted within sports coach education programmes in the UK. Indeed, Galvin (1998, p. 5) suggested:

> A gap of form and context between a coach education course and the actual practice of sports coaching then exists. Things which seemed to make complete sense at the coach education course suddenly become more complex and difficult when coaches attempt to implement them with their own performers or team.

Craft knowledge is developed from practice experience and interaction with other coaches, however, there was still the problem of how coaches *learn* from their practice without the development of underpinning skills to facilitate this process (Knowles et al., 2001). Reflective practice has been discussed as a strategy that could help practitioners to explore their decisions and experiences and so increase their understanding and management of themselves and their practice (Anderson et al., 2004). The literature demonstrated that reflective practice had been adopted by several domains, including nursing and education (e.g., Ghaye & Lillyman, 2000; Johns, 2000; Osterman & Kottkamp, 1993). Knowles et al. (2001) 'borrowed' practice from teaching and nursing and adapted these to sports coaching in view of context-specific factors such as the coach's role, coaching environment and coach education practices. The result was a redevelopment of the core strand of a BSc (Hons) Coaching Science Programme that consisted of a 120-hour sports coaching placement with accompanying learning contract, individual journal writing, reflective workshops (with peers and experienced facilitator) and the completion of a post-placement reflective writing exercise. The post-course evaluation of this programme was documented in a previous paper (i.e., Knowles et al., 2001). At the time of writing the 2006 paper, the literature had yet to explore the extent to which those who had engaged in reflective practice as part of their education programme had continued to apply it outside the confines of a supported reflective based curriculum. Consequently, the research question responded to these sentiments by focusing on how coaching science graduates employed reflective processes in their coaching practice three years following completion of a reflective practice based training curriculum. Specifically, the main purpose of the project described within this chapter was to identify what strategies coaches use to facilitate reflection in their 'real world' setting with a second purpose of establishing how teaching reflective practice could be adapted to reduce the variance between the undergraduate programme and the post-programme reality of sports coach employment.

Choice of method (Matching the method to the research question)

A qualitative methodology was considered appropriate to address the research question. Specifically, to answer *how* reflective practice had been used and to gain insight into *what* strategies had been employed by the graduates, it was necessary to use an open-ended method of enquiry. We envisaged analysing the data through content analysis but also representing examples of good practice through verbatim quotations and this was unlikely to be captured though the more onerous written questionnaire. The researcher conducting the data collection was also a programme graduate (two years after the participants) and therefore had credibility and knowledge about the programme, yet no knowledge of the cohort and was thus deemed suitable for data collection. Data collection in person through interview at the participants' convenience for time and location as opposed to self-completed written replies was considered appropriate to maximise participation with a low maximum sample of twelve.

Data collection

Ethical issues and approval

During this stage we attempted to identify the possible social, psychological and physical risks of harm that the researcher or potential participants may face during interview. The key concerns were:

1   That the participants would name places, events or persons that would identify themselves or indeed others (including minors) that were not party to the research.
    - Such identification cannot occur without prior signed consent. For minors (and age range may vary across countries) this must include parental consent. Offering assurances on the consent form together with a reminder at the start *and* conclusion of the interview (should anything have 'slipped' out) is good practice.
2   That the coaches would disclose examples of practice that were considered dangerous, unethical or morally challenging that as a coach the researcher would deem necessary to report.

- You should be clear on what your position is as regards dealing with these issues and advice should be taken from a supervisor. This must then be communicated to the participants in advance of the interview.
3   That in recommending the interview be at a place and time convenient to the participant and without a prior visit the venue would be unsuitable.
    - A poor audio recording with background noise means transcription is difficult and aspects of conversation are missed. Doing a quick 'sound-check' even when you are limited by time will prevent this and allow you to relax and not worry about the quality of the recording.

In view of these issues all potential participants were provided with a participant information sheet and voluntary informed consent form which highlighted the following:

1   Participation is purely voluntary and the voluntary informed consent form must be completed prior to interview.
2   The main purpose of the study and the types of questions they (the participants) would be asked, and would also inform them that they did not have to answer any question and could stop the interview at any point.
3   Inform each participant as to my position within the overall project team, background and position of objectivity (stating relationship to any of the participants, links with organisation(s) and stating any benefits/rewards expected from the research).
4   The participants' role in checking accuracy of transcription and that text can be removed at that point and not used for analysis.
5   Inform the participants that a participant number will be allocated to identify them in the analysis, all identifying characteristics will be removed and get expressed permission for use for verbatim quotations.
6   Suggest the participant liaise with me to identify an appropriate interview venue that would be comfortable for me and the participant, and that would not be too distracting.

The interview guide

Due to the focus of the inquiry an interview guide was developed through drafting amongst the research team. In total six drafts were made (and this is typical) and with each draft came an increasing sense of creating an efficient set of coherent questions in a pre-determined order linked with statements to 'open' and 'close' sections of the interview. Questions asked must be clearly linked to the research questions. Any questions that do not relate in this way should be discarded. The following must be checked in the drafting process:

1   Write out statements for introduction, checking the audio recording, moving between sections and closure on the script.

2   Ensure the minimum number of questions are asked to answer the research questions. This will make the interview efficient to participate in and for you to transcribe.

3   Have prompts and clarification points on the script for when questions are not understood or responses are limited.

4   Ensure questions are open ended where practically possible, although a closed question may be followed up with an open question.

5   Ensure language/terminology is appropriate and use colloquial terms with care.

6   Ensure the thematic aspects of the interview (focus of the questions) flow easily for the interviewee and have statements to indicate moving on and closure. Aim to ask 'easier' or less challenging questions first, then move to the more challenging and return to easier questions to close.

7   Ensure the dynamic aspects of the interview (how questions are asked) flows from short and concise, to more in depth and then short and concise to finish.

8   Finally, practise sufficiently so that you spend more time engaging with the interviewee and less time looking at the script!

The interview process used was retrospective and reflective in nature and was based on Gibbs' (1988) six-stage reflective model. This model was introduced as an example of a reflective guide within the curriculum at academic Year 2. All participants had used this model to facilitate their reflection in their journal writing and course assessment. Furthermore, the interview structure was developed in accordance with the established principles of staged reflection (Knowles et al., 2001). Together, the model and principles of staged reflection provided a useful framework to shape the dynamic aspects or flow of the interview and also instilled a sense of familiarity. Thematic aspects of the interview were based on the reflective process and contemporary research in the topic area. In order to be transparent to the reader, the interview guide with question probes and rationale was included in the appendix of the published article (see Appendix 1).

Prior to interview, participants were asked to revisit reflective journals, end-of-year reflective reports and any reflections since graduation in order to inform their interview. Participants were told they may bring and refer to these documents if they felt it appropriate. The interviews were scheduled to last between 30 and 45 minutes. Participants were asked to be available and uninterrupted for one hour to ensure that they were not rushed. Saturation of data was used as an indictor of interview progression and accounted for variation in interview duration. As a researcher you need to be aware when you have exhausted a question and this may be indicated through prolonged silence or repetition of information. Silence can often be misread as saturation and may actually be a period of thought, so check with the interviewee before moving on.

Key message: When designing an interview, focus on being efficient and ensure all questions asked link clearly to the research question. Alongside this, consider the flow of the questions and practise being aware of approaching and dealing with saturation points.

Pilot interviews

Author 2 (Gareth) conducted the data collection for the research project. A pilot interview was conducted with a peer who was a practising coach and graduate of the programme after 2001. For Gareth, this was his second interview-based study and thus the pilot interview allowed refinement of skills associated with the dynamic aspects of the interview and familiarity with new audio equipment acquired by the school. The audio was listened to by all the members of the research team and adjustments were made to a few questions. Concern was raised as to the use of closed questions (e.g., question 6), however (as mentioned previously) these were justified as, in effect, they were introductory questions to more in-depth probes and successive questions.

Participants

The twelve graduates of 2001 from the BSc (Hons) Coaching Science degree at Liverpool John Moores University were approached by letter to participate. Inclusion criteria for the study included graduation prior to January 2002 (to allow for any deferral/referral awards), possession of a valid NVQ level 3 coaching award, and to be coaching on a regular basis. Contact details for potential participants were retained from the 2001 study. Two students were out of the UK, two unreachable and two excluded as they did not meet the coaching related criteria. Three sports were represented across the six participants, football ($n = 4$), hockey ($n = 1$) and tennis ($n = 1$). All participants had been exposed to two academic cycles of the curriculum that housed a core strand of reflective practice and had graduated three academic cycles prior to the start of the project.

Key message: If you intend to do a follow-up/retention study, ensure you get full contact details, permission to store these on the consent form and the most appropriate method to contact participants.

Interviews

Participants were contacted to arrange a suitable time and venue for the research interview. Individual semi-structured interviews were conducted by Gareth to ensure consistency. Geographically the participants lived some distance apart and the researcher had to plan effectively and make appropriate travel and contact arrangements. Conducting the interviews raised a number of issues for the researcher, firstly that of efficiency. When conducting research with elite/busy practitioners or athletes there is a need to be efficient with time you are requesting from them. You must give a realistic estimation of the time expected for the data collection in the pre-study information. In essence, if you are asking for over 90 minutes of their time, it is unlikely you will recruit and a 20-minute slot may render little meaningful information for analysis. The researcher needs to be armed with an *efficient* interview guide and be disciplined enough to adhere to timings (not easy when the participant is 'senior' or an icon!) when conducting the interview, both of which can be helped by a series of pilot interviews with debriefing. Secondly, it is important that there is a theme of commonality between the researcher and the participant. In this case, both had studied the same degree course, so there is potential to 'drift' to irrelevant conversation or 'chat' at the expense of project focused data collection. The researcher must, therefore, remain objective and resist the urge to comment on common themes, discuss their own experiences or convey opinion. The interview has to be transcribed in its entirety and irrelevant wordage can not only be time consuming, but found to be at the expense of project-relevant, rich information. In the present study the interviews were transcribed verbatim, yielding 61 pages of single-spaced transcript. Primary screening was undertaken to remove references to other sports coaches, practice venues and identities of any other persons who had not been informed of the project. Transcripts were then sent to the participants for their approval and they were requested to highlight any text to be deleted or provide amendments/additions. No transcripts were adjusted. In line with Lincoln and Guba's (1985) trustworthiness criteria, the above process represents 'referential adequacy', a means of credibility whereby recorded data is reviewed.

Key message: Be efficient as regards your instrument/guide, use pilot interviews with debriefing and be realistic with the expectations of time required by the participant.

Data analysis

Data was analysed through content analysis guided by the procedure of Gould et al. (1993) and Patton (1990). It is deemed important for researchers to state within their methodology which protocol is being used/adapted as there are many different interpretations of content analysis. For the purposes of this paper the stages were as follows:

1   Gareth and I repeatedly read the interview transcripts to generate familiarity with the data.
2   The analysis was performed by hand and in the first instance the transcript data was reviewed for emergent themes from which meaningful quotes

of varying length were extracted for analysis. The quotes omitted any unnecessary repetitive words and the irrelevant sentence content seen in conversation (e.g., 'Erm…er…umm' etc.).

3   These quotes generated raw data themes (RDTs), which appear to the left of the content analysis table/figure. It is important that raw data themes are self-explanatory and no more than 6–7 words in length. This may involve paraphrasing or abbreviating but must not lose the essence of the quotation. When read in conjunction with the title of the content analysis table/figure the text must be clear to the reader. Alongside each RDT, frequency data (illustrated by a list of participant numbers) is added to demonstrate the 'strength' or popularity of the theme amongst the participants. Participant numbers are the assigned ID numbers from their consent forms. This process helps to ensure that readers can associate data with specific participants, whilst helping to sustain the 'context' of the data.

4   The analysis process continued across to a single higher order theme (HOT), which represents a clustering of raw data themes under a common heading of approximately 4 words.

5   General dimensions (GD) are located on the right of the table and link one or more HOTs. In some instances RDTs can be taken directly to the GD level.

6   Any unallocated quotes are revisited and the process was continued until all thematic links had been identified and theoretical saturation occurred. Should any quotes remain, these may reflect a deviation from the interview question, be deemed irrelevant or be treated as emergent in nature and acknowledged separately within the results.

Researcher triangulation (a form of credibility within 'trustworthiness' criteria) occurs at each stage of the analysis process. In this project, this was achieved through consultation and agreement between all four researchers.

For the student researcher, the triangulation process should also take place despite it being an individual piece of work and it is recommended that your supervisor(s) and a peer (outside the rubric of the project) take on this role independently followed by a meeting to discuss, achieve and justify consensus. In accordance with Lincoln and Guba's (1985) trustworthiness criteria, this analysis procedure ensures a high level of 'dependability'. Some studies may also warrant a further level of triangulation with the participants. Whilst this adds to the credibility of the analysis, the researcher must be aware of timescales involved in sending and receiving approval from participants. Sports coaches/athletes may well, at times, be unreachable and thus a delay may incur in the project. If this is a foreseen stage in the analysis, researchers should plan the timing and means by which to send documents/receive approval. 'Conceivability' (or the believable nature of the analysis process) was achieved through the presence of an audit trail through all stages of data analysis. Researchers should always have draft work and interim stages of analysis available for scrutiny.

Patton (1990) stated that 'sufficient quotational data should be presented to illuminate and support whatever analysis the evaluator provides in narrative form' (p. 420), and, alongside the only content analysis table in the paper, transferability was achieved by providing thick description through descriptive quotes from the sports coaches to illustrate significant findings from the content analysis. Seventeen quotations were used in the paper (taken from meaningful quotes stage) and thus there was a significant emphasis on these extracts providing scope for analysis and discussion in the remainder of the paper. Quotations must be justified for inclusion and this can be agreed within the triangulation process, and used sparingly to ensure that they are not at the expense of synthesis or discussion.

Data presentation

Only one content analysis table was presented providing a composite overview of the sports coaches' perceptions of reflective practice (Figure 7.1). The content analysis process elicited 121 raw data quotations, which were represented within 27 RDTs, 16 HOTs and 5 GDs. The dimensions were: the definition of reflection, the rationale for reflection, overcoming barriers of reflection, issues regarding written reflection and finally reflection with others. The dimensions provided the subheadings for the remainder of the results and discussion section, which offered quotations as illustration to the results in the content analysis figure.

Key message: Ensure you offer the reader a clear structure for results and discussion section to allow them to follow large amounts of qualitative data.

The inclusion of the verbatim quotations was to expand the reader's awareness of the contexts and depth of the responses, which, by the reduction-based process of content analysis, are somewhat lost. The results section offered quotes of support and contrasts interspersed with interpretive commentary. The journal format required quotes to be separated from the main text and indented with no quotation marks added. An example of this is below but is somewhat truncated here for reasons of brevity. The interested reader is directed to pages 170–171 of the published paper.

The main barrier to reflection was seen to be a lack of time:

> I can think about it in that hour journey but I might not be able to jot anything down, I obviously can't while I'm driving and when I get back it's late and it's whether I can write things down. (Coach 2)

> Even after the session you're driving home and then it's late at night and you just go to bed and you couldn't fit it in. (Coach 4)

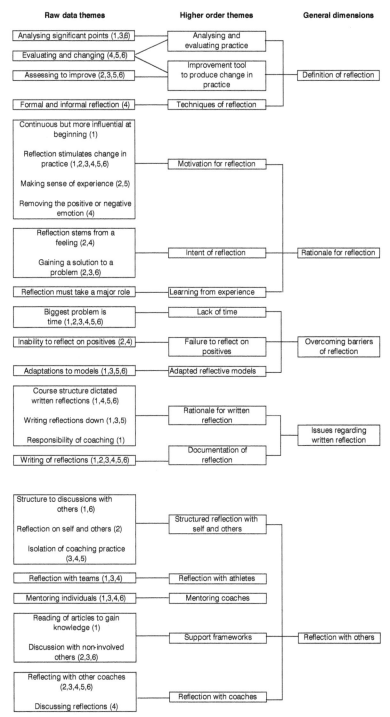

FIGURE 7.1 Coaches perceptions of reflective practice

The interpretation of reflection was also seen as having a negative focus, principally coaches would reflect on experiences that went wrong.

> Although sometimes when things are just going good, sometimes you don't even think about it, you just think that was ok...In reality sometimes you might get in feeling good and turn the radio on and that stops those thought processes going on. (Coach 2)

> It's like anything; if something is going right then you don't need to sort something out that has gone right, do you? It's a case that reflection would be a method to solve things that have gone wrong... when something has gone right I don't tend to think about it much. (Coach 4)

However, some coaches had started to develop and adapt their own reflective models and reflective process to assist in overcoming the barrier of time. One subject discussed the interpretation of dual-staged reflection (Knowles et al., 2001):

> Yeah I think when you're leaving a training session I would think about it, have a break and then later on in the evening when I've had a chance to take my mind off it and go back in again I might sit down for longer and think about it. (Coach 3)

Finally the subjects provided interesting details of how they facilitate the process of reflection with particular interest to the dissemination of knowledge amongst others and vice versa:

> Definitely we (myself and other coaches) talk loads on the phone and through text messages about what is happening and that can be quite a broad thing like the culture of the club and what's going on at the club to small details about a little tactic that worked or someone did against us. This can be initiated by either of us. (Coach 2)

Other examples included reflecting with athletes, mentoring to pass on knowledge to other coaches, reflecting with non-involved others and also reflecting with other coaches.

Contribution to knowledge

The discussion section of the paper took the structure of the results section, using the same subheadings to ease clarity for the reader. In this section the aim was to compare the current study findings with that of previous research. Although context-specific research (i.e., reflective practice in sports coaching), was at that time limited to that work undertaken by the authors themselves (Knowles et al., 2001), a wider focus to other fields more accustomed to reflective practice was used. For example:

> The sports coaches reported that reflection is a cognitive process influenced by the prime barrier of time. Practically, the sports coaches reported difficulties in both making time to reflect due to the unsociable hours and being able to reflect on continuous hours of sports coaching. The process of dual staged reflection (Knowles et al., 2001) was seen as important to minimize the barrier of time, particularly in relation to the hours that are implicit to the sports coaching role. Reference to non-sport reflective literature offers some solutions. For example, Tribble and Newburg (1998) and Titchen and Binnie (1993) have both outlined how time allocated to medical personnel encourages formal reflection. Teams of surgeons attend scheduled weekly meetings in order to reflect on operations. In contrast, within the isolated context of sports coaching, the tendency towards hourly contact pay and a lack of demand for accountability (required to maintain qualified status) does not readily encourage structured reflection opportunities. (p. 174)

Reference to our own previous work (self-citation) to demonstrate an extension or report new findings is an important aspect of the discussion section, as are recommendations for improving practice. The following extract from the discussion demonstrates this:

> A further barrier was identified as reflective practice having a 'negative focus' (Knowles et al., 2001) and was manifested as an inability/failure to reflect on positives. Furthermore, whilst sports coaching is a complex activity that manages not only the demands emanating from the needs of the performer, but also those contained within the performance environment, it appears almost exclusively focused on competitive outcome as an index of effectiveness. What results is a biased reflection that is too narrow in its orientation. Coaches should be encouraged to reflect on both positive and negative experiences that also consider the competitive process and their role within it. Reflecting on 'negative' experiences is not a barrier to reflection per se, but rather a barrier to a 'rounded' reflective experience.

Focusing now on the contribution to knowledge, before the current study was undertaken it was deemed that little was known about the use of reflective practice once a facilitated learning programme (like the BSc coaching core strand) had been completed. Results suggest that post-course reflection still exists as an important element of coaching practice. However, despite all participants receiving the same training in reflective techniques, the research noted changes in the nature and methods of reflection being deployed in the workplace. Indeed, by this very nature of 'standardised' training with little room for 'personalised learning' methods within the confines of an academic programme this may well have influenced the adaptation of techniques seen at postgraduate level. The paper was clear in its intention to offer recommendations for future coaching education programmes and several were proposed at the end of the discussion section and via the conclusion. Here, the authors recommended change at a delivery and support level but also a called for a change in wider policy (in this case sports governing bodies responsible for education and training) to support this. Papers often conclude by offering a wider perspective on the research outcomes or recommendations for future research. For example:

> In a similar way, strategic change at governing body level may also facilitate more systematic reflection through the adoption of reflective bridging programmes and associated mentoring. A strategic influence on the use and development of reflective practice within sports coaches would appear critical, particularly if practitioner accountability to their client is to be enhanced.

Key message: The discussion section should reflect back to the literature and forward to future research, providing suggested changes to practice or policy. Keep the key messages brief and as late in the paper as possible (i.e., 'leave' them with the reader at the conclusion).

Impact on practice

In an applied sense, this research was undertaken to allow exploration of post-course reflective practice and thus allow a more relevant and appropriate education programme to be offered that would be workable and not at variance to post-course practice. The research was sympathetic to the demands of the coaching environment and allowed the researchers to once again note which techniques previously 'borrowed' from educare professions were effective to inform further education programmes. We recommended revisions and considerations for the practitioner, the educator and the policy maker. For example, it was proposed that for the educator curricular procedures may need to be more sensitive to the realities of the post-graduation workplace. In a similar way, strategic change at governing body level (policy maker) may also facilitate more systematic reflection through the adoption of reflective bridging programmes and associated mentoring. The journal article may well be read by all of these individuals and thus it was important to offer a focus for each but also emphasise the need for co-ordination across practice, education and policy. The paper concludes with a statement noting its contribution to the evidence base and offering support to the claims that reflective practice is an effective practitioner development tool. Typically, a call for further research (and often specific directions for this) is made and in the case of the present paper this was to explore the uptake and use of reflective practice in the coaching community more generally as opposed to those who had undertaken the 2001 programme.

The conscious choice of the *Reflective Practice* journal as opposed to a sport-based journal also meant that by its very nature it would be *reviewed* in the first instance and subsequently *read* by researchers/educators from other disciplines. With this in mind and given the emergence of reflective practice techniques and principles into sport being 'borrowed' from other professions, there was the hope that they would be able to draw from our conclusions and recommendations.

Reflection

The strengths of this study lie in its ability to document the retention and role of reflective practice in post-course education. Thus this research adds support to the previously somewhat unsubstantiated claim that reflective practice is of *value* to the coach in post-education-based practice. The research methods employed have allowed an in-depth exploration of adaptations to the skills/techniques and these were demonstrated through a reduction/summary of data (content analysis) and specific examples (verbatim quotations). The study has finally contributed to the topical and cyclical nature of curriculum/educational policy for sports coaches and hopefully stimulated thought and change at practice, education and policy levels.

To focus on what could be done differently, it is apparent now that the reductionist approach of content analysis can offer only a 'snapshot' of the data and an overuse of quotations can appear descriptive and lacking analysis. Since this study was conducted, the authors have been developing a pen-profile approach to analysis which combines content analysis procedures but which is represented in a more visually appealing 'map' demonstrating themes, frequency and example quotations. Under rigorous peer review (and not without its challenges) this had been accepted (Ridgers et al.,2012) and is now gathering momentum as a technique which, although content analysis in origin, is presented in a more 'reader-friendly' format. The aim is to engage the reader in the data headlines and reduce the need for pages and pages of tables. Likewise a dissatisfaction with the presentation of discrete quotations and a need to offer 'more' of the participants' experience through extended prose/stories, has led the authors towards more alternative approaches to representation, for example ethnographic approaches (see Knowles & Gilbourne, 2010; Knowles et al., 2011). The confidence gained for exploring practice and theory from outside the confines of sport in this study has proved beneficial in the subsequent quest for research and representation techniques. Ethnographic and alternative forms of representation embrace a number of creative, literary, dramatic and media related fields that we as researchers have become accustomed and excited by as regards their potential. For the researcher, representing the experiences of others will remain a contentious issue, however our more recent research is perhaps testimony to the importance and scope of widening methodological focus to perhaps the most unlikely of fields.

Key message: Outcomes of research can also be a critique/development of methodological/analysis techniques not just outcomes associated with proving/disproving hypotheses or answering research questions.

> If you liked this chapter, you should read Chapters 5, 11 and 13, where the authors use interviews to address the given research question.

References

Abraham, A. & Collins, D. (1998) Examining and extending research in coach development, *Quest, 50*, 59–79.

Anderson, A., Knowles, Z. & Gilbourne, D. (2004) Reflective practice for applied sport psychologists: a review of concepts, models, practical implications and thoughts on dissemination, *The Sport Psychologist, 18*, 188–201.

Côté, J., Salmela, J.H., Trudel, P., Baria, A. & Russell, S.J. (1995) The coaching model: a Grounded assessment of gymnastics coaches' knowledge, *Journal of Sport & Exercise Psychology, 17*, 1–17.

Galvin, B. (1998) *A Guide to Mentoring Sports coaches.* Leeds: National Coaching Foundation.

Ghaye, T. & Lillyman, S. (2000) *Reflection: Principles and Practice for Healthcare Professionals.* Salisbury: Quay Books.

Gibbs, G. (1988) *Learning by Doing: A Guide to Teaching an Learning Methods.* Oxford: FE Unit, Oxford Polytechnic.

Gould, D., Ecklund, R.C., Jackson, S.A. & Finch, L.M. (1993) Coping strategies used by elite US Olympic wrestlers, *Research Quarterly for Exercise and Sport, 64*, 83–93.

Johns, C. (2000) *Becoming a Reflective Practitioner: A Reflective and Holistic Approach to Clinical Nursing, Practice Development and Clinical Supervision.* London: Blackwell Science.

Knowles, Z. & Gilbourne, D. (2010). Aspiration, inspiration and illustration: Initiating debate on reflective practice writing, *The Sport Psychologist, 24*, 505–520.

Knowles, Z., Gilbourne, D., Borrie, A. & Nevill, A. (2001) Developing the reflective sports coach: a study exploring the processes of reflective practice within a higher education coaching programme, *Reflective Practice, 2*, 186–201.

Knowles, Z., Borrie, A. & Telfer, H. (2005). Towards the reflective sports coach: Issues of context, education and application, *Ergonomics, 48*, 1711–1720.

Knowles, Z., Tyler, G., Gilbourne, D. & Eubank, M. (2006). Reflecting on reflection: Exploring the practice of sports coaching graduates, *Reflective Practice, 17*, 163–179.

Knowles, Z., Gilbourne, D. & Niven, A. (2011). Thoughts on writing reflectively: steering reflective practice towards the 'narrative turn' In M. Anderson & D. Gilbourne (Eds). *Critical essays in sport psychology,* pp. 59–73. Champaign, IL: Human Kinetics.

Lincoln, Y. & Guba, E.G. (1985) *Naturalistic inquiry.* Newbury Park: Sage.

Osterman, K. & Kottkamp, P. (1993) *Reflective practice for educators.* Newbury, CA: Corwin Press.

Patton, M.Q. (1990) *Qualitative evaluation and research methods* (2nd edn). Newbury Park, CA: Sage Publications.

Ridgers, N., Knowles, Z. & Sayers, J. (2012). Play in the natural environment: a child-focused evaluation of Forest School, *Children's Geographies, 10*, 55–71.

Salmela, J.H. (1995) Learning from the development of expert coaches, *Coaching & Sport Science Journal, 2*, 3–13.

Titchen, A. & Binnie, A. (1993) Research partnerships: collaborative action research in nursing, *Journal of Advanced Nursing, 14*, 403–410.

Tribble, C. & Newburg, D. (1998) Learning to fly: teaching mental strategies to future surgeons, *The Journal of Excellence, 1*, 8–21.

Appendix 1

TABLE 7.1   Study interview guide

Question	Probe	Theoretical rationale
Description		
1. Describe your coaching experience.	1a. Recent coaching.	1b. Start off with something they are the expert with.
2. What does the term reflection mean to you?	2a. Use previous definitions.	2b. There is no clear definition (Knowles et al., 2001)
Feelings		
3. What did you learn from the course? Map out feelings that were experienced about reflective practice.	3a. 25% towards degree i.e. 1st sessions, final thought in 3rd yr. 75% after degree.	3b. Pre-service teaching and pre-registration nursing use reflection to improve.
Evaluation		
4. How do you evaluate the effectiveness of reflection since leaving university?	4a1. Benefits & barriers since leaving university and why?	4b. Negative focus (Knowles et al., 2001)
	4a2. What is the value of reflective practice in your practice?	4b1. Accountability (Knowles et al. 2001 & Anderson et al. 2004)
		4b2. Working in isolation or working in a reflective culture for a change in practice or development or theory (Ghaye & Lillyman 2000).

Question	Probe	Theoretical rationale
What sense can you make		
5. Therefore what is your ideal reflective process?	5a. Techniques/models used with adaptations?	5b. 5 guides/models used – Anderson et al. 2004 use of John's 21 questions to suit psychology practice.
	5a1. Use of reflective journal links to value of RP. In degree it was necessary for completion of course.	5b1. Accountability (Knowles et al. 2001 & Anderson et al. 2004)
What else can we do?		
6. Have you discovered an alternative way of learning from practice?		
7. Have you ever facilitated the process of reflection?	7a. Sharing reflection. 7a1. Supervising/ mentoring. 7a2. Publication in academic journals.	7b. Dissemination (Knowles et al. 2001 & Anderson et al. 2004)
What would you do next time?		
8. What recommendations would you suggest to coaches to prepare them for the applied setting?	8a. Any improvements/ adaptations to any of the above.	8b. All of the above – conclusion to interview.
9. Is there anything that you may be able to take away from this interview for your own future practice?	9a. Another time to reflect on what has been reflected.	9b. Meta reflection (Ghaye & Lillyman 2000)/ staged reflection (Knowles et al. 2001).

8

STRENGTH AND CONDITIONING

Influence of recovery time on postactivation potentiation in professional rugby players

Liam Kilduff

Article reference

Kilduff, L.P., Owen, N., Bevan, H., Bennett, M., Kingsley, M.I.C., & Cunningham, D. (2008). Influence of recovery time on postactivation potentiation in professional rugby players. *Journal of Sports Science, 26,* 795–802.

Article summary

Postactivation potentiation (PAP) can be harnessed to improve acute and chronic (through training) performance in explosive type sports. However, at the time this article was published very little was known about the impact recovery would have on an athlete's ability to utilise PAP. Following a bout of heavy resistance training (HRT) the muscle is in both a fatigued and potentiated state with subsequent muscle performance depending on the balance between these two factors and there was no uniform agreement about the optimal recovery required between the HRT and subsequent muscle performance to gain performance benefits through PAP. Therefore, the main purpose of this study was to determine the recovery time required to observe enhanced muscle performance following a bout of HRT. Twenty professional rugby players performed a countermovement jump (CMJ) at baseline and ~15 s, 4, 8, 12, 16, 20 and 24 min following an HRT bout (3 sets of 3 repetitions at 87 per cent 1 RM of squat). Despite an initial decrease in CMJ performance following the HRT ($p < 0.001$), subjects' performance increased significantly following 8 min recovery between the HRT and the CMJ ($p < 0.001$) (e.g., jump height increased by 4.9 ± 3.0 per cent). Muscle performance during a CMJ can be significantly enhanced following bouts of HRT providing adequate recovery (~8 min) is given between the HRT and the explosive activity.

Related author publications

Bevan, H., Owen, N., Cunningham, D., Cook, C.J., Tooley, E. & Kilduff, L.P. (2010). Influence of postactivation potentiation on sprinting performance in professional rugby players. *Journal of Strength & Conditioning Research*. *24*, 701–705.

Bevan, H., Owen, N., Cunningham, D., Kingsley, M.I.C., & Kilduff, L.P. (2009). Complex training in professional rugby players: Influence of recovery time on upper body power output. *Journal of Strength & Conditioning Research*, *23*, 1780–1785.

Personal prologue

My primary research interests are centred on athlete preparation, monitoring, and recovery. Within this, the current research study and a number of additional studies from our research group focus on the application of postactivation potentiation (PAP) to elite sport. The main driver behind this series of studies came from extensive interaction with applied practitioners in the area of performance physiology and strength and conditioning. It was very clear that despite the widespread application of PAP within the applied environment very little was known about the optimal programme variables (e.g., intensity and recovery) to evoke the greatest performance improvement. In addition, there was a lack of scientific literature in this area with only two studies examining this issue indirectly with no studies specifically looking at this extremely important area. Based on the above issues a clear research question was developed. Specifically, we deemed it important to identify the optimal recovery time between the completion of a bout of heavy resistance training (HRT) and the subsequent muscle performance in a group of elite athletes, as understanding this aspect of PAP would allow performance scientists and strength and conditioning coaches to apply this information to both the training (termed complex training) and competition environment (as part of the warm-up).

Moving from a research problem to a research question

As mentioned in the previous section, the primary research problem that we aimed to answer within this study was born from applied practice, in that many performance scientists were utilising PAP as part of their athletes' training and in some cases as part of the athletes' pre-competition strategy (built into the warm-up) with limited research to guide their decisions.

Over the years, sports scientists have examined the effectiveness of various training methods proposed to enhance muscular power, which is considered an essential component of success in many team sports. These training methods have included athletes trying to develop power while working against their body mass (e.g., plyometrics) and also while working against external loads that equate to various intensities of their 1 repetition maximum (RM), between 40 to 70 per cent during upper body exercises (e.g., Baker et al., 2001; Newton et al., 1997), between body mass to 60 per cent for lower body exercises (e.g.,

Izquierdo et al., 2002; Stone et al., 2003) and between 80 to 100 per cent for Olympic-style weightlifting movements (e.g., Kawamori et al., 2005; Kilduff et al., 2007). Recently, a training method that requires an athlete to work against a heavy load (> 80 per cent 1 RM) followed by a light load has been proposed to be effective for enhancing power output in athletes (e.g., Gossen & Sale, 2000; Baker, 2003).

It has been shown that the ability of a muscle group to produce force can be positively or negatively influenced by the contractive history of that muscle group. For example, following heavy resistance training (HRT) (> 80 per cent 1 RM) subsequent muscle performance has been demonstrated to decrease (e.g., Ebben et al., 2000; Gossen & Sale, 2000; Jones & Lees, 2003), while other studies have reported increases in performance (e.g., Baker, 2003; Chiu et al., 2003). The observed decrease in performance can be attributed to muscle fatigue associated with the HRT (e.g., low intramuscular stores of phosphocreatine), while the increase in muscle performance observed has been attributed to a condition referred to as postactivation potentiation (PAP) (e.g., Gullich & Schmidtbleicher, 1996). PAP can be defined as an acute enhancement of muscle function following an intense muscle activity (Hodgson et al., 2005). Current research indicates that both fatigue and PAP can coexist in skeletal muscle, and muscle performance following HRT depends on the balance between muscle fatigue and muscle potentiation (Rassier & MacIntosh, 2000).

The conflict in the literature regarding an athlete's ability to harness PAP can in part be explained by numerous methodological differences in published studies (e.g., intensity of preload used) (Hodgson et al., 2005). While the majority of methodological limitations (e.g., preload intensity, type of movement used to induce PAP) can be overcome by careful study design, there is no uniform agreement about the optimal recovery time between the HRT and subsequent explosive activity, with studies reporting recovery periods ranging from 0 to 18.5 min (Baker, 2003; Brandenburg, 2005; Chiu et al., 2003; Comyns et al., 2006; Duthie et al., 2002; Young et al., 1998). To date, only two studies have attempted to directly examine the optimal recovery time between the HRT and subsequent explosive activity. Jensen and Ebben (2003) and Comyns et al. (2006) investigated short recovery periods between the HRT and the subsequent explosive activity. Jensen and Ebben (2003) examined recovery periods of 10 s, 1, 2, 3 and 4 min between the HRT and the subsequent explosive activity (countermovement jump; CMJ), while Comyns et al. (2006) utilised recovery periods of 30 s, 2, 4 and 6 min. Both these studies concluded that there was no effect on jump performance following the HRT at any of the specified recovery periods. However, they both used relatively short recovery periods, which may indicate that greater than 6 min of recovery might be needed to see a performance enhancement.

Therefore, due to the conflicting research concerning appropriate recovery periods between the HRT and the subsequent explosive exercise, the aim of our study was to determine the optimal recovery time for maximal benefits between the HRT (3 sets of 3 repetitions at 87 per cent 1 RM) and the explosive activity in a group of professional rugby players using a more robust and specific study design to answer this important question.

Choice of method (Matching the method to the research question)

In the current study we decided on a within-subject study design where the same group of subjects were exposed to each condition (e.g., time frame). We decided on this design for a number of reasons: firstly as we are dealing with an elite population, numbers will always be limited (sample size) and a within-subjects design generally requires half the numbers of subjects compared with a between-subjects design. A within-subject design can also minimise errors associated with individual differences which is an important consideration in these types of studies as the results may be biased by individual differences. So having each player serve as their own baseline reduces this potential source of error.

Data collection

Ethical approval

Prior to ethical approval, the research team met with the management staff of the team where we recruited the players to conduct a risk assessment on the project. This meeting was also used to discuss any concerns the management might have had. The risk assessment process is used to identify potential issues that may occur as a result of carrying out this study. The primary risks in the current study was the potential risk of injury from asking the players to perform an HRT and a number of CMJs, however due to the nature of the players training both the research team and management believed the risk associated with this was minimal.

Other potential ethical issues associated with this type of study are:

*   Age range of subjects: In the current study all subjects were 18–35 years of age, however in some cases subjects may be 16 years of age and therefore would need parental consent.
*   Data storage and protection: In the current study all subjects were assigned a number to ensure their data sets could not be identified by anybody outside the research team and all data was stored on password protected computers.

All the above-mentioned concerns were incorporated into the ethical application and study design to ensure we gained ethical approval and 'buy-in' from the teams' players and management. The main ethical issues involved in this study are common to all studies in this area and therefore ethical approval was granted and all subjects completed a medical questionnaire and gave the research team their informed consent. The medical questionnaire was used to ensure all subjects were in a suitable condition to take part in the current study. If subjects indicated any medical issues in the questionnaire that may inhibit their ability to perform during our testing, additional information was required from the medical team. Following this consultation, a decision was then made to include or exclude the subject.

Familiarisation

Prior to the commencement of the main experimental trial, we visited the team's training facility in order to familiarise the players with the testing methods and testing team. During this familiarisation session subjects also practised performing the countermovement jump with the aim to maximise jump height for the experimental trials. In addition, during this session each player's 3 RM squat was measured. We decided to use a 3 RM method of strength testing to minimise the risk of injury from 1 RM testing and also players perform 3 RM testing routinely as part of their normal testing and training. Forty-eight hours after the familiarisation and strength-testing period, all subjects performed the testing session to ensure any soreness associated with the previous testing had subsided.

Subjects

Twenty professional rugby players volunteered to take part in the study and provided written informed consent before participation. Subjects were recruited on the basis that they were engaged in a structured weight-training programme for at least 2 years prior to the start of the study and were able to complete the CMJ with correct technique as assessed by a qualified strength and conditioning coach.

Experimental procedures

Following the measurement of each subject's stature and body mass (measurements used as descriptive characteristics for the subjects), subjects underwent a standardised warm-up that comprised 5 min on a rowing ergometer, followed by a series of dynamic stretches with an emphasis on stretching the musculature associated with the squat and CMJ. Following the warm-up, subjects completed a baseline CMJ. After a recovery period subjects completed the HRT on the squat (3 sets of 3 repetitions at 87 per cent 1 RM). Immediately following the HRT (within 15 s) and every 4 min after the HRT up to 24 min (e.g. at 4, 8, 12, 16 and 20 min) the subjects repeated the CMJ.

Measurements

Countermovement jump (CMJ)

For the measurement of lower body power, subjects completed a CMJ on a portable force platform. In order to isolate the lower limbs, subjects stood with arms by their sides. After an initial stationary phase of at least 2 s in the upright position, for the determination of body weight, the subjects performed a CMJ, dipping to a self-selected depth and then exploding upwards in an attempt to gain maximum height. Subjects landed back on the force platform and their arms were kept akimbo throughout the movement.

Force platform

A Kistler portable force platform with built-in charge amplifier (type 92866AA, Kistler Instruments Ltd, Farnborough, UK) was used for data collection of the ground reaction force (GRF) time history of the CMJ. A sample rate of 1,000 Hz was used for all jumps and the platform's calibration was confirmed pre- and post-testing. Force platforms allow for accurate and valid measurements of a number of key performance variables such as force, velocity, power and rate of force development.

Data calculation

As measures of PAP, the main dependent variables in the current study were peak power and maximal jump height.

The vertical component of the GRF as the subject performed the CMJ was used in conjunction with each subject's body weight to determine the instantaneous velocity and displacement of the subject's centre of gravity (CG) (Hatze, 1998). Instantaneous power was determined using the following standard relationship:

Power (W) = vertical GRF (N) $\times$ vertical velocity of CG (m.s^{-1})

In order to determine the velocity of the subject's CG, numerical integration was performed using intervals equal to the sample rate. Using the relationship that impulse equals change in momentum, each sample rate area was then divided by the subject's mass to produce a value for the change in velocity for the centre of gravity (it was assumed that the subject's mass remained constant throughout the jump). This change in velocity was then added to the CG's previous velocity to produce a new velocity at a time equal to that particular interval's end time. This process was continued throughout the jump. As this method can only determine the change in velocity it was necessary to know the CG's velocity at some point in time. For this purpose, the velocity of the CG was taken to be zero prior to the initiation of the jump (during the period of body weight measurement) and specifically at the point identified as the start of the jump. The start point was defined as the time when the subject's GRF exceeded the mean ± 5 standard deviations from the values obtained in the second (of the stationary body weight measuring phase) immediately prior to the command to jump, in a fashion similar to Vanrenterghem et al. (2001). Integration started from this point. This start point has previously been shown to give a repeatable start time to allow for accurate calculation of the performance variables.

Vertical displacement was determined by a second integration. The instantaneous velocity time history was numerically integrated (in the same way as described above) from the start point of the jump. The height (vertical displacement) of the centre of gravity at the start point of the jump was defined as zero. Jump height was then defined as the difference in the vertical displacement of the CG, between take-off (toes leave the force plate) and maximum vertical displacement achieved.

Test-retest reliabilities (intraclass correlations) for peak power, peak rate of force development and maximum jump height were 0.979, 0.890 and 0.976, respectively.

Data analysis

The primary aim of our study was to determine the optimal recovery period between heavy resistance training and subsequent explosive activity. As with all quantitative studies, the first stage of the analysis was to accurately identify the relevant dependent and independent variables. In this instance we measured three dependent variables: power output, peak rate of force development, and maximum jump height. The only independent variable was time, which included a baseline measure prior to the resistance training, a measure at 15 seconds post-resistance training, and then a measure every 4 minutes thereafter up to and including 24 minutes. The nature of this independent variable necessitated a repeated measures approach to analysis, because all participants provided data at all time points.

The second stage of the data analysis was to screen the data to ensure suitability for parametric statistical tests. Parametric stats tests are preferred as they have more *power* to test or detect an effect size of a given value (see Field, 2009). The assumptions for use of parametric tests are that the data is: i) measured at least at the interval level; ii) independent (i.e., data points from one participant are not influenced by data points from other participants); iii) normally distributed; and, iv) it has homogeneity of variance. In our study, all the data collected was ratio level data (scaled units with a true fixed zero point), which exceeds the criteria for interval level data. In terms of independence, our force platform data was collected in such a way that the participants could not influence each other's measures physically. However, it is worth noting that independence is often assumed too easily in experimental designs and in reality there are very few data sets that are truly independent. For example, in our study, as all participants were trained by the same strength and conditioning coach, their CMJ scores were more likely to be similar to each other than to CMJ scores from another team trained by another coach (i.e., higher intra-class correlation) and hence non-independent.

The third assumption, *normality*, assumes that all the data is evenly distributed (symmetrically) around the mean and this is often graphically represented as a bell-shaped curve. Data that is non-normal is described as skewed and/or kurtosed. Positive skewness is where the graph indicates that the majority of data points are stacked up on the left-hand side of the graph, whereas negative skewness is observed when data points are stacked up on the right-hand side of the graph. Similarly, positive kurtosis indicates peaked distribution of scores, whereas negative kurtosis indicates a flat distribution of scores.

Generally speaking, if data is not normally distributed it can cause problems with the analysis, increasing the chances of a type 1 error (false positive finding) occurring. In reality there is no such thing as perfectly distributed data (i.e., skew = 0, kurtosis = 0) and therefore we examine our data to see if it falls within acceptable limits. SPSS (the software package used in our study) provides skewness and kurtosis statistics that can be used to examine the assumptions of normality. The significance of skewness and kurtosis values can be assessed by converting them into z-scores or standard scores. This can be done by dividing the skewness and kurtosis values by their associated standard errors (also provided by SPSS). Values greater than 1.96, 2.58, and 3.29 reflect significant skewness/kurtosis at the $p < .05$, $p < .01$, and $p < .001$ levels respectively. SPSS also produces two tests for normality (Kolmogorov–Smirnov and Shapiro–Wilks) where a significant result indicates that the data departs sufficiently from normality to be a concern. In our study, the data was found to be distributed within these limits and was therefore deemed as 'normal'.

In repeated measures designs, the fourth and final assumption of parametric data, *homogeneity of variance*, is tested in a slightly different manner to between-group designs. In fact, it relates more to the independence of the data than homogeneity of variance per se. Specifically, in repeated measures designs the notion of independence is always violated because scores from the different experimental conditions (e.g., the different time points in our study) come from the same participant and therefore will be related. Therefore, in repeated measures designs we try to ensure that our data has *sphericity*. Simply described, sphericity assumes that the differences between pairs of scores (e.g., time 1 and time 2, time 1 and time 3 etc.) have similar variances. In SPSS, you can test for sphericity using Mauchly's test, where a significant result indicates that the differences in variance between data points is significantly large enough to be a concern (see Field, 2009, for an account of how to treat this data). In our study, Mauchly's test was non-significant and therefore it was assumed that the data was sufficiently spherical. Having confirmed that our data matched the requirements for parametric data analysis, we proceeded with the next part of the analysis.

Parametric data collected using a repeated measures design is most often analysed using repeated measures ANOVA. This type of ANOVA tests for differences in within-subject variances, such that, when scores across conditions (e.g., the time points in our study) differ consistently across participants this indicates that these changes are a function of our experimental design rather than error (e.g., something outside our control or outside the manipulation used in the experiment). In our study, we completed three separate repeated measures ANOVA for each of the dependent variables measured. These ANOVA tested whether there was an effect for time on the dependent variables. These tests indicated that for all three dependent variables there was a significant effect for time (i.e., scores on the dependent variables differed as a function of time). Once a significant effect was established, we wanted to ascertain specifically where (i.e., between which time points) these differences occurred. Pairwise comparisons are used to compare all of the time points with each other to indicate where the differences identified by the ANOVA occurred. For our study, this meant completing a total of 28 pairwise comparisons. Unfortunately, when you complete this many comparisons you increase the likelihood of a Type 1 error. The logic of hypothesis testing means that we should reject the null hypothesis in favour of what are rare events. However, when we complete multiple comparisons we increase the chance of identifying rare events that are in fact false (Abdi, 2010). In statistical terms this is referred to as *inflation* of alpha (p), and we used the Holm–Bonferroni method to correct the p-values to account for this.

The final part of our data analysis examined the relationship of strength (3 RM) and changes in peak power output following PAP. This analysis was included as previous research indicates that training history and strength of participants has an effect on the outcome of PAP studies (see Hodgson, Docherty, & Robbins, 2005 for a review). As our repeated measures and multiple comparisons had revealed that PAP occurred at 8 min of recovery time, we sampled changes in peak power from this point (power output at 8 min – power output at baseline). A Pearson correlation was used for this analysis as this measures the linear relationship between two variables. In this instance we chose a 1-tailed test (i.e., we hypothesised that the linear relationship would be positive), as previous research indicated that stronger athletes show greater changes in peak power output following PAP. Our results ($r = 0.489, p < .05$) provided some support for this idea. However, to examine this notion further, we concluded this analysis by looking more carefully at the individual participant data to examine where peak power outputs occurred. With experimental designs with relatively small sample sizes, examining the data set can provide useful extra information regarding the pattern of results observed. In this instance it became clear that although the majority of participant peaked in performance in all three dependent variables at 8 minutes (hence the significant finding) the remaining six participants peaked either earlier (4 min) or later (12 min). Scrutinising the data in this way allowed us to make important inferences regarding the individualistic nature of PAP.

Data presentation

This study was published in the *Journal of Sports Science*, which is the journal of the British Association of Sports and Exercise Science. This journal is seen as one of the primary journals for publishing Sports Science related papers in the UK. In addition to publishing the paper here, this data was also presented at a number of Strength and Conditioning conferences and practical workshops in order to ensure that practitioners working in the elite environment were aware of this data and had the opportunity to discuss its practical significance. Presentations at the conferences comprised of invited keynote presentations which presented the current findings in context with already existing literature whereas the presentations to elite teams and practitioners took the form of more practical workshops showing how to incorporate the current findings into their current training and competition practices.

When preparing an experimental manuscript for publication, it is important to consider how best to present the results of the experiment. The results section should be meaningful and directly address the original research question presented in the introduction. In addition, decisions need to be made about the manner in which the data is described or illustrated (e.g., within text, tables or figures/graphs), and repetition (i.e., presenting means in both graphs and tables) should generally be avoided. In our experiment, we decided to use a combination of written description and graphical figures. The written description was used to explain the results of the inferential statistics (i.e., the repeated measures ANOVA and correlations) (Table 8.1), while the graphs were used to display the longitudinal trends in the data over time (i.e., from baseline through to 24 minutes post-intervention) (see Figure 8.1).

Contribution to knowledge

The following is an extract from the discussion section of the published paper, which gives our results context within the literature and also clearly shows what this study added to the knowledge base within this area:

> The results of the present study indicate that the optimal recovery to maximise the effect of PAP on CMJ performance was 8 min in professional rugby players (Figure 8.1A–C). In addition, the present study highlights that when the CMJ was performed immediately after (~15 s) the HRT performance was decreased compared with the same exercise performed with no HRT.

Previous studies have used recovery periods ranging from 0 to 18.5 min (Young et al., 1998; Duthie et al., 2002; Baker, 2003; Chiu et al., 2003; Gourgoulis et al., 2003; Brandenburg, 2005) with no uniform agreement to date on the optimal time required. The majority of the studies have used recovery periods

TABLE 8.1 Tests of within-subjects effects

Source		Type III sum of squares	df	Mean square	F	Sig.	Partial eta squared
Time	Sphericity assumed	173.279	7	24.754	19.633	.000	.508
	Greenhouse–Geisser	173.279	4.445	38.979	19.633	.000	.508
	Huynh–Feldt	173.279	5.971	29.018	19.633	.000	.508
	Lower bound	173.279	1.000	173.279	19.633	.000	.508

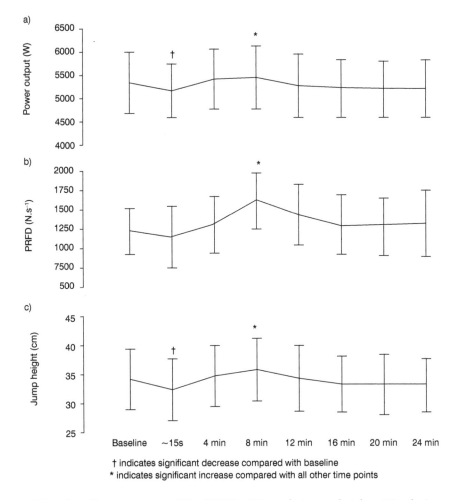

† indicates significant decrease compared with baseline
* indicates significant increase compared with all other time points

FIGURE 8.1 Power output (A), PRFD (B) and jump height (C) during countermovement jumps before and after HRT

of approximately 4 min, presumably to allow for PCr resynthesis following the HRT (e.g. Young et al., 1998; Duthie et al., 2002; Baker, 2003; Brandenburg, 2005). In the present study we allowed 4 min recovery between the HRT and the CMJ and found no significant difference between this time point and baseline. However, we did observe an initial drop in performance when the CMJ was performed immediately after the HRT; consequently, the finding that performance was similar between baseline and 4 min after the HRT did in fact reflect that replenishment of PCr stores had occurred after 4 min of recovery (e.g. Nevill, Jones, McIntyre, Bogdanis & Nevill, 1997) which is in agreement with the findings of Jensen and Ebben (2003).

Only two studies have examined the effectiveness of longer than 6 min recovery between the preload and subsequent exercise (Chiu et al., 2003; Jones & Lees, 2003). For example, Chiu et al. (2003) reported that average force, average power and peak power were significantly greater at 18.5 min postactivation compared with 5 min postactivation. However, as measurements were only taken at these time points, the optimal recovery period could be anywhere between 5 and 18.5 min. The results of the current study help clarify the recovery period needed in order to achieve maximal increases in CMJ performance in well-trained athletes. Our results indicate that 8 min of recovery is required to achieve maximal increases in power output (PO), maximum jump height and peak rate of force development (PRFD). Furthermore, 70 per cent of the subjects performed their best jump at the 8 min time point with the remaining 30 per cent performing better at the 4 min (15 per cent) and 12 min (15 per cent) time points.

Impact on practice

Prior to the completion of this study there was minimal data published on the influence of recovery time on athletes' ability to harness PAP; we feel this study has significantly added to the training science model in that it shows that individual determination of the optimal recovery rest interval is necessary to induce PAP. Not only does the study's findings add to the training science model but as many practitioners now utilise PAP as part of their athletes warm-up we feel that these findings have further application to elite sport in that it now better informs practitioners and athletes when to incorporate PAP into their warm-up strategy.

Dissemination

The results from the above study were presented at numerous academic and applied conferences. From the academic conference perspective presentations took the normal format of basically providing an overview of the study rationale, design, analysis and interpretation. However this style of presentation does not always suit practical setting. Results that were fed back to the club's management included a very simple overview of why power is important and the key findings and meaning (from a training perspective) of the data. Within this presentation players asked a number of very insightful questions which led to further studies in this area such as Bevan et al. (2009, 2010).

Reflection

The primary strengths of the current study were that it was a research question driven by applied practice and that it was carried out in an elite group of athletes to allow the findings to have real transferable impact to this population. However working in the elite environment also brings constraints on the study design; for example, ideally we would have carried out each test on a separate day as opposed to all testing on the one day to ensure no interference from the previous jumps performed.

However, due to time constraints with regard to access to the athletes this was not possible. To minimise this as a potential covariate we examined what impact each previous CMJ would have on the subsequent jump. In order to ensure that any effect observed during this experiment was due to the HRT, 10 subjects were required to complete 7 CMJs following a standardised warm-up with 4 min recovery between each one. This was carried out to ensure that during the main experimental trial there was no warm-up effect or fatigue effect from the subsequent CMJ. A repeated measures one-way analysis of variance revealed no significant time effect over the duration of the study ($ES = 0.78, P = 0.759$).

> If you liked this chapter, you should read Chapters 2, 4 and 12 as the authors describe research processes that focus on furthering knowledge in physiology, exercise and health.

References

Abdi, H. (2010). Holm's sequential Bonferroni procedure. In N. Salkind (Ed.), *Encyclopaedia of Research Designs.* Thousand Oaks, CA: Sage.

Baker, D. (2003). Acute effects of alternating heavy and light resistances on power output during upper-body complex power training. *Journal of Strength and Conditioning Research, 17,* 493–497.

Baker, D., Nance, S., & Moore, M. (2001). The load that maximizes the average mechanical power output during explosive bench press throws in highly trained athletes. *Journal of Strength and Conditioning Research, 15,* 20–24.

Brandenburg, J.P. (2005). The acute effects of prior dynamic resistance exercise using different loads on subsequent upper-body explosive performance in resistance-trained men. *Journal of Strength and Conditioning Research, 19,* 427–432.

Chiu, L.Z.E., Fry, A.C., Weiss, L.W., Schilling, B.K., Brown, L.E., & Smith, S.L. (2003). Postactivation potentiation response in athletic and recreationally trained individuals. *Journal of Strength and Conditioning Research, 17,* 671–677.

Comyns, T.M., Harrison, A.J., Hennessy, L.K., & Jensen, R.L. (2006). The optimal complex training rest interval for athletes from anaerobic sports. *Journal of Strength and Conditioning Research, 20,* 471–476.

Duthie, G., Young, W.B., & Aitken, D. (2002). The acute effects of heavy loads on jump squat performance: An evaluation of the complex and contrast methods of power development. *Journal of Strength and Conditioning Research, 16,* 530–538.

Ebben, W.P., Jensen, R.L., & Blackard, D.O. (2000). Electromyographic and kinetic analysis of complex training variables. *Journal of Strength and Conditioning Research, 14,* 451–456.

Field, A. (2009). *Discovering statistics using SPSS.* London, UK: Sage.

Gossen, E.R. & Sale, D.G. (2000). Effect of postactivation potentiation on dynamic knee extension performance. *European Journal of Applied Physiology, 83,* 524–530.

Gourgoulis, V., Aggeloussis, N., Kasimatis, P., Mavromatic, G., & Garas, A. (2003). Effect of a submaximal half-squat warm-up program on vertical jumping ability. *Journal of Strength and Conditioning Research, 17,* 342–344.

Gullich, A. & Schmidtbleicher, D. (1996). Short-term potentiation of power performance induced by maximal voluntary contractions. *XVth Congress of the International Society of Biomechanics,* pp. 348–349.

Hatze, H. (1998). Validity and reliability of methods for testing vertical jumping performance. *Journal of Applied Biomechanics, 14,* 127–140.

Hodgson, M., Docherty, D. & Robbins, D. (2005). Post-activation potentiation. *Sports Medicine, 35,* 585–595.

Izquierdo, M., Hakkinen, K., Gonzalez-Badillo, J.J., Ibanez, J. & Gorostiaga, E.M. (2002). Effects of long-term training specificity on maximal strength and power of the upper and lower extremities in athletes from different sports. *European Journal of Applied Physiology, 87,* 264–271.

Jones, P. & Lees, A. (2003). A biomechanical analysis of the acute effects of complex training using lower limb exercises. *Journal of Strength and Conditioning Research, 17,* 694–700.

Jensen, R.L., & Ebben, W.P. (2003). Kinetic analysis of complex training rest interval effect on vertical jump performance. *Journal of Strength and Conditioning Research, 17,* 345–349.

Kawamori, N., Crum, A.J., Blumert, P.A., Kulik, J.R., Childers, J.T., Wood, J.A., Stone, M.H. & Haff, G. (2005). Influence of difference relative intensities on power output during the hang power clean: Identification of the optimal load. *Journal of Strength and Conditioning Research, 19,* 698–706.

Kilduff, L.P., Bevan, H., Owen, N., Kingsley, M.I.C., Bunce, P., Bennett, M., & Cunningham, D. (2007). Optimal loading for peak power output during the hang power clean in professional rugby players. *International Journal of Sports Physiology and Performance, 2,* 260–269.

Nevill, A.M., Jones, D.A., McIntyre, D., Bogdanis, G.C., & Nevill, M.E. (1997). A model for phosphocreatine resynthesis. *Journal of Applied Physiology, 82,* 329–335.

Newton, R.U., Murphy, A.J., Humphries, B.J., Wilson, G.J., Kraemer, W.J., & Hakkinen, K. (1997). Influence of load and stretch shortening cycle on the kinematics, kinetics and muscle activation that occurs during explosive upper-body movements. *European Journal of Applied Physiology. 75,* 333–342.

Rassier, D.E. & MacIntosh, B.R. (2000). Coexistence of potentiation and fatigue in skeletal muscle. *Brazilian Journal of Medical and Biological Research, 33,* 499–508.

Stone, M.H., O'Bryant, H.S., McCoy, L., Coglianese, R., Lehmkuhl, M., & Schilling, B. (2003). Power and maximal strength relationships during performance of dynamic and static weighted jumps. *Journal of Strength and Conditioning Research, 17,* 140–147.

Vanrenterghem, J., DeClercq, D., & Van Cleven, P. (2001). Necessary precautions in measuring correct vertical jumping height by means of force plate measurement. *Ergonomics, 44,* 814–818.

Young, W.B., Jenner, A., & Griffiths, K. (1998). Acute enhancement of power performance from heavy load squats. *Journal of Strength and Conditioning Research, 12,* 82–84.

9

SPORT PSYCHOLOGY

An examination of hardiness throughout the sport injury process

Ross Wadey

Article reference

Wadey, R., Evans, L., Hanton, S., & Neil, R. (2012). An examination of hardiness throughout the sport injury process. *British Journal of Health Psychology*, *17*, 103–128.

Article summary

This study examined the effect of hardiness on the prediction of, and athletes' responses to, sport injury. A two-year longitudinal design was conducted with a baseline sample of 694 asymptomatic participants (389 men, 305 women; *M* age = 19.17, *SD* = 1.69 years), 104 of whom subsequently became injured. Logistic regression, Pearson product-moment correlations, and Preacher and Hayes's (2008) bootstrapping procedure were used to analyse the data. Findings revealed a direct and moderating effect of hardiness on the prediction of injury. Hardiness was also found to correlate positively with desirable, and negatively correlate with undesirable, post-injury psychological responses and coping strategies over time. Finally, problem-focused coping was found to mediate certain effects of hardiness on injured athletes' psychological responses. These findings have important implications for practitioners who have a vested interest in the health and well-being of those who participate in sport in terms of minimising rates of injury occurrence and promoting recovery from injury.

Related author publication

Wadey, R., Evans, L., Hanton, S., & Neil, R. (2012). An examination of hardiness throughout the sport injury process: a qualitative follow-up study. *British Journal of Health Psychology*, *17*, 872–893.

Personal prologue

For as long as I can remember I have been fascinated by adversity. Perhaps emanating from my own personal experiences inside and outside of sport, I have always been intrigued why some people are resilient in the face of adversity, whereas others struggle to manage or even succumb to stress. One common type of adversity experienced by sports performers during their competitive career is injury, which was formally introduced to me by Dr Lynne Evans during my studies. When I came to read the psychology of sport injury literature, I was surprised to find that the majority of the research had explored factors that 'predict' injury occurrence and 'exacerbate' negative responses following injury. With this knowledge in mind and my interest in personal resilience, Dr Lynne Evans, Professor Sheldon Hanton, Dr Rich Neil and I had a number of in-depth discussions, which led to the development of a PhD programme of research investigating whether having a resilient disposition (i.e., personality trait of hardiness) can 'prevent' injury occurrence and 'attenuate' negative responses following injury. The significance of this area of research, and the reason why it excited me, was that sport-related injuries at the time were emerging as a public-health concern. This programme of research, therefore, had the potential to inform professional practice by providing practitioners with evidence-based strategies that athletes could use to lower their risk of, and expedite their recovery from, injury. The purpose of this chapter is to describe and explain the processes I went through, guided by the supervisory team, to generate the first study of this programme of research, from developing the research question to utilising the appropriate methods to collect, analyse, and present the data.

Key message: Being a researcher can be challenging at times, which is why it is important to understand and remind yourself of the theoretical and/or practical significance of your study. Taking the time to think about your question and its importance is time well spent.

Moving from a research problem to a research question

Although research devoted to the psychology of sport injury can be dated back to the late 1960s, its most significant development has occurred in the past 20 years. Indeed, scholars in this field of research have made a number of important conceptual, theoretical, and methodological advances to aid our understanding of the biological, psychological, and social factors that prevent and promote recovery from injury (Brewer, 2010; Wiese-Bjornstal, 2010). Of the theories and models used to guide research to date, Williams and Andersen's (1998) stress-based model of the prediction of injury and Wiese-Bjornstal et al.'s (1998) integrated model of injury response have received the most research attention and empirical support. Put simply, the models suggest that personal factors (e.g., personality), situational factors (e.g., social support received from others), and environmental demands (e.g., major life events) can affect one's risk of, and responses and recovery outcomes from, injury. Some consistent findings that had emerged from the literature before I developed my research questions were:

- Major life events predicted injury occurrence (i.e., as the number of major life events increased, the likelihood of injury occurrence increased).
- Certain personal (e.g., optimism) and situational (e.g., social support) factors moderated the positive relationship between major life events and injury occurrence. For example, as social support increased, the strength of the relationship between major life events on injury occurrence decreased.
- Injured athletes' thoughts, feelings, and behaviours had been found to change over time, from injury onset, throughout rehabilitation, and subsequent return to competitive sport.
- Certain personal (e.g., injury severity) and situational (e.g., emotional climate) factors affected athletes' responses to injury. For example, as the severity of injury increased, the level or intensity of injured athletes' reactions increased.

Although these findings greatly enhanced my knowledge and understanding of the psychology of sport injury, from reviewing the literature I identified two main concerns. My first observation was that the literature could be divided into two broad domains: (a) prediction of sport injury, and (b) responses to sport injury. This observation was in contrast to Wiese-Bjornstal et al.'s (1998) integrated model which suggests that pre-injury factors (e.g., major life events and personality) can affect post-injury responses and recovery outcomes. With this knowledge in mind, my initial plan was to extend the literature by conducting a study that integrated these two distinct bodies of research. Indeed, Brewer (2007) reported, 'By integrating research on the causes and consequences of sport injury, a more complete picture of sport injury is likely to result' (p. 418). But although I had decided that I wanted to examine the entire sport injury process (i.e., the prediction of, and response to, injury), I still had not decided on what specific variable(s) to explore. Upon re-examining the literature, my second observation was that it was dominated by negative concepts, in particular stress, anxiety, grief, and depression. Although examining these concepts had provided important insights towards helping practitioners understand how to alleviate the distress athletes' experience pre- and post-injury, I felt it did not provide a complete understanding of the sport injury experience. Drawing from my reading of positive psychology (see Seligman & Csikszentmihalyi, 2000) and a number of anecdotal reports of positive responses and outcomes from injured athletes (see Wilkinson, 2004), I felt there was a need for researchers to investigate positive subjective experiences and positive individual traits that promote positive adjustment following sport injury. This observation excited me at the time; I was excited that if I started to address this gap in the literature it may provide important insights into how injured athletes could capitalise on their strengths to prevent experiencing distress as well as promoting their psychological and physical recovery from injury and their general well-being.

One positive individual trait that had received limited research attention in a sport injury context, and one that I had a great deal of personal interest in, was resilience. I found this omission to be particularly surprising, especially considering that resilience has often been suggested to be associated with 'bouncing back' from various forms of adversity, which can include negative major life events (i.e., a significant predictor of injury) and injury itself. For example, the terms, 'resilient, resilience, and resiliency are often used by coaches and the media to describe favourable responses of athletes or teams to incidents such as catastrophic injuries' (Galli & Vealey, 2008, p. 316). One pathway to resilience according to Bonanno (2004) is what Kobasa (1979) conceptualised as the personality trait of hardiness, which my supervisors were examining at the time (Hanton, Evans, & Neil, 2003). Specifically, hardiness is 'a pattern of attitudes and actions that helps in transforming stressors from potential disasters into growth opportunities' (Maddi, 2005, p. 261). After exploring this disposition in greater depth, and several weeks of extensive discussions with my supervisory team, I decided that the central purpose of my programme of research would be to examine the personality trait of hardiness throughout the sport injury process. My reasoning for selecting the personality trait of hardiness was threefold. First, Williams and Andersen's (1998) and Wiese-Bjornstal et al.'s (1998) models of prediction and response suggest that hardiness could prevent, and facilitate recovery from, injury. Second, hardiness had been shown to lower the risk of physical disorders (e.g., cardiovascular diseases, obesity, cancer, and Alzheimer's disease) and mental health problems such as depression and anxiety (Maddi, 2005); therefore, I felt it may have an important role throughout the sport injury process. Finally, I found that more than two decades have passed since the first call for researchers to examine hardiness in the context of sport injury (Andersen & Williams, 1988), and despite a repeated call (Williams & Andersen, 1998) this construct had yet to be examined systematically.

In line with Williams and Andersen's (1998) and Wiese-Bjornstal et al.'s (1998) theoretical models, my research question was to examine the direct (i.e., the relationship between hardiness and injury occurrence) and moderating (i.e., the influence of hardiness on the strength of the relationship between major life events and injury occurrence) effect of hardiness on the prediction of injury occurrence, and the direct (i.e., the relationship between hardiness and post-injury responses) and indirect (i.e., whether coping explained the relation between hardiness and post-injury responses) effect of hardiness on athletes' responses to injury. In order to guide my study, my next task was to generate a number of hypotheses (i.e., specific, testable predictions about what you expect to happen in your study) that were driven by my research question. The hypotheses I developed were:

- *Hypothesis 1:* An increase in hardiness will decrease the likelihood of injury occurrence.
- *Hypothesis 2:* Hardiness will moderate (weaken rather than strengthen) the relationship between major life events and injury occurrence.
- *Hypothesis 3:* Hardiness will positively correlate with desirable, and negatively correlate with undesirable psychological responses and coping strategies at injury onset, rehabilitation, and return to competition.
- *Hypothesis 4:* The relationship between hardiness and psychological responses will be mediated by coping and this will be determined by problem-focused coping (i.e., strategies to deal with environmental demands) and emotion-focused coping (i.e., strategies to deal with emotional responses) strategies rather than avoidance coping (i.e., strategies to disengage).

Choice of method (Matching the method to the research question)

Given that the research area was reasonably well established, standardised measures of the key concepts had previously been developed, and the research question had a clear theoretical underpinning that aimed to identify relationships between the independent (e.g., hardiness) and dependent variables (e.g., responses to injury), I felt a quantitative approach best fitted my research question. The appropriateness of this approach, and in particular embracing a prospective longitudinal research design (i.e., where one studies a group of people over time to see how suspected risk factors affect a future outcome of interest), was further reinforced by a number of recommendations in the literature:

- Petrie and Falkstein (1998) recommended that future research should use prospective rather than retrospective research designs to examine the prediction of sport injury;
- Evans and Hardy (1999) recommended future research should account for the temporal changes in athletes' responses to injury;
- Brewer (2007) recommended that future research should account for the full temporal sport injury process (i.e., the prediction of, and response to, sport injury).

Data collection

Ethical issues and approval

I researched and discussed all the possible psychological, social and physical risks of harm that the athletes may experience from participating in this study. The two key concerns that we highlighted were: (a) whether completing the pre-injury questionnaires (e.g., major life events) and post-injury measures (e.g., psychological responses) would bring up sensitive issues which could cause the participant to feel anxious or depressed, and (b) ensuring the anonymity of the participants. To address these issues and gain approval from the university's Research Ethics Committee, we made sure that the project was designed according to British Psychological Society ethical guidelines for research with human participants. In particular, all participants were 18 years or older, gave their consent to participate prior to commencing the study, and were informed that participation was entirely voluntary and they had the right to withdraw. This project used standardised, published measures only. Following the questionnaire pack on the debrief form, I also gave the participants the number of the Samaritans, just in case they did feel anxious or depressed following the completion of the measures. To ensure anonymity, questionnaires were kept anonymous but participants were given a 3-digit code (e.g., 123) on their questionnaire pack – which they kept a copy of. Published results also only comprised data derived from descriptive and inferential statistical analyses, no individual results were published.

Questionnaires

One of the most challenging aspects of this research process was deciding on what measures to use. At first, this process involved reviewing the literature and identifying all the potential measures I could use to account for major life events, hardiness, psychological responses, and coping. I found this task particularly challenging because some of the measures were unpublished, developed only for specific studies, difficult to gain access to, and/or had a financial cost (e.g., commercial instruments). Once I had identified all possible questionnaires, I then compared across the measures, paying particular attention to item selection (e.g., how were the items developed?), scale construction (e.g., what statistical analysis was used?), reliability (i.e., test–retest and internal consistency), and validity (i.e., content, criterion, and construct-related validity). All these factors can influence the quality of the data you obtain. To clarify, test–retest and internal consistency are common methods of estimating reliability. Test–retest involves administering a questionnaire to the same set of participants on two different occasions, and calculating the correlations between the scores obtained. High test–retest correlations indicate a more reliable scale. In contrast, internal consistency refers to the degree to which the items that make up the scale are measuring the same underlying construct. The most commonly used statistic to assess internal consistency is Cronbach's coefficient alpha, with values ranging from 0 to 1 (higher values indicate greater reliability). With regard to validity, content validity refers to evidence that the content of a questionnaire corresponds to the construct that it was designed to measure (e.g., having experts in sport injury to assess the items of a questionnaire designed to measure the coping strategies used by injured athletes); criterion validity refers to evidence that scores from a questionnaire correspond with or predict measures conceptually related to the measured construct (e.g., the degree of the correlation between the scores on a questionnaire [sport-confidence] and an outcome that it is designed to predict [successful sporting performance]); and construct validity refers to evidence which shows that the test really is a measure of what it claims to measure (e.g., correlations between theoretically similar measures should be high [mental toughness and resilience] while correlations between theoretically dissimilar measures should be low [optimism and neuroticism]).

Overall, the objective I set myself throughout this process was to identify and employ population-specific measures where possible that had a clear conceptual underpinning and desirable psychometric properties. By desirable psychometric properties, I mean acceptable procedures and values in relation to the construction and validation of the questionnaires (for more specific information regarding measurement in sport and exercise psychology, see Tenenbaum, Eklund, & Kamata, 2012).

Although learning the previous terms and values was not the most exciting thing I have ever done, I cannot stress enough the importance of using well-designed and validated measures. Indeed, it is important that new researchers are aware that not all measures have been systematically developed; making predictions or drawing inferences on the basis of these questionnaires therefore would be misleading and unethical. To shed some light on the process of selecting valid and reliable measures, the following subsections provide insights into the process and specific criteria I used for each measure in my study.

Major life events

Major life events are stressors (e.g., death of a close family member, being fired from job, and marriage), which potentially require a substantial amount of physiological, psychological, and behavioural readjustment (Holmes & Rahe, 1967). Researchers examining major life events within the psychology of sport injury literature have employed a number of measures. The measures used include the Social Readjustment Rating Scale (SRRS; Holmes & Rahe, 1967), Social and Athletic Readjustment Rating Scale (SARRS; Bramwell et al., 1975), Social Readjustment Rating Questionnaire (SRRQ; Coddington, 1972), Life Experiences Survey (LES; Sarason et al., 1978), Athletic Life Experiences Survey (ALES; Passer & Seese, 1983), Life Event Questionnaire (LEQ; Lysens et al., 1986), Adolescent Perceived Experiences Survey (APES; Compas et al., 1987), Sport Experiences Survey (SES; Smith et al., 1992), Life Events Survey for Collegiate Athletes (LESCA; Petrie, 1992), Athletic Experiences Survey (AES; Kerr & Goss, 1996), and Life Events List (LEL; Van Mechelen et al., 1996). Once I had compiled this list of measures and retrieved copies of most of them, I remember sitting at my desk in a complete state of confusion. I just could not understand why so many measures had been developed, especially considering the similarities between them. It was not until about two weeks later, after reading and re-reading the papers and familiarising myself with the content of the questionnaires, that I became aware of the differences between them.

On closer inspection, it was clear that a number of the aforementioned measures were not developed for use with athletic populations. For example, the items within the APES were derived from non-athletic adolescents; the items within the SRRQ were derived from teachers, paediatricians, and mental health workers for non-athletic children; and the items in the LES were developed for the general population. The content validity of these measures, therefore, with regard to athletic populations must be questioned. Indeed, Turner and Wheaton (1997), in their review of measures of major life events, recommended that researchers should ensure the relevance and sensitivity of measures for the population being studied. However, although the items within the SARRS, ALES, AES, and LEQ were derived from athletic samples, they were either developed for male athletes, gymnasts, or first year physical education students. In contrast, the items within the LESCA were derived from a diverse sample of athletes, including both males and females from a variety of sports. Considering that I was interested in generating a number of findings that could be generalised across sex and sports, my initial appraisal was that the LESCA was the most appropriate for my study.

With regard to the psychometric properties of the major life event measures, the majority of them failed to establish any evidence of validity or reliability, including the SARRS, ALES, LEQ, AES, SES, and LEL. In contrast, Petrie (1992) provided some evidence of criterion-related validity and reliability of the LESCA. He found a significant positive relationship between the LESCA and SARRS as well as the LESCA and future injury for males and females across sports. Furthermore, the LESCA was shown to demonstrate adequate test–retest reliability over two different time periods: 1-week and 8-week test–retest reliability for total major life events were .83 and .72, respectively. These findings are satisfactory in that they suggest that the LESCA is relatively stable over time. However, researchers should be aware of the problems with using test–retest correlations with measures of major life events. Indeed, Herbert and Cohen (1996) reported that they 'only indicate whether there is stability in overall scores, not whether specific events are reliably reported over time' (p. 303). Turner and Wheaton (1997) elaborated on this point by discussing their concerns when using test–retest correlations for major life events questionnaires:

> We question the use of test–retest correlations based on total events scores. The practice allows a score of 2, constituted by reporting a job loss and a divorce, to be consistent with a later score of 2 after reporting an assault and a family member dying. The reliability of the total is important, but it is better to achieve that reliability by investigating the consistency of reporting individual items on inventories. (p. 46)

Overall, although I had a few concerns with the LESCA (i.e., the manner in which some of the psychometrics were established, limited evidence of construct validity, and that it is dated), I came to the conclusion that the LESCA was the most appropriate measure to use in my study for two main reasons: (a) the items had been generated from a similar sample pool to my study, and (b) it was the most valid and reliable measure of major life events in a sporting context. Specifically, the LESCA is comprised of 69 major life events. Participants are requested to rate the perceived impact and desirability of each event they had encountered in the last 12 months on an 8-point Likert scale, anchored at −4 (extremely negative) and +4 (extremely positive). The LESCA provides three outcomes: scores for positive major life events, negative major life events, and total major life events. Positive and negative major life event scores reported by the participants were calculated by summing the respective impact scores, whereas the total major life event score was derived by totalling the absolute values for positive and negative major life events.

Hardiness

Hardiness was conceptualised by Kobasa (1979) as the composite of three interrelated resilient attitudes: commitment, control, and challenge (i.e., the 3Cs of hardiness). Individuals high in hardiness feel deeply involved in or committed to the activities in their lives, believe that they can at least partially control events they experience, and consider change as an exciting challenge to further development.

Despite the plethora of research that has examined hardiness and its implications for health and performance outcomes (for a review, see Maddi, 2002), the one question that has continued to plague researchers, in particular myself, is which scale is the most valid and reliable indicator of hardiness? From my reading of the hardiness literature, it appeared that the main shortcoming of the research was the manner in which hardiness had been operationalised. For example, early researchers integrated pre-existing scales of similar concepts to create a measure of hardiness, with some reporting the use of up to 19 subscales. Rather than measuring hardiness directly, the scales also used negative indicators of hardiness (i.e., high scores indicating an absence of hardiness). A measure of alienation, for example, was often used to assess commitment, or powerlessness was used to assess control. What is still unclear is whether these negative indicators are valid reverse-coded measures of the attitudes of hardiness. Adding further to my confusion surrounding the measurement of hardiness was that the number of subscales used varied across studies, with some studies even using the same subscale to assess different attitudes. For example, whereas the powerlessness scale was used to indicate commitment in some studies, it was used to indicate control in others. All in all, and even after reading and re-reading the early literature focusing on hardiness, I found it extremely challenging to draw up a definitive list of hardiness measures, largely because so many variations had been used. To use Hull et al.'s

(1987) words, 'Unfortunately, there now exist nearly as many ways to measure hardiness and its subcomponents as there are people conducting research on the topic. Obviously if progress is to be made in this area, this practice must stop' (p. 521). Still to this day, I could not agree more with their observation. For me, it did not demonstrate an effective approach for developing a robust and unified body of literature. Indeed, the use of multiple and contrasting subscales created a body of research that was difficult to draw any conclusions from.

Encouragingly, one decade after Kobasa introduced the concept of hardiness, and to account for the previous measurement issues, the next generation of measures started to emerge: Dispositional Resilience Scale (DRS; Bartone et al., 1989), Personal Views Survey (PVS; Maddi & Khoshaba, 1994), Personal Views Survey-II (PVS-II; Maddi, 1997), and Personal Views Survey-III (PVS-III; Maddi & Khoshaba, 2001). For example, despite some concerns (e.g., the majority of the items are negative indicators and there is no information on its test–retest reliability), the DRS demonstrated several advantages over previous scales: (a) it includes some positive indicators of hardiness; (b) it uses equal numbers of items to measure commitment, control, and challenge; and (c) the items and scoring of the scale are readily available (see Bartone et al., 1989, pp. 327–328). With regard to the latter point, the PVS and its subsequent editions are only available through the Hardiness Institute as commercial psychometric instruments; this frustrated me at the time, perhaps being a relatively inexperienced researcher, I just could not understand why the authors would not want to publish the measures in the public domain, thereby enabling researchers to use them (without charge) to increase our understanding of the effect of hardiness on important health outcomes. In addition, another drawback of these measures was that there was limited information regarding their development and psychometric properties. In contrast, Bartone et al. (1989) demonstrated evidence of criterion (e.g., the DRS was highly correlated with previous hardiness measures) and construct-related validity (e.g., statistical analysis supported the three factors of commitment, control, and challenge subscales). High internal consistency for the composite hardiness score and its subscales were also found, with Cronbach alpha coefficients all being above .85 for hardiness, .75 for commitment, .66 for control, and .62 for challenge (Bartone et al., 1989). For these reasons I chose to use the DRS in my study. Specifically, the DRS consists of 45 statements about life in general that individuals often feel differently about (15 items per subcomponent). Participants are asked to indicate the truthfulness of each statement on a 4-point Likert scale anchored at 0 (*not at all true*) and 3 (*completely true*). Scores for each subcomponent range from 0 to 45. The composite hardiness score ranges between 0 and 135.

Psychological responses

Researchers interested in the psychology of sport injury have largely focused on injured athletes' psychological responses to date, in particular the emotions and mood states they experience throughout their recovery. Due to the importance placed on injured athletes' psychological responses in the literature, I decided to also read the research focusing on emotions and moods in other contexts (e.g., Lazarus, 2000). At first, I regretted it, because as I soon realised, it was another significant body of the literature for me to get my head around; but as I read on, a number of interesting insights emerged, in particular the difference between emotion and mood. Indeed, a shortcoming of research in the context of sport injury is that the terms emotion and mood are often used interchangeably. For example, researchers who have embraced a quantitative approach to measure athletes' emotional responses to injury have frequently used the Profile of Mood States (POMS; McNair et al., 1971) as the primary measurement tool, which measures six dimensions of mood: anger, confusion, depression, fatigue, tension, and vigour. Although studies generally demonstrate that athletes' mood states shift from a negative to a more positive mood state over time (see Evans et al., 2006), researchers and practitioners need to interpret these findings with caution with regard to how athletes' *emotionally* respond to injury.

From my reading of the literature on emotions and mood at the time, I identified a number of problems with researchers using the POMS to assess injured athletes' emotional responses to injury. Firstly, the POMS is a measure of mood rather than emotion. Indeed, Jones et al. (2005) reported in relation to the mood states assessed by the POMS, 'Fatigue is not an emotion, confusion would probably best be considered a cognitive state, and depression is fraught with clinical connections, which can confuse researchers and athletes' (p. 408). Secondly, Evans et al. (2006) reported that the POMS failed to demonstrate support for the oscillation between highs and lows in athletes' responses to injury. A potential explanation that I found from my reading for this is that mood is proposed to be an 'enduring' low-intensity state in which an individual does not know the causes of the feelings experienced, whereas emotion is proposed to be a more 'transient' high-intensity state that is triggered by an event or stimulus (Jones et al., 2005). Thirdly, the POMS was designed to primarily measure negative rather than positive mood states (Leunes & Burger, 2000), which may help to explain why Appaneal et al. (2009) reported that, 'the majority of research thus far has focused on negative postinjury reactions' (p. 60). For example, the POMS does not account for potential positive emotional responses that may be experienced throughout one's recovery from injury (e.g., happiness, relief, pride, hope, gratitude, and compassion; Lazarus, 2000). Finally, Evans and Hardy (1999) suggested that since the POMS was not developed to measure or predict variables derived from any psychological response model of injury, its content and criterion-related validity with regard to injured populations must be questioned. In summary, although I am not disputing the potential role mood may play in athletes' recovery from injury, an important lesson I learned from reading this literature was the importance of developing and employing population-specific and conceptually accurate measures.

With my concerns about the POMS at the forefront of my mind, I went to speak to my director of studies, Dr Lynne Evans, who specialised in the area of injured athletes' psychological responses. She informed me of a measure she had under review in the *Journal of Sports Rehabilitation* at the time (now published, Evans et al., 2008), which addressed the need for a theoretically-derived and population-specific measure of injured athletes' psychological responses. Using confirmatory factor analysis procedures, Lynne and her colleagues developed the Psychological Responses to Sports Injury Inventory (PRSII). Although the measure did not distinguish between emotion and mood (it operated at a broader level of abstraction), one of its key strengths for me was that all the items were representative of the responses of injured athletes based on a review of clinical, medical, and sport psychology literature and reinforced by a panel of sport psychologists ($N = 6$) who possessed appropriate subject expertise, thereby supporting the content validity of the scale. Results from the confirmation factor analysis also supported the construct validity of the scale by demonstrating good factor loadings and fit statistics (see Evans et al., 2008, p. 31). Evidence of criterion-related validity and reliability were not provided. Despite these shortcomings, it is clear that the PSRII offered a significant improvement over the POMS in that it was theoretically derived, population-specific, and possessed appropriate levels of content validity. From my discussions with Lynne, I felt that these characteristics were essential if researchers and applied practitioners are to accurately assess injured athletes' psychological responses to injury in order to design and implement effective interventions that can expedite athletes' successful return to competitive sport. For these reasons, I chose to use the PRSII in my study. Specifically, the PRSII comprises six subscales: devastation, dispiritedness, reorganisation, isolation, feeling cheated, and restlessness. Each subscale has four items each, apart from reorganisation which consists of three items. Participants are asked to indicate the extent to which each statement reflects how they presently feel on a 5-point Likert scale anchored at 1 (strongly disagree) and 5 (strongly agree). Each subscale score (with the exception of reorganisation) ranges from a low of 4 to a high of 20. For reorganisation, this equates to a low of 3 and a high of 15.

Coping strategies

Coping was the last concept I had to get to grips with before I could even consider data collection. Frustratingly, limited research had focused on coping with injury; therefore I drew heavily from research outside the psychology of sport injury literature. The first book I read was by Lazarus and Folkman (1984), which gave me an excellent grounding of the concept. According to these authors, coping represents a process of constantly changing cognitive and behavioural efforts to manage specific external and/or internal demands appraised as taxing or exceeding one's resources. I then went on to read a few more review papers and specific studies, before I searched for the measures that had been used previously in the sport injury literature. These measures were the Coping with Health and Injury Problems (CHIP; Endler et al., 1998), Coping Orientation to Problems Experienced (COPE; Carver et al., 1989), Coping Response Inventory Adult Form (Moos, 1994), and the Sports Inventory for Pain (Meyers et al., 1992). On closer inspection, I found that none of these measures were developed specifically to assess the coping strategies used by injured athletes throughout their recovery. Once again, to my frustration, there was not a clear choice. Because I did not have sufficient time to develop my own population-specific measure, I decided that the best approach would be to review and synthesise the qualitative literature that had explored injured athletes' use of coping strategies in order to compare the findings with the items on the aforementioned scales to identify which scale possessed the highest level of content validity.

Consistent with other conceptual frameworks (e.g., Lazarus & Folkman, 1984), I found the findings from the qualitative studies (e.g., Gould et al., 1997) could be divided into three dimensions: problem-focused coping (i.e., where an individual attempts to deal with the environmental demands he or she encounters), emotion-focused coping (i.e., where an individual attempts to deal with his or her emotional responses to stressors), and avoidance coping (i.e., where an individual disengages from the task and redirects attention to task-irrelevant cues). When I compared this finding with the measures of coping that had been used in the literature, it was clear that they best aligned with the subscales of the COPE and CHIP. For example, consistent with a series of second-order factor analyses (Lyne & Roger, 2000), which involves grouping subscales rather than individual items, the subscales within the COPE have been found to collapse into problem-focused coping (e.g., planning and active coping), emotion-focused coping (i.e., seeking social support for emotional reasons and focus on and venting of emotions), and avoidance coping (i.e., behavioural and mental disengagement). Furthermore, considering the COPE was among the most commonly used measures in coping research, it had previously been used in the context of sport injury (Quinn & Fallon, 1999), Carver et al. (1989) found that it possessed desirable psychometric properties in terms of validity (i.e., construct validity) and reliability (i.e., test–retest), and Gould et al. (1997) recommended its use based on their qualitative findings, I chose to use the COPE in my study. Specifically, I used the situational-specific version where participants are required to respond to each item on a 4-point Likert scale anchored at 1 (*I am not doing this at all*) and 4 (*I am doing this a lot*). Cronbach's alpha coefficients are generally above .70 (Carver et al., 1989).

Injury

Injury is commonly defined as a medical problem that requires the athlete to miss at least one day of practice and/or competition (Petrie & Falkstein, 1998). For example, a simple count of the number of days the athlete has missed due to injury – generally referred to as 'time-loss' as an indirect measure of injury severity – has been used as an outcome measure. However, from familiarising myself with the psychology of sport injury literature, I found that not only are definitions based on time-loss inconsistent with Williams and Andersen's (1998) model that predicts the greater likelihood of injury as opposed to severity of injury, but according to Johnson et al. (2005), 'This fact has problems. For example, is 6 days missed due to three separate injuries the same as 6 days missed due to one injury?' (p. 34). For this reason, I used number of injuries as the dependent variable in this study. To quantify as an injury, however, I used the following definition: an injury was defined as a medical problem resulting from sport participation that prevented normal training and competition for a minimum period of two weeks. The reason why I used two weeks' time-loss rather than one day was because I was interested in examining athletes' responses to injury over time. Minor scrapes and bruises that may require certain modifications (e.g., strapping or protective garments) for training and competition purposes were not classified as injuries (Andersen & Williams, 1999).

Participants

Sampling in injury research invites a playoff between size and composition. In pursuit of larger sample sizes, researchers have used heterogeneous samples (i.e., where the sample pool is made up of athletes with different characteristics), whereas those interested in sample composition have utilised homogenous smaller samples (i.e., where the sample pool is made up of athletes with similar characteristics). Considering the prospective nature of my study and that I was interested in generalising my results to a broad sample of competitive athletes, I decided to 'cast my net' as wide as possible so to speak to increase the likelihood of identifying injured athletes. Specifically, my sample pool consisted of 694 athletes that were asymptomatic, which Williams and Roepke (1993) defined as 'free from any time-loss injury or restrictions on any type of participation' (p. 21). These participants were drawn from five sports institutions based within the United Kingdom and represented eight team and 18 individual sports. The competitive level at which they participated ranged from recreational to international, with an average of three years' experience at their current level. The mean age of participants was 19.17 (SD = 1.69 years) and 56 per cent of the sample was male. The injury status of the participants was monitored for 2 years. From the original sample of 694, 104 participants incurred an injury, which included fractures, dislocations, strains, and sprains of different body parts. All injuries were diagnosed by a doctor, nurse, or physiotherapist, and the resulting time-loss from training and competition ranged from 14 to 504 days (M days = 49.90; SD = 81.35). The injured participants represented eight team and 10 individual sports from recreational to international standards of competition. Participants had an average of 3 years' experience at their current competitive level. The mean age of participants was 19.22 (SD = 1.10 years) and 53 per cent of the sample was male.

Procedure

Once ethical approval, participant identification, and informed consent had finished, the athletes who agreed to participate were asked to complete a demographic data sheet and pre-injury baseline questionnaires (i.e., LESCA and DRS).

In what was then the most frustrating period of this study, I had to wait for the participants to become injured! I monitored the participants' injury status for two years by contacting them on a weekly basis after scheduled training sessions or competitions. But, days soon turned into weeks, weeks soon turned into months, and still no one had experienced an injury. It was an extremely frustrating position to be in and I started to doubt whether I would ever have sufficient numbers to complete this study. Then to my relief, after several months, a number of athletes informed me they had experienced an injury. I had mixed emotions; on the one hand, I was excited to have participants, whereas on the other I felt bad that I felt so happy about someone experiencing an injury! From that point on, I typically had at least one participant contact me each week. Each participant was requested to complete the PRSII and COPE at three time points: Time 1 was within the first week of injury onset, Time 2 was midway through their rehabilitation, and Time 3 was within the first week of their return to competitive sport. During the first time point, four other details were also recorded: (a) date of injury occurrence, (b) type and location of the injury, (c) who diagnosed the injury, and (d) estimated duration for recovery (i.e., the approximate number of weeks the athlete would be injured and unable to participate in normal training and competition). The latter information was used to estimate the subsequent two time points (i.e., rehabilitation and return to competitive sport), which I monitored as the participants rehabilitation progress unfolded.

Key message: It is important to maintain control over the data collection process to make sure the questionnaires are completed accurately. Petrie and Falkstein (1998) recommended either (a) collecting the data yourself or (b) providing standardised instructions for others who will administer the questionnaires.

Data analysis

It is true what they say, 'if you don't use it, you'll lose it'! When I came to analyse my data, I could not remember how to run a few of the tests. The book that I turned to in order to refresh my memory was Field's (2009) book *Discovering Statistics*. In line with Hypotheses 1 and 2 and my definition of injury (i.e., frequency), I worked out that I needed to use logistic regression. Put simply, logistic regression is multiple regression but with a dependent variable that is categorical (i.e., you are either injured or you are not injured) and independent variables that are continuous (e.g., major life events and hardiness) or categorical (e.g., sex and sport type). In contrast, I used correlations and regression for Hypotheses 3 and

4. Specifically, Pearson product-moment correlation was used to describe the strength and direction of the linear relationship between hardiness and post-injury responses at each time point (Hypothesis 3). For example, this analysis examined whether hardiness was positively or negatively correlated to feeling dispirited at injury onset. But although this analysis described the relationship between two variables, it did not explain how they relate. For this reason, I used Preacher and Hayes's (2008) bootstrapping procedure to examine total (i.e., the effect of all the mediators [coping]) and specific (i.e., the effect of each mediator [problem-focused coping, emotion-focused coping, and avoidance coping]) indirect effects of hardiness on psychological responses (i.e., Hypothesis 4). Another reason why I used the bootstrapping procedure was because Hypothesis 4 involved mediation by multiple potential mediators. For a discussion of some of the advantages of using multiple mediation (i.e., simultaneous mediation by multiple variables) rather than simple mediation (i.e., mediation involving one mediator at a time) see Preacher and Hayes (2008, pp. 881–882).

Data presentation

It was a good feeling when I got to this phase in the research process, because, for me, the hard work was done! The only slight issue I had was that logistic regression had not been used a great deal in the sport psychology literature; therefore, it was difficult to find guidelines about how to present the findings. From reviewing a number of other resources however (e.g., Jaccard, 2001), it soon became clear to me that it is important to present certain values (e.g., Wald test, odds ratio, and confidence intervals). The key value I was interested in was the odds ratio (OR), which represented, 'the change of odds of being in one of the categories of outcome when the value of a predictor increases by one unit' (Tabachnick & Fidell, 2007, p. 461). In my study the odds ratio represented the odds of being injured vs. noninjured relative to a score on an independent variable. If the value is greater than 1 then it indicates that as the independent (predictor) variable increases, the odds of injury occurring increase. Conversely, a value of less than 1 indicates that as the predictor increases, the odds of injury occurring decrease. To provide an example, I found that negative major life events (Wald test $= 84.591$, $p < .001$; OR $= 1.070$, CI $= 1.054$, 1.085) significantly contribute to the prediction of injury status (Hypothesis 1). That is, as negative major life events increased, the likelihood of injury occurrence also increased (odds ratio great than 1). Finally, Jaccard (2001, pp. 53–58) recommended using tabular and/or graphical methods that will assist in the presentation of interaction effects. In terms of my findings, for example, I found a two-way interaction term between negative major life events and hardiness (Wald test $= 24.100$, $p < .001$; OR $= 0.996$, CI $= 0.994$, 0.997). That is, as hardiness and its components increased, the effect of negative major life events on injury status decreased (Hypothesis 2). Moving beyond the mere presentation of these values, I illustrated the interaction effect using a graph (see Figure 9.1).

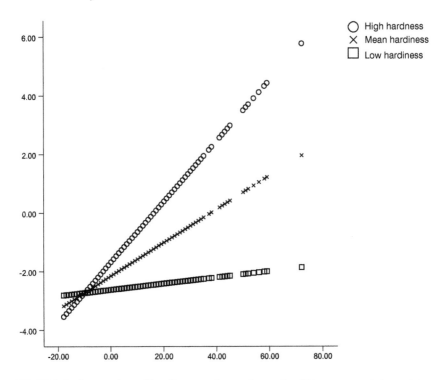

FIGURE 9.1   Interaction of hardiness and negative major life events on injury status

In terms of Hypothesis 3, I presented the Pearson correlation coefficients (*r*) for each recovery phase separately (i.e., injury onset, rehabilitation, and return to competitive sport). To provide an example, I found hardiness to positively correlate with reorganisation (*r* = .29), problem-focused coping (*r* = .27) and emotion-focused coping (*r* = .21), and to negatively correlate with devastation (*r* = –.23) and dispiritedness (*r* = –.28) at injury onset. Although significant (*ps* < .05), all these coefficients reflect a small correlation. Follow-up multiple mediation models at injury onset to examine Hypothesis 4 showed that the total indirect effects for coping mediating the relationship between hardiness and psychological responses were non-significant (*ps* > .05). However, Preacher and Hayes (2008) reported, 'It is entirely possible to find specific indirect effects to be significant in the presence of a nonsignificant total indirect effect' (p. 882). Upon examination of the specific indirect effects, they indicated that problem-focused coping mediated the relationship between hardiness and reorganisation at injury onset (indirect effect = .01). Put simply, athletes high in hardiness used more problem-focused coping, which in turn increased feelings of reorganisation. In line with recommendations (Preacher & Hayes, 2008), I reported this finding in a table (see Table 9.1) and figure (see Figure 9.2), making sure we presented key values (i.e., bootstrap effect, normal effect, normal theory tests, and bias-corrected and accelerated confidence).

TABLE 9.1 Indirect effects of hardiness on psychological responses through proposed mediators at injury onset

	Bootstrap effect	Normal effect	Normal theory tests			Bias corrected and accelerated CIs	
			SE	Z	P	Lower	Upper
Hardiness and reorganisation							
Total effect	.01	.01	.01	1.22	.22	-.00	.02
PFC	.01	.01	.01	2.22	.03	.00	.03
EFC	-.01	-.01	.00	-1.53	.13	-.02	.00
AC	.00	-.00	.00	-0.10	.92	-.00	.00
Contrasts for indirect effects							
PFC vs. EFC	.02	.02	.01	2.31	.02	.00	.04
PFC vs. AC	.01	.01	.01	2.32	.02	.00	.03
EFC vs. AC	-.01	-.01	.00	-1.39	.16	-.02	.00

Note. PFC = Problem-focused coping; EFC = Emotion-focused coping; AC = Avoidance coping; Significant (p < .05) effects indicated in bold.

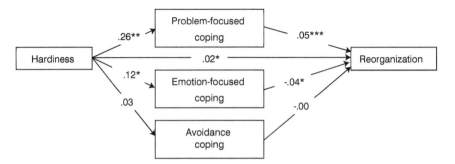

FIGURE 9.2 Coefficients representing effects of hardiness on coping and reorganization at injury onset. $* p < .05$, $** p < .01$, $*** p < .001$. The multiple mediator model was significant, $F(4, 95) = 6.24$, $P < .001$, accounted for 21% of the variance (Adj. R2 = . 17)

Contribution to knowledge

The main contribution I think my study has made to knowledge development was being the first to explore the full-temporal sport injury process (i.e., pre- and post-injury). Therefore, it can provide a useful template for future research to examine the relationships between Williams and Andersen's (1998) and Wiese-Bjornstal et al.'s (1998) models and also how they could be integrated to create a comprehensive theoretical model that describes and explains the sequence of events, responses, and outcomes that encapsulate the injury process. Another way I feel my study has contributed to this field of research is by supporting Williams and Andersen's (1998) and Wiese-Bjornstal et al.'s (1998) models. My findings demonstrated that negative major life events predicted injury occurrence, hardiness predicted injury occurrence and moderated the relationship between major life events and injury occurrence, pre-injury variables affected post-injury responses, and post-injury coping strategies indirectly affected athletes' psychological responses to injury. A final contribution of this study is that it accounted for a number of future research recommendations, including using a prospective research design to examine the prediction of sport injury (Petrie & Falkstein, 1998) and examining the effect of hardiness on the prediction of sport injury (Andersen & Williams, 1988). It also investigated the effect of hardiness on responses to injury (Grove & Creswell, 2007), illuminating the mechanisms by which hardiness operates (Maddi, 2002), utilised population-specific measures that possess appropriate levels of content validity (Evans et al., 2006), and accounted for the temporal changes implicit in response models to injury by using longitudinal (rather than cross-sectional) designs (Evans & Hardy, 1999).

Impact on practice

Encouragingly for athletes, coaches, and practitioners, researchers have demonstrated that hardiness can be learnt and developed (Maddi, 1987; Maddi et al., 1998). Maddi (1987) was the first to develop, implement, and evaluate the efficacy of a hardiness training programme. Unfortunately, the specifics of the intervention programme are only available through the Hardiness Institute (i.e., through their workbooks that contain narratives, examples, exercises, and checkpoints). The programme aimed to transform stressful situations into opportunities for personal development (e.g., turning something bad into something good). Using a waiting-list control group, Maddi (1987) evaluated the efficacy of the training programme on 27 middle-level managers at the Illinois Bell Telephone company. Findings revealed a significant increase in hardiness and job satisfaction as well as a significant decrease in strain (e.g., anxiety, depression, and blood pressure) in the hardiness training group compared with the waiting-list control group of 19 middle-level managers. Extending this study by using relaxation and passive listening control groups, Maddi et al. (1998) also evaluated the efficacy of Maddi's (1987) hardiness training programme. Using 46 lower, middle, and upper level managers of a utilities company, they reported that the 18 managers who received the hardiness training showed significantly greater increases in hardiness, job satisfaction, and perceived levels of social support, along with significant decreases in subjective strain and illness severity compared with those in the relaxation ($N = 12$) and passive listening control groups ($N = 16$).

Despite the fact that researchers have yet to observe the effect of hardiness training programmes in the context of sport injury, for me the previous findings are encouraging in that if athletes can increase their hardiness, they may not only reduce their likelihood of incurring an injury (through psychosocial mechanisms), but also be in a better position to expedite the rate and quality of their recovery if they do get injured through other mediums (e.g., overuse, fatigue, or improper technique). These findings are even more pertinent considering that sport-related injuries have become a public-health concern.

Reflection

Reflecting on this study, I take great pride in the way it has shaped me as a researcher. I became aware of the importance of the research process; the process of generating a research question, planning and implementing a methodology that was driven by the aims of the study, and utilising the most appropriate methods to collect, analyse, and present the data. For me though, the aspect of this study that I am most proud of is that it did not focus on a 'safe' question that was limited in scope and did not challenge existing scientific research. Rather, this study emanated from considerable thought and planning of the most critical question in need of study and how it will contribute to the advancement of knowledge and understanding in the psychology of sport injury literature. Despite evoking considerable uncertainty and discomfort in me from not having a 'blueprint' to work from and having no control as to whether the participants became injured or not, I now strongly believe that by going where researchers have not gone before has ultimately enhanced the quality of this paper and its contribution to the literature. Furthermore, this study fell under the characteristics of significant or high impact studies, which are (a) asking important questions, (b) conducting studies which are part of a line of systematic research, and (c) using and striving for theory development.

In hindsight, would I have done anything differently? In all honesty, probably not. That is not to say that there are not issues with my study, there are several; I was just very fortunate that I had a great deal of time to spend planning this study and I had an experienced supervisory team to guide and challenge me. I guess there have been times though, when I looked back and wished I had incorporated other variables into the study; however, I am aware that this was largely because my interests have changed over time, which is a direct result of the findings from this study. On a related note, another lesson I have learned from going through this research process was that there is only so much you can accomplish in one study; that is why at the end of each paper you see future research directions! I remember one time during the start of this research project when I wanted to incorporate every variable in order to find answers to every possible question. But from going through this research process, I realised that it is important not to be too greedy! What I mean by this point is not asking too much from the participants (e.g., do not ask them to fill out too many questionnaires), otherwise they will get bored and either drop out or provide incomplete or invalid data. My approach now is, 'Only ask participants to do what you would be willing to do yourself.' Another similar lesson that I learned is that research takes a great deal of time; it operates at a very slow pace. A quote from Gandhi that I've always liked is, 'Whatever you do will be insignificant, but it is very important that you do it.' I now know I am never going to solve everything, although I am going to give it a good try, but this quote illustrates to me that it is important for the discipline of sport psychology, which I have become very fond of, that I play my part by contributing at least 'one piece of the giant jigsaw'.

My mind-set now as a researcher is very different from when I started (and I'm sure it will no doubt change again with time), and this study has had a significant contribution to that change. Although it is always important to look at the bigger picture and to have a relatively clear long-term vision to build a body of literature, my approach now is concentrated far more on the process: the process of making sure there is a clear alignment, from the research question to the methodology and methods. But ultimately what it comes down to is that I set myself the same goal for each study: make sure the study achieves its aim(s). It is a lesson I teach all my students now; I always bring them back to their aim(s). I do not profess to be a 'good' researcher, whatever that means, and I am fully aware I will always still have a lot to learn.

On a final note, another lesson I have learned from this study that I teach to my MSc and PhD students, and constantly remind myself of, is to be aware of your strengths and areas in need of improvement as a researcher. Although

I have an appreciation of a number of methodologies, for example, there will always be gaps in my knowledge. The important thing is that I am aware of these gaps and that I do not shy away from them; I do not want to be a 'one-trick pony'. I learned this lesson from my supervisory meetings for this study. Today, I try and work with as many researchers as possible, especially those with strengths that I do not possess, as I know they can provide me with new insights, and hopefully I can offer them something in return.

> If you liked this chapter, you should check out Chapter 13 that conducts a qualitative approach to furthering knowledge within the sport psychology field and Chapters 8 and 12 that adopt statistical tests to analyse research data.

References

Andersen, M.B., & Williams, J.M. (1988). A model of stress and athletic injury: Prediction and prevention. *Journal of Sport and Exercise Psychology, 10*, 294–306.

Andersen, M.B., & Williams, J.M. (1999). Athletic injury, psychosocial factors and perceptual changes during stress. *Journal of Sports Sciences, 17*, 735–741.

Appaneal, R.N., Levine, B.R., Perna, F.M., & Roh, J. (2009). Measuring postinjury depression among male and female competitive athletes. *Journal of Sport and Exercise Psychology, 31*, 60–76.

Bartone, P.T., Ursano, R.J., Wright, K.M., & Ingraham, L.H. (1989). The impact of a military air disaster on the health of assistance workers. *The Journal of Nervous and Mental Disease, 177*, 317–328.

Bonanno, G.A. (2004). Loss, trauma, and human resilience: Have we underestimated the human capacity to thrive after extremely aversive events? *American Psychologist, 59*, 20–28.

Bramwell, S.T., Masuda, M.D., Wagner, N.N., & Holmes, T.H. (1975). Psychosocial factors in athletic injuries: Development and application of the social and athletic readjustment rating scale (SARRS). *Journal of Human Stress, 1*, 6–20.

Brewer, B.W. (2007). Psychology of sport injury rehabilitation. In G. Tenenbaum & R.C. Eklund (Eds.), *Handbook of sport psychology* (3rd Edition) (pp. 404–424). Hoboken, NJ: Wiley.

Brewer, B.W. (2010). The role of psychological factors in sport injury rehabilitation outcomes. *International Review of Sport and Exercise Psychology, 3*, 40–61.

Carver, C.S., Scheier, M.F., & Weintraub, J.K. (1989). Assessing coping strategies: A theoretically based approach. *Journal of Personality and Individual Differences, 2*, 267–283.

Coddington, R.D. (1972). The significance of life events as etiologic factors in the diseases of children. *Journal of Psychosomatic Research, 16*, 7–18.

Compas, B.E., Davis, G.E., Forsythe, C.J., & Wagner, B. (1987). Assessment of major and daily stressful events during adolescence: The adolescent perceived events scale. *Journal of Consulting and Clinical Psychology, 55*, 534–541.

Endler N.S., Parker J.D., & Summerfeldt, L.J. (1998). Coping with health problems: conceptual and methodological issues. *Canadian Journal of Behavioral Sciences, 25*, 384–399.

Evans, L., & Hardy, L. (1999). Psychological and emotional response to athletic injury: Measurement issues. In D. Pargman (Ed.), *Psychological bases of sport injuries* (pp. 49–66). Morgantown, WV: Fitness Information Technology.

Evans, L., Mitchell, I., & Jones, S. (2006). Psychological responses to sport injury: A review of current research. In S. Hanton & S.D. Mellalieu (Eds.), *Literature reviews in sport psychology* (pp. 289–319). New York: Nova Science.

Evans, L., Hardy, L., Mitchell, I., & Rees, T. (2008). The development of a measure of psychological responses to sport injury. *Journal of Sport Rehabilitation*, *16*, 21–37.

Field, A. (2009) *Discovering statistics using SPSS* (3rd Edition). London, UK: Sage.

Galli, N., & Vealey, R.S. (2008). 'Bouncing back' from adversity: Athletes' experiences of resilience. *The Sport Psychologist*, *22*, 316–335.

Gould, D., Udry, E., Bridges, D., & Beck, L. (1997). Coping with season-ending injuries. *The Sport Psychologist*, *11*, 379–399.

Grove, J.R., & Creswell, S.L. (2007). Personality correlates of appraisal, stress, and coping during injury rehabilitation. In D. Pargman (Ed.), *Psychological bases on sport injuries* (3rd Edition), pp. 53–79. Morgantown, WV: Fitness Information Technology.

Hanton, S., Evans, L. & Neil, R. (2003). Hardiness and the competitive trait anxiety response. *Anxiety, Stress, and Coping: An International Journal*, 16, 167–184.

Herbert, T.B., & Cohen, S. (1996). Measurement issues in research on psychosocial stress. In H.B. Kaplan (Ed.), *Psychosocial stress: Perspectives on structure, theory, life course and methods* (pp. 295–332). New York: Academic.

Holmes, T.H., & Rahe, R.H. (1967). The social readjustment rating scale. *Journal of Psychosomatic Research*, *11*, 213–218.

Hull, J.G., Van Treuren, R.R., & Virnelli, S. (1987). Hardiness and health: A critique and alternative approach. *Journal of Personality and Social Psychology*, *53*, 518–530.

Jaccard, J. (2001). *Interaction effects in logistic regression*. Thousand Oaks, CA: Sage Publications.

Johnson, U., Ekengren, J., & Andersen, M.B. (2005). Injury prevention in Sweden: Helping soccer players at risk. *Journal of Sport and Exercise Psychology*, *27*, 32–38.

Jones, M.V., Lane, A.M., Bray, S.R., Uphill, M., & Catlin, J. (2005). Development and validation of the sport emotion questionnaire. *Journal of Sport and Exercise Psychology*, *27*, 407–431.

Kerr, G., & Goss, J. (1996). The effects of a stress management program on injuries and stress levels. *Journal of Applied Sport Psychology*, *8*, 109–117.

Kobasa, S.C. (1979). Stressful life events, personality, and health: an inquiry into hardiness. *Journal of Personality and Social Psychology*, *37*, 1–11.

Lazarus, R.S. (2000). How emotions influence performance in competitive sports. *The Sport Psychologist*, *14*, 229–252.

Lazarus, R.S., & Folkman, S. (1984). *Stress, appraisal, and coping*. New York: Springer.

Leunes, A., & Burger, J. (2000). Profile of mood states research in sport and exercise: Past, present, and future. *Journal of Applied Sport Psychology*, *12*, 5–15.

Lyne, K., & Roger, D. (2000). A psychometric re-assessment of the COPE questionnaire. *Personality and Individual Differences*, *29*, 321–335.

Lysens, R., Vanden Auweele, Y., & Ostyn, M. (1986). The relationship between psychosocial factors and sports injuries. *Journal of Sports Medicine and Physical Fitness*, *26*, 77–84.

Maddi, S.R. (1987). Hardiness training at Illinois Bell Telephone. In J. Opatz (Ed.), *Health promotion evaluation* (pp. 101–115). Stevens Points, WI: National Wellness Institute.

Maddi, S.R. (1997). Personal Views Survey II: A measure of dispositional hardiness. In C.P. Zalaquett & R.J. Woods (Eds.), *Evaluating stress: A book of resources* (pp. 293–310). New York: University Press.

Maddi, S.R. (2002). The story of hardiness: Twenty years of theorizing, research, and practice. *Consulting Psychology Journal: Practice and Research*, *54*, 175–185.

Maddi, S.R. (2005). On hardiness and other pathways to resilience. *American Psychologist*, 60, 261–262.

Maddi, S.R., & Khoshaba, D.M. (1994). Hardiness and mental health. *Journal of Personality Assessment, 63*, 265–274.

Maddi, S.R., & Khoshaba, D.M. (2001). *Personal Views Survey III-R: Internet instruction manual*. Newport Beach, CA: Hardiness Institute.

Maddi, S.R., Kahn, S., & Maddi, K.L. (1998). The effectiveness of hardiness training. *Consulting Psychology Journal: Practice and Research, 58*, 78–86.

McNair, D.M., Lorr, M., & Droppleman, L.F. (1971). *Manual for the Profile of Mood States*. San Diego, CA: Educational and Industrial Testing Service.

Meyers, M.C., Bourgeois, A.E., Stewart, S., & LeUnes, A. (1992). Predicting pain response in athletes: Development and assessment of the Sports Inventory for Pain. *Journal of Sport & Exercise Psychology, 14*, 249–261.

Moos, R.H. (1994). *Coping Response Inventory Adult Form: Professional manual*. Odessa, FL: Psychological Assessment Resources.

Passer, M.W., & Seese, M.D. (1983). Life stress and athletic injury: Examination of positive versus negative events and three moderator variables. *Journal of Human Stress, 9*, 11–16.

Petrie, T. (1992). Psychosocial antecedents of athletic injury: The effects of life stress and social support on female collegiate gymnasts. *Journal of Behavioral Medicine, 18*, 127–138.

Petrie, T., & Falkstein, D.L. (1998). Methodological, measurement, and statistical issues in research in sport injury prediction. *Journal of Applied Sport Psychology, 10*, 26–45.

Preacher, K.J., & Hayes, A.F. (2008). Asymptotic and resampling strategies for assessing and comparing indirect effects in multiple mediator models. *Behavior Research Methods, 40*, 879–891.

Quinn, A.M., & Fallon, B.J. (1999). The changes in psychological characteristics and reactions of elite athletes from injury onset until full recovery. *Journal of Applied Sport Psychology, 11*, 210–229.

Sarason, I.G., Johnson, J.H., & Siegel, J.M. (1978). Assessing the impact of life changes: Development of the life experiences survey. *Journal of Consulting and Clinical Psychology, 46*, 932–946.

Seligman, M.E.P., & Csikszentmihalyi, M. (2000). Positive psychology: An introduction. *American Psychologist, 55*, 5–14.

Smith, R.E., Ptacek, J.T., & Smoll, F.L. (1992). Sensation seeking, stress, and adolescent injuries: A test of stress buffering, risk-taking, and coping skills hypotheses. *Journal of Personality and Social Psychology, 62*, 1016–1024.

Tabachnick, B.G., & Fidell, S.L. (2007). *Using multivariate statistics*. Boston, MA: Pearson Education.

Tenenbaum, G., Eklund, R.C., & Kamata, A. (2012). *Measurement in sport and exercise psychology*. Champaign, IL: Human Kinetics.

Turner, R.J., & Wheaton, B. (1997). Checklist measurement of stressful life events. In S. Cohen, R.C. Kessler, & L.U. Gordon (Eds.), *Measuring stress: A guide for health and social scientists* (pp. 29–58). New York: Oxford University Press.

Van Mechelen, W., Twisk, J., Molendijk, A., Blom, B., Snel, J., & Kemper, H.C.G. (1996). Subject-related risk factors for sports injuries: A 1-yr prospective study in young adults. *Medicine and Science in Sports and Exercise, 28*, 1171–1179.

Wiese-Bjornstal, D.M. (2010). Psychology and socioculture affect injury risk, response, and recovery in high intensity athletes: A consensus statement. *Scandinavian Journal of Medicine and Science in Sports, 20*, 103–111.

Wiese-Bjornstal, D.M., Smith, A.M., Shaffer, S.M., & Morrey, M.A. (1998). An integrated model of response to sport injury: Psychological and sociological dynamics. *Journal of Applied Sport Psychology*, *10*, 46–69.

Wilkinson, J. (2004). *My world*. London: Headline Book Publishing.

Williams, J.M., & Andersen, M.B. (1998). Psychosocial antecedents of sport injury: Review and critique of the stress and injury model. *Journal of Applied Sport Psychology*, *10*, 5–25.

Williams, J.M., & Roepke, N. (1993). Psychology of injury and injury rehabilitation. In R. N. Singer, M. Murphy, & K. Tennant (Eds.), *Handbook of research on sport psychology* (pp. 815–839). New York: Macmillan.

10

PERFORMANCE ANALYSIS

The development of position-specific performance indicators in professional rugby union

Nic James

Article reference

James, N., Mellalieu, S.D., & Jones, N. (2005). The development of position-specific performance indicators in professional rugby union. *Journal of Sports Sciences, 23,* 63–72.

Article summary

The aim of this study was to construct a valid and reliable methodology for the analysis of performance profiles of individual playing positions within rugby union. Twenty-two matches were sampled from the domestic season of a professional male rugby union team. Key performance indicators for individual positions were developed and notated using a computerised behavioural analysis system. Performance profiles of playing positions containing data from one or more individuals were then constructed to compare intra-positional differences. Significant differences (chi square) were observed between individuals within all the tested playing positions for the principal performance indicators (i.e., passing, carrying and tackling for the forward positions, and passing, carrying, tackling and kicking for the backs). For example, the difference between the two outside halves in the study ($p < 0.001$) was illustrated by one of the players having a median of 6 successful carries for the season (95 per cent confidence limits of 13 and 3), whereas the other had a median of 2 successful carries (95 per cent confidence limits of 5 and 1). The findings suggest that while general positional performance profiles appear to exist, intra-positional differences may occur due to variations in an individual's style of play, the decision-making demands of the position and the effects of potential confounding variables. Multiple profiles may therefore be necessary for some playing positions to account for variation in factors such as playing conditions and the strength of the opposition.

Related author publications

Jones, N.M.P., James, N. & Mellalieu, S.D. (2008). An objective method for depicting team performance in elite professional rugby union. *Journal of Sports Sciences, 26*, 691–700.

Jones, N.M.P., Mellalieu, S.D. & James, N. (2004). Team performance indicators as a function of winning and losing in rugby union. *International Journal of Performance Analysis in Sport, 4*, 61–71.

Personal prologue

I became interested in performance analysis as an undergraduate student in 1988 when my focus for dissertation was on analysing my own squash performance. I was ranked number 50 in Wales and wanted to work out what I needed to improve during match play. I wrote a BASIC program for a BBC Microcomputer and inputted data using a Concept keyboard. My data was a comparison of 12 of my games with the same number of games played by the World ranked number 50. This analysis identified over 20 things that he was doing that I was not and in 6 months of training to improve these parts of my game I had risen to number 12 in the Welsh rankings. Performance analysis at the time was not well known, but as luck would have it, my dissertation supervisor, Peter Treadwell, was working for the National Coaching Foundation and he wanted me to write software to analyse different sports for the Welsh National teams. This led me to work with rugby, hockey, netball and judo – but I was keen to pursue further study. Peter and I wrote a research proposal submitted to the School of Psychology at Cardiff University, which suggested that a coach viewing a rugby match was akin to an eyewitness to a criminal event; the credit for this insight belongs to Professor Ian Franks, who has since become a friend, and who wrote a paper "Eyewitness testimony in sport". As luck would have it (again!) the head of school, Professor Haydn Ellis, was a rugby fanatic and expert in eyewitness testimony! Unsurprisingly he was enthused by the proposal and took me on as a research student, waiving the fees in the process! To assist my development as a researcher he suggested that I take a statistics course with Dr John Patrick, who I went to see immediately. More luck, he was a squash player and once I had shown off my talents we became great friends and he took me on as a PhD student studying Applied Cognitive Psychology. This led to my first job as a teaching assistant in Psychology at Swansea University and my final bit of luck (for this story anyway): the University's decision to start a Sports Science course. I beat off an international field of candidates to land the first lecturing post and was in the fortunate position of helping design the course and write modules. Consequently, I wrote and developed a course in Performance Analysis, Psychology and Statistics from first year to postgraduate level. My first student to complete a PhD was Nick Jones and it is some of the work that we did together, assisted by Dr Stephen Mellalieu, that is the focus of this chapter. Nick was a semi-professional rugby player who had heard of me from another player, Neil Hennessy, who was studying for an MPhil at Swansea University. Whilst he was not very focused on what he wanted to study, I suggested it should be something he was interested in and preferably to do with rugby. I suggested performance analysis and gave him some papers to read.

Key message: To some extent you make your own luck in life, but more prophetically, as Arnold Palmer famously said, "It's a funny thing, the more I practise the luckier I get."

Moving from a research problem to a research question

The *research problem* I suggested to Nick was performance analysis of rugby, simply because I thought this would motivate him, a major goal for somebody about to spend three years studying. As a supervisor I wanted him to review the literature and come up with an action plan. However, it is not always the case that a student goes off, reads some papers and returns with a PhD study all mapped out. It is more usual that lots of conversations take place between supervisors and student where ideas are discussed, amended, discarded and finally a plan of action emerges. In this instance, I simultaneously approached a professional rugby team to see if I could get them to pay some money for some performance analysis support. This approach was successful and the money was used to pay Nick's tuition fees and expenses. Working for a rugby team also meant that Nick's source of data was in place.

A review of the relevant literature suggested the need to focus on the development and utilisation of performance indicators (Hughes and Bartlett, 2002), where a performance indicator was referred to as, "a selection, or combination, of action variables that aims to define some or all aspects of a performance" (p. 739). The development of performance indicators can subsequently lead to the creation of performance profiles which were suggested to be a description of a pattern of performance from a team or individual analysed, typically created from collected frequencies of a combination of key performance indicators (e.g., scrum success, turnovers), that offer some prediction of future performance (Hughes et al., 2001). The literature was thus telling us that if we collected data on what players actually did during matches we could use this data to estimate what these players would do in future matches. In doing so we felt that strengths and weaknesses of future opponents could be elucidated and consequently strategies derived to potentially overcome these opponents.

Based on these issues, a clear *research question* was justified. Specifically, we (the research team) deemed it important to provide a detailed analysis of the observable key performance indicators for each playing position within a rugby union team and examine the performance indicators of different individuals from the same playing position to determine whether any potential intra-positional variations may exist. Although previous research had identified some inter-position skill differences, this was not complete and the extent to which these skills varied between games and between players who played in the same position was not known. This was the first step towards making predictions regarding future playing behaviours. There were four reasons why we thought this was necessary:

1   Although a clear picture of certain skill demands of individual playing positions in rugby had already been presented (Parsons and Hughes, 2001; Vivian et al., 2001), common and specific positional profiles had not been constructed.

2   There was little guidance in the extant literature on how to develop a performance profile (the only one at the time being Hughes et al., 2001). In particular, what was the number of samples of performance required before a representation of typical performance could be generated? Logic suggested the greater the number of matches, the more accurate the performance profile, but as Hughes et al. (2001) pointed out, as a database of matches increases in size it becomes more insensitive to changes in playing patterns. This is because a relatively large data set will not be dramatically altered when the data from one match is added. However, when selecting a data set one also has to consider the appropriateness of the data. That is, last season's data may be inappropriate, the last 5 matches may be appropriate for current form, whereas last 10 matches may not. We also recognised that fluctuations in performance were inevitable as performance in rugby union could be dependant upon external factors such as the strength of the opposition, previous performances of the team or individual, the dynamics of the analysed team, and the changing environmental conditions.

3   It was clear that the literature provided little detail as to how or why relevant behaviours were selected, defined and coded by the researcher. We decided that we would also provide validation procedures to ensure that the performance behaviours selected were accurately identified and measured, something not always provided in previous studies.

4   A further methodological limitation with the existing notational analysis literature at the time was that the procedures and measures adopted by researchers often failed to adequately assess reliability (Hughes et al., 2001; Nevill et al., 2002). The research undertaken prior to 2002 was at a time when performance analysts in general had not adequately considered which were the most appropriate methods to use to assess reliability. Consequently, many studies used techniques that have subsequently been shown to be inappropriate (e.g., using ANOVA or t-tests). A special edition of the *International Journal of Performance Analysis in Sport* was published (volume 1, 2007) that focused solely on reliability.

Choice of method (matching the method to the research question)

The first task was to devise a mechanism for translating the game events into a format that could be analysed to satisfy both the rugby team and the PhD. This involved the three members of the research team identifying the key behaviours. We thought we could do this reasonably well since we had a combined experience of 40 years in performance analysis, 50 years in rugby union and knowledge of the existing literature within the field. However, we validated our selection by asking the coaches of the professional team (with a combination of 50 years playing and coaching experience at the elite level) to comment upon, clarify and add to the list if they felt it necessary. This gives the analysis face validity (i.e., on the face of it the people who should know about analysing rugby agree that the techniques employed measure what they are supposed to be measuring). Appropriate changes or alterations were subsequently made. These changes were typically minor (e.g., the definition of a successful kick was changed slightly). Whilst this particular change could have had a dramatic or insignificant effect on the subsequent results, the main point is that the definition was deemed as the most appropriate at that point in time and the definition was made available to other researchers so that if they subsequently wish to compare their results with those of the study they can make a fair comparison. If two studies used the same definition then differences could be due to factors unique to each study, whereas if different definitions had been used then differences may have simply been due to the different definitions used. We recognised that as some behaviours could occur in combination (e.g., passing and tackling), and sometimes were related to specific positions (e.g., a hooker's throw-in to the lineout), both common and specific performance indicators were identified for each position. Our intention was not to produce an exhaustive list of all behaviours but merely to identify the most important (or key) behaviours that define successful or unsuccessful performance for each playing position.

To ensure consistent coding of behaviours, operational definitions for each performance indicator were formulated (Partridge and Franks, 1989). These definitions provided the analyst (and trained researchers for reliability purposes) with fixed parameters to reduce uncertainty or confusion about a code. For example, a successful pass was defined as a throw of the ball from one player's hands to another player of the same team and the pass went straight to the receiving player's hands (regardless of whether or not the ball was caught). All definitions were subject to separate verification by the research team and the panel of elite coaches, with changes made in response to specific feedback where appropriate. This process was very rigorous because the operational definitions effectively determine how reliable the study is. For example, in the example definition above if we had not included the word "straight" then a pass that bounced on the floor before being caught by the receiving player may or may not have been coded as successful. If the operational definition does not include some information and ambiguity exists then different analysts are likely to code the same event differently, hence the low reliability. Of course there can be instances where analysts disagree with what should be classed as a successful pass for example. Sometimes it is not possible to determine what is the correct definition and so by providing the readers with the operational definitions used in the study, the readers can at least determine whether their definitions are the same or otherwise so that fair comparisons can be made.

Having determined the behaviours that we were going to record, we needed some mechanism for achieving this. The Noldus 'Observer Video Pro' behavioural measurement software package (Noldus Information Technology, 1995) was selected as it enabled us to create a unique coding structure that translated the specific rugby behaviours into codes for later analysis. The complexity of the data inputting, and hence the time required, meant that coding would need to take place post-event.

Data collection

Ethical issues and approval

Analysis of sports events that have been broadcast on television have fewer ethical issues than collecting data from participants in a laboratory for example. It is deemed that the participants have consented to their performance being watched and therefore being analysed, although issues relating to storing electronic data can still be relevant. However, when working with a team, and filming specifically to provide an analysis for that team, confidentiality can be an issue. In this situation an analyst may have access to material that is not broadcast (e.g., training sessions), for which participant consent cannot be assumed. Also if a team is paying for the analysis then they have rights over the results and may prefer to keep them away from their competitors, at least during the time when this information could be potentially useful. For this reason we decided to keep the name of the team and its players anonymous. We then gained informed written consent from all participants that they were happy for the results to be published in an anonymous manner. Given the turnaround time from submission to publication for international journals, this effectively meant that the published paper related to data that was too old to be of use to opponents even if they could work out which team had been analysed. Finally we submitted our proposal to a university ethics committee for approval, which was approved.

Participants

Participants were elite, male rugby union players ($N = 22$) from the squad of a professional European rugby union team during the 2001–2002 season. Although a total of 40 players represented the team throughout the season, based upon the findings from previous performance profiling studies in rugby, only individuals who had played more than five whole games were utilised (cf. Vivian et al., 2001; Hughes et al., 2001). Seventy per cent of the full squad had represented their country at international level with a sum of 295 appearances. Sample selection, based upon the availability of match footage, resulted in 22 matches being analysed, 11 were played at home and 11 away, with the team winning a total of 10 and losing 12, scoring a total of 465 points for and 439 against with an average score of 21 points for and 20 against. We felt it important to add these details as they indicated that the sample was fairly balanced in terms of the number of matches played home and away and won and lost. If this had not been the case then any results may have been subject to location or score-line effects.

Procedure

Recorded matches were transferred from VHS to writeable compact discs in MPEG format using the Clipmaster software package (Fast Multimedia AG, 1999). Each video file was viewed within the Observer software and coded so that single key presses translated to specific behaviours. In order to allow a detailed analysis, several codes were entered for certain behaviours. For example, if the playing position of outside-half kicked the ball, the individual's squad number would be inputted followed by the codes for a kick, a descriptor for the type of kick and finally an indicator of the kick's outcome. Once a match was coded, the raw data (> 11,000 rows) was transferred into the SPSS v10.0 statistics package (SPSS Inc., 2000) for analysis.

Reliability

Each operational definition had to enable the person coding the match to be clear as to what any behaviour should be recorded as. If the operational definitions were not clear and ambiguous then the same behaviour could be coded differently by different people or the same person could over time change their view of a behaviour and code it differently. To ensure that this did not happen, both intra- and inter-observer reliability tests were calculated with percentage errors for each variable (Hughes et al., 2001). For intra-observer procedures, the main analyst (Nick, with over 100 hours experience on the analysis system) viewed three randomly selected matches twice over a four-week period under the same conditions. This resulted in a low percentage of errors for all variables (mean $\pm$ s: 1.97 per cent $\pm$ 3.14 per cent). For inter-observer procedures, two researchers (Nic and Steve) with a combined rugby experience of 22 years and a basic knowledge of the system also analysed the same matches. Each output was then compared with that of the main analyst. Both observers demonstrated relatively high error levels for many variables (mean $\pm$ s: 11.09 per cent $\pm$ 8.61 per cent). When all differences were examined in detail to identify reasons for a discrepancy, it was apparent that mistakes were made by the observers with a limited knowledge of the system. Hence key press mistakes and observational errors were made as a consequence of not having had substantial specific training on the behavioural analysis system (cf. James et al., 2002). However, since the study was reliant solely on the main analyst for data input, the reliability results confirmed acceptable levels of error.

Key message: To improve the chances of acceptable reliability in the data, substantial specific training on behavioural analysis systems is required.

Data analysis

Data transformation

One issue that we spent a number of hours thinking about was the fact that individual players often do not play the full match due to substitution or injury. We realised that when constructing a performance profile for each position (using frequencies of behaviours performed during each match) a decision had to be made to account for these individual contributions. For example, although an individual may make five tackles in one half of a match, it is not certain whether this will equate to ten tackles in a whole match. The question was, could we use data from a player who had played an incomplete match or did we discard it? Discarding it seemed intuitively wrong as we realised that this might result in us not having data for some players. In this situation we would be unable to provide information to a coach and this would be unacceptable to us. Alternatively we could use the data but when data is collected from different matches and then simply added up to form one total value (e.g., adding up all of the values for all home matches), the random error associated with each individual measurement (from each match) would be subsumed within the cumulated data (one total value). In this situation all of the variability in the data set would be lost and any subsequent data analysis compromised. So we had to decide how to treat data collected from an individual playing, say, 40 or 20 minutes as opposed to the whole match. In addition, if a large amount of injury time was allowed during a match by the official an adjustment should take place to the data to reflect this extra playing time. Our solution was to transform the data to account for the number of minutes an individual player was on the field, which, according to Howell (1992, p. 316), is appropriate as long as the nature of the transformation is sensible.

The simplest way of dealing with data from an incomplete match is to take the raw frequency data and transform it into a proportionate value related to the time the player spent on the pitch. Here the frequency of the behaviour is multiplied by 80 (total match time) and divided by the number of minutes on the pitch. This transformation is exponential in nature. That is, for low playing times of less than 10 minutes the value of the multiplication is very

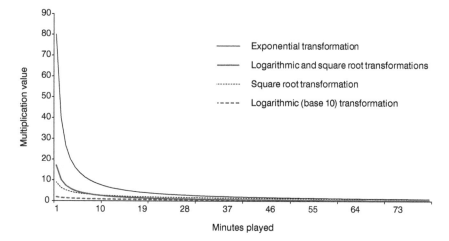

FIGURE 10.1 Multiplication values for different transformations tried

large (between 8, for 10 minutes, and 80, for 1 minute) whereas all values are between 2 and 1 when playing 40 minutes or more (see the black continuous line on Figure 10.1).

Logically, an exponential transformation made sense as we thought that data collected from small playing times were weaker predictors of full match performance than data from larger playing times. We considered this as the "certainty" of the data as we thought that chance factors (e.g., irregular ball bounces, incorrect referee decisions, or slipping on a wet patch of ground) would have more of an effect on the observed frequencies for small playing times than large playing times. We tested the transformation with data and had a situation where a player came off the replacements bench in the latter stages of a match and played only 4 minutes, during which time the team was constantly defending. The tackle rate was high ($n = 5$) due to the team defending for the period the individual was on the pitch but when transforming this value to a full 80 minutes play, an unrealistically high rate ($n = 100$) was created (as the frequency was multiplied by 20). We thought therefore that while the values obtained by the transformation existed in the correct pattern, an exponential curve, the weighting of the transformation for small periods of the match played by an individual was too high. This led us to think about the magnitude of the transformation and so we tried other transformations to see which fitted the data best.

1   The first we tried was the square root transformation (black dashed line, Figure 10.1), as this would lower the magnitude of the transformation for the small playing periods whilst maintaining the integrity of the shape of curve. We again tested this transformation and felt that the resultant value did not appropriately credit performances for small playing times, the example of 5 tackles would result in 10 tackles for the 80 minutes.

2   We also tried a logarithmic (base 10) transformation (grey dashed line, Figure 10.1) as this has the effect of reducing large values dramatically in comparison to small values, with a similar outcome. For our example we would have 2 tackles for the 80 minutes.

3   Finally we multiplied the logarithmic and square root transformations (grey continuous line, Figure 10.1) to come up with what we considered a reasonable multiplication value for any time played; our example results in 20 tackles for the 80 minutes. This approach was based on intuition and logic, as opposed to hard rules, and as such should be considered a solution that requires evidence from future research to assess its robustness.

Whilst we were pretty happy with the transformation, we recognised that a small value for a particular behaviour may also under-represent typical performance. This can also occur when a behaviour is absent from the performance and in this situation all transformations will underestimate full match performance. One solution is to use the mean value previously calculated for a single behaviour. This can be problematical, however, as previous data may be unavailable or unreliable due to an exceptional previous performance. It should also be noted that even in a full match players may not undertake specific behaviours and so values of zero can be expected. Consequently, where behaviours were absent no effort was made to increase them as no general rule could be formulated that accounted for all eventualities. The resultant predictability of the performance behaviours should therefore be interpreted with respect to the possibility of small underestimations in certain, but rare, instances. Coaches may therefore consider the possibility of making ad hoc adjustments for these situations.

Development of performance profiles

In order to assess whether data collected is representative of a performance profile, previous researchers (e.g., Hughes et al., 2001) have suggested assessing the 'stability' of profiles by comparing sample data with sample means from similar distributions (either from other research or the same data set) collected over larger periods. However, this procedure is impossible when collecting data for the first time and is limited in its applicability in many cases due to fluctuations in factors such as team changes, maturation and the fact that some performances never stabilise. We suggested an alternative approach whereby the specific estimates of population medians were calculated from the sample data through confidence limits (CLs). We used median values as opposed to means because the data distributions were typically non-normal, suggesting a non-parametric approach (Zar, 1999). CLs represent upper and lower values between which the true (population) median is likely to fall based on the observed values collected. Non-parametric confidence limits can only be calculated with 6 or more data observations (as these are the only values computed by Zar, 1999) and so this

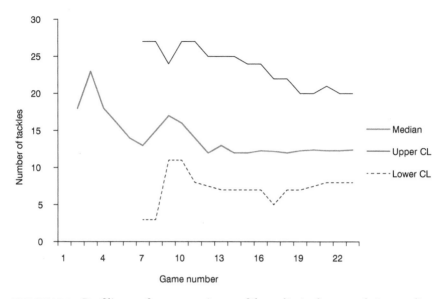

FIGURE 10.2   Profiling performance using confidence limits for a population median

approach can only be used with data from 6 matches or more. Calculated CLs naturally change as more data is collected, typically resulting in the confidence interval (upper CL minus lower CL) decreasing, known as regression to the mean (see, for example, Figure 10.2). We suggested that confidence intervals (CIs) were a more appropriate guide to performance compared with using just the mean, as used by some previous researchers, although the median is a more appropriate measure of central tendency from a statistical perspective, as suggested above. We thought that one value (i.e., a mean or median) would be too constrained due to potential confounding variables that typically affect performance. Rather the upper and lower CIs provide more realistic high and low values for predicting future performance.

To calculate the CL and median values for number of tackles made in Figure 10.2 we simply used a spreadsheet and recorded the value for a performance indicator (using the data transformation technique described above) in chronological order for matches 1 to 22. The median value for the data sample was calculated for matches 1 and 2, matches 1 to 3 and so on up to matches 1 to 22 (green line on Figure 10.2). The upper and lower CLs were similarly calculated although this was only possible for matches 1 to 6, 1 to 7 and so on up to matches 1 to 22 (blue and red lines on Figure 10.2). In order to get the correct values for the lower and upper CLs the data had to first be ordered in magnitude (lowest to highest) which meant that this sorting (achieved in Excel using the sort function) had to be done each time a new data point was added (i.e., once the calculation was done for matches 1 to 6 the data had to be re-ordered for matches 1 to 7). Once the data was sorted, Table 10.1 (order and probability values for calculating confidence limits of a population median) was

TABLE 10.1 Lookup table for CLs (taken from Zar, 1999)

Sample size	Place in order for lower CL	Place in order for upper CL	Exact level (> 95%)
6	1	6	96.9
7	1	7	98.4
8	1	8	99.2
9	2	8	96.1
10	2	9	97.9
11	2	10	98.8
12	3	10	96.1
13	3	11	97.8
14	3	12	98.7
15	4	12	96.5
16	4	13	97.9
17	5	13	95.1
18	5	14	96.9
19	5	15	98.1
20	6	15	95.9
21	6	16	97.3
22	6	17	98.3
23	7	17	96.5
24	7	18	97.7
25	8	18	95.7

consulted to determine which values were to be used for the CLs. For example, for the data for matches 1 to 6, the sample size was 6, the value for the lower CL was then the lowest value (data value for the first number in the order) and the value for the upper CL was then the highest value (sixth in the order; Table 10.1). Note the probability levels (i.e., the probability that the confidence limits calculated are the true values) used were always better than the 95 per cent level of statistical significance, the common level used in published scientific studies.

Since this procedure appears complex I will provide a simple example to try to help you navigate your way through the process. Suppose we had collected data relating to tackles made in rugby matches and the frequency of tackles for the first 6 matches of the season were 12, 14, 10, 6, 18 and 11. First we would re-order the values from low to high (i.e., 6, 10, 11, 12, 14 and 18). Using Table 10.1 we know that the sample size is 6 and so we therefore take the first and sixth values from the ordered data (i.e., 6 and 18). We have thus ascertained that the lower confidence interval is 6 and the upper is 18. Suppose in the next match the player made 15 tackles. The data is now 12, 14, 10, 6, 18, 11 and 15. We need to re-order the values from low to high (i.e., 6, 10, 11, 12, 14, 15 and 18). Using Table 10.1 we now know that the sample size is 7 and so we therefore take the first and seventh values from the ordered data (i.e., 6 and 18). In this example the upper and lower confidence intervals have not changed although this is obviously dependent on the data sample.

Analysis of intra-position differences

We wanted to analyse the performance indicators of different individuals from the same playing position to investigate intra-positional variations within the team. At the outset we had discussed whether players played in a way that suited the team or whether the team's performance changed with the introduction of different players. This is fundamental to how effective substitutions would be and we could not find this type of analysis in the literature. To facilitate comparisons, the 15 positions of a rugby union team were split into groups known as positional clusters (Bracewell, 2003). The original nine clusters (i.e., prop, hooker, lock, openside flanker, blindside flanker and number 8, half-back, first five-eighth, midfield back, outside back) described by Bracewell (2003) were amended to ten after consideration of the positional profiles (i.e., prop, hooker, lock, openside flanker, blindside flanker, number 8, scrum-half, outside-half, centre and outside-back – incorporating the two wings and full-back). Chi square tests were used to examine for significant differences between the behaviours of individuals from the same playing position (Nevill et al., 2002). This test is non-parametric and appropriate for frequency data, hence its use here. We used SPSS but the chi square test can be calculated quite simply in Excel. When comparing individuals, only principal performance indicators were selected for analysis due to the low occurrence (frequency) of certain behaviours – recall that one of the assumptions of the chi square test of independence is that the data comes from a random sample where there are adequate (at least 5) expected cell counts. This meant that behaviours that occurred infrequently would violate the expected count assumption for chi square tests and were consequently not used for analysis. Specifically, passing, carrying and tackling were selected for the forward positional clusters, while passing, carrying, tackling and kicking were selected for the backs. Alpha levels were set at the 95 per cent level of statistical significance.

Data presentation

In order to present the findings of this study we wanted to use a method that best presented the data for interested parties from both the sports and academic fields. This meant that whilst we had to use the appropriate statistical measures from the academic perspective, we also needed to provide something visual so that a non-academic could see and understand the data easily. As a consequence, in this paper we presented both tables of summary statistics for the relevant behaviours for specific positional clusters and figures illustrating both inter-positional comparisons. That is, between the scrum-half and outside-half, and intra-positional comparisons of the positional clusters (i.e., between two outside-halves). In both instances we used the median frequencies and 95 per cent confidence limits for the population median, as described above.

The presentation of summary information in table form allows a lot of information to be presented in a manner that enables the interested person to derive any specific information that they require. However, many readers will not be interested in this data other than for the methodology used, so that they can reproduce them with their own data. Hence, tables are recommended in circumstances where there is a lot of specific data of value to some readers. They can look in detail at the values as they require, everyone else can pay cursory attention and move on.

When the data analysis is fundamental to the paper, in this case to show how our methods had enabled a comparison between or within positional clusters, it is more important to present the data in a way that facilitates the reader "seeing" the data comparison. In this case the use of a figure is more advisable as it is visual. Here we used a line graph with error bars as this allowed us to present the median and the 95 per cent confidence limits (the error bars). We decided that a line was appropriate, rather than plotting the data not joined together with a line, as there was a natural link between the behaviours being presented (i.e., they were all behaviours performed by an individual player or positional cluster).

Contribution to knowledge

The aim of this study had been to construct a rigorous methodology for the analysis of individual performances within rugby union, which enhanced the methods presented in previous studies. This was achieved through the development of validated key performance indicators (Hughes and Bartlett, 2002), the adoption of appropriate reliability procedures (Hughes et al., 2001) and the use of appropriate statistical techniques to determine individual player performance profiles and make intra-positional comparisons. We thus presented an explicit process for identifying key performance behaviours, together with suitable descriptions of these behaviours, verified by individuals with considerable coaching and playing experience in the sport.

At the time of writing this paper the notational analysis literature was divided on how to construct a performance profile and the amount of data required for the analyst to be confident that the number of behaviours recorded were truly representative of an individual's performance of that behaviour. Two viewpoints were prevalent at the time; Hughes et al. (2001) had suggested that without achieving a stable profile for a set of performance behaviours, any inferences regarding an individual or team performance can be taken as somewhat spurious; O'Donoghue (2004), on the other hand, argued that performances might never stabilise for some performance indicators as he found that within-player variability (between soccer matches or even within the same match) could exceed the differences between different positional groups. We introduced the use of confidence limits to represent upper and lower limits for the population median of performance behaviours as we thought this was the most applicable methodology, particularly to the applied practitioner, for producing performance profiles which could be established after the collection of relatively few data sets ($n = 6$). We noted, in a similar manner to O'Donoghue (2004), that some performance profiles may never "stabilise" or become consistent due to the variability or unpredictability of the individual. Therefore, the use of confidence limits, as opposed to a single measure such as a mean value, provides an appropriate process for assessing whether there is consistency or inconsistency in performance.

Impact on practice

The development of an objective performance analysis system that presents relatively consistent (or inconsistent) values for performance behaviours of individual positions allows the coach/sports scientist to monitor the impact of any intervention strategy (technical, tactical, mental or physical) upon the team or individual with an increased degree of confidence. It is only by recording and assessing behaviour over time that changes in performance can be adequately determined; this can then lead to establishing why these changes have occurred (e.g., a positive consequence of an intervention or training, fatigue effects, opposition quality, match location).

The focus of this paper had been on the development of a rigorous methodology for analysing rugby union performance. We had presented some profiles for some performances but felt that this was only the beginning in terms of the types of profile that could be presented. As this work had to satisfy both the rugby team that was paying for performance analysis support and the PhD study, there was both a theoretical and applied perspective to fulfil. Of particular interest was an applied development of this methodology that came about as a consequence of trying to determine what strengths and weaknesses the rugby team being worked for had in comparison to their main rivals for a league competition they were competing in. These two teams were about to play each other in a crucial match that was likely to determine the outcome of the league competition. To assess the strengths and weaknesses of both teams the median values of 12 performance indicators (taken from the team's previous five matches) were compared with the same performance indicators for the opposition team in their previous five matches (presented at an international conference). The previous five matches of both teams were closely matched

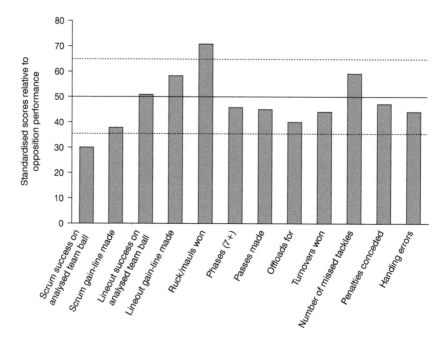

FIGURE 10.3 Form chart comparing the median performances for the analysed team (previous 5 matches) relative to the prior performance (previous 5 matches) by their next opponents

as they had been against almost identical opposition and played in similar conditions with the same home/away ratio. We hypothesised that the resulting profile (Figure 10.3) would indicate where the teams differed in performance and this was used as a basis for predicting how the subsequent match between the two teams would unfold.

The method for constructing the form chart was presented in Jones et al. (2008) but in simple terms we used the median value for each performance indicator for our team and compared this with the median and interquartile range for the opponents. Standardised values were calculated so that all performance indicators could be viewed on one scale using the formula:

$$\text{Transformed score} = (15)\left(\frac{X - Mdn}{IQR}\right) + 50$$

where X is the median value of our team's five-match sample, Mdn and IQR are the five-match sample median and interquartile range for the opposition team. This formula was derived from the formula for calculating z scores (also known as standard scores) where the z score for an individual score is equal to the score minus the mean value for a distribution divided by the standard deviation for the distribution. We changed the mean and standard deviation to the median and interquartile range (for the reasons explained above). Standard scores have the effect of converting any distribution to a standard distribution with a mean of zero and a standard deviation of one. If the standard score is then multiplied by a value, that value becomes the new standard deviation for the distribution (since one multiplied by x is always x). In the same way, adding a value to the equation changes the mean from 0 to the new value. In essence the values we used would create a distribution which would have lowest scores of around 5 and highest scores of around 95, although these extreme values would rarely be seen. This is not exact but essentially performances on any performance indicator would range between values of 5 and 95 (close to 0 and 100) and hence we have created a scale which is well known to most people (a score out of 100) with average performance at 50. Consequently performance indicators whose better performances were represented by lower scores were reverse scored so that high transformed scores always reflected better performance. Thus, performance indicators which had values greater than the median line ($y = 50$) indicated that the analysed team had produced better average performances compared with the opposition team, whilst those falling below 50 indicated poorer performance (Figure 10.3). On this basis we predicted that in the subsequent match between the two teams our team would perform worse on some behaviours (e.g., scrum success on analysed team ball) and better on others (e.g., rucks/mauls won). When this prediction was assessed by comparing the form chart with the data from the match between the two teams we found that we had correctly predicted the team's performance relative to the opponents for 10 of the 12 performance indicators (lineout success on the analysed team's ball and handling errors were erroneous). Whilst this outcome tends to support the usefulness of the form chart it should be noted that this was one comparison and as such may not be representative of future comparisons. However, we think that this development of our methodology shows great promise as the form chart presents data in a visually simple and comparable manner. Coaches and players alike can instantly pinpoint specific areas where performance is below set standards or vice versa.

Reflection

Looking back, it is clear that the strengths of this paper lie in the robust methodology and the presentation of new statistical procedures. Whilst the main audience for this paper has been in academic circles it has been gratifying that performance analysts working for professional teams (in sports other than rugby also) have asked for advice on how to undertake some of these procedures. This suggests that the work could be described as "real world" sports science of practical relevance to both academics and practitioners. For example, these procedures can help performance analysts assess whether performances are poor or good in relation to prior performances and hence help make informed coaching decisions both during and post-event. At the time of writing this paper we were grappling with applied questions related to how to present behaviour data but more importantly what do to with this data. To this end we successfully developed a method for presenting the data but there remain to this day a large number of questions related to what to do with the data. Fundamentally, we observed that while differences existed in some of the positions analysed in our study (e.g., outside-half), more research was required to determine whether a single profile for a position could be created or whether two or more profiles were required to account for potential confounding variables such as the time of day, match venue, officials, weather conditions, the effect of injured players and the nature and strength of opposition (Taylor et al., 2008). This need has, to some extent, been embraced by the research community although not specifically in rugby.

The successes in producing consistent performance profiles (i.e., with relatively small confidence intervals), will aid the ability to predict future performance as if performance is consistent then we have some degree of certainty as to what is likely to happen in a future match. Inconsistent profiles on the other hand do not allow for precise estimates of future performance. We speculate that repeatable performance exists to some extent (i.e., if x happens then y will follow), and the construction of profiles using the methods described in this paper will facilitate finding them. However, what we did not do in this paper, and is critical in the future, is to produce profiles of performance that are specific to certain aspects of play. For example, it is obvious that a rugby team's performance is affected by the playing conditions when comparing performance on a very wet pitch to a dry one. It seems sensible therefore to construct profiles for behaviours on wet and dry pitches separately. This would reduce the variability evident in one profile undertaken on both wet and dry pitches. To accurately achieve this goal, profiles would need to be constructed at each level of all independent variables that affect performance, itself a very time-consuming task. For this reason this paper did not attempt to present a comprehensive profile of the analysed team's performance, rather exemplars were given. In the future it is hoped that better statistical techniques will be presented that can simplify the rationalisation of independent variables so that more accurate profiles can be produced which have better predictive validity.

If you liked this chapter, you should check out Chapter 6 where Marianne Gittoes describes a research process that focuses on developing a biomechanical model to understand physical demands in sport and Chapters 8 and 12 that use figures to visually represent research findings.

References

Bracewell, P.J. (2003). Monitoring meaningful rugby ratings. *Journal of Sports Sciences, 21,* 611–620.

Fast Multimedia AG (1999). *Fast Multimedia Clipmaster, Software User's Guide.* Munich, Germany: Fast Multimedia AG.

Howell, D.C. (1992). *Statistical Methods for Psychology – Third Edition.* California, USA: Duxbury Press.

Hughes, M.D. and Bartlett, R.M. (2002). The use of performance indicators in performance analysis. *Journal of Sports Sciences, 20,* 739–754.

Hughes, M.D., Evans, S. and Wells, J. (2001). Establishing normative profiles in performance analysis. *International Journal of Performance Analysis in Sport, 1,* 1–26.

James, N., Jones, N.M.P. and Hollely, C. (2002). Reliability of selected performance analysis systems in football and rugby. Research paper presented at the 4th International Conference on Methods and Techniques in Behavioural Research. Amsterdam, The Netherlands, August.

Jones, N.M.P., James, N. and Mellalieu, S.D. (2008). An objective method for depicting team performance in elite professional rugby union. *Journal of Sports Sciences, 26,* 691–700.

Nevill, A.M., Atkinson, G., Hughes, M.D. and Cooper, S.M. (2002). Statistical methods for analysing discrete and categorical data recorded in performance analysis. *Journal of Sports Sciences, 20,* 829–844.

Noldus Information Technology (1995). *The Observer Version 3.0, Base Package for Windows Reference Manual.* Wageningen, The Netherlands: Noldus Information Technology.

O'Donoghue, P.G. (2004). Sources of variability in time-motion data; measurement error and within player variability in work-rate. *International Journal of Performance Analysis of Sport, 4,* 42–49.

Parsons, A. and Hughes, M.D. (2001). Performance profiles of male rugby union players. In *Pass.com: Fifth World Congress of Performance Analysis of Sport* (edited by M.D. Hughes and I. Franks), pp. 129–136. Cardiff, UK: Centre for Performance Analysis, University of Wales Institute, Cardiff.

Partridge, D. and Franks, I.M. (1989). A detailed analysis of crossing opportunities from the 1986 World Cup (Part I). *Soccer Journal,* May/June, 47–50.

SPSS Inc. (2000). *SPSS for Windows Version 10: User's Guide.* Chicago, USA: SPSS Inc.

Taylor, J.B., Mellalieu, S.D., James, N. and Shearer, D.A. (2008). The influence of match location, quality of opposition, and match status on technical performance in professional Association Football. *Journal of Sports Sciences, 26,* 885–895.

Vivian, R., Mullen, R. and Hughes, M.D. (2001). Performance profiles at league, European Cup and international levels of male rugby union players, with specific reference to flankers, number 8s and number 9s. In *Pass.com: Fifth World Congress of Performance Analysis of Sport* (edited by M.D. Hughes and I. Franks), pp. 137–143. Cardiff, UK: Centre for Performance Analysis, University of Wales Institute, Cardiff.

Zar, J.H. (1999). *Biostatistical Analysis,* 4th edn. Englewood Cliffs, NJ: Prentice-Hall.

11

SPORT DEVELOPMENT

Volunteers in sport, and social inclusion: Manchester Event Volunteers

Geoff Nichols and Rita Ralston

Article reference

Nichols, G. and Ralston, R. (2011) Social inclusion through volunteering – a potential legacy of the 2012 Olympic Games. *Sociology, 45*, 900–914.

Article summary

Considerations of Olympic Games' legacies have focused on economic benefits, with little consideration given to the potential legacy from the substantial number of volunteers involved. This paper examines the experiences of volunteers in a programme established as a legacy of the 2002 Commonwealth Games. Its results challenge the dominant social inclusion discourse in showing that volunteering provides social inclusion benefits beyond employability by enriching volunteers' lives and empowering them to make new choices. Recognising and valuing this would have enabled 'social inclusion' programmes promoting volunteering at major events, such as the 2012 Olympics, to broaden their objectives.

Related author publications

Nichols, G. and Ralston, R. (2011b) *Manchester Event Volunteers: a role model and a legacy.* University of Sheffield Management School.
http://www.shef.ac.uk/polopoly_fs/1.227269!/file/MEV_2012_with_cover.pdf.
Nichols, G. and Ralston R. (2011c) Lessons from the volunteering legacy of the 2002 Commonwealth Games. *Urban Studies, 49*, 165–180.

Personal prologue

Building on our previous research on volunteering in sport, this chapter presents some of our work with Manchester Event Volunteers (MEV). Geoff had researched volunteering in sport since 1996. He had been involved in teams conducting national surveys of sport volunteers in 1996 and 2002 (for Sport England), and a national survey of sport clubs for the Sport and Recreation Alliance in 2009. In 2003 he also reviewed the contribution of the voluntary sector in sport to the Agenda of the Home Office Active Communities Unit for the Central Council for Physical Recreation, and later, in 2008, he contributed to a report for sportscotland on the effect of child protection legislation on volunteers. Most relevant to the research reported in this chapter, in 2007 Geoff instigated research into Newham Volunteers (Nichols and Ojala, 2009; Nichols, 2009) because this volunteer broker organisation appeared to offer a model for developing a volunteering legacy for the 2012 Olympics. Although Geoff did not realise it at the time, Newham Volunteers was modelled almost exactly on MEV. For two years prior to this Geoff, Rita and two other researchers had been attempting, unsuccessfully, to gain access to the 2012 Olympic volunteering programme with a view to conducting action research and informing the development of the programme.

Rita led a team in the UK Sport funded study into volunteers at the 2002 Commonwealth Games. This resulted in a series of publications (Downward and Ralston, 2006; Ralston et al., 2005; Ralston et al., 2004), as well as reports for UK Sport (Ralston et al., 2003a; 2003b; 2004; Games Final Report, undated). Rita also had continued a close involvement with event volunteers in Manchester, and had personal contacts with MEV management who were the critical 'brokers' for providing access to the organisation, and were also 'stakeholders' in that they had an interest in the outcome of the research. The politics of research, access and interest groups are very important to appreciate, especially in management research (Easterby-Smith et al., 2008). Thus, for both Geoff and Rita, the work with MEV built on considerable previous experience and their previous collaboration in attempting to develop a programme of research around volunteers at the 2012 Olympics. At the time, MEV was probably the best example of a volunteering legacy organisation developed from a mega-sports event.

The study that is the focus of this chapter was therefore a natural extension of our interests, we had access through personal contacts, and the study was of topical interest. Our previous research work gave us credibility with MEV, and beyond that, we were both genuinely interested in promoting sport volunteering. Perhaps if our approaches to the London Olympics had been successful, Geoff would not have developed the work with Newham Volunteers, and together we might not have had the capacity to research MEV. But MEV offered a very topical case study as it illustrated the potential volunteering legacy from the London Olympics.

Although we had shared interests we were working in quite different institutions. Geoff was in a 'research led' university, where he was expected to undertake research and, in theory, this accounted for 40 per cent of his workload. In contrast, Rita was working in a 'new university' where there was an extremely heavy teaching and administration load with no time allocated for research. This meant that Rita's research was in practice an addition to her 'normal' working hours, requiring considerable commitment. Some working environments offer much more scope for conducting research than others! Geoff's managers tried to dissuade him from working with colleagues from new universities as they would not have the capacity or inclination to aim for publication in top-level journals. (We discuss the implications for research outputs of the Research Excellence Framework and the journal hierarchy within management studies later.) However, an important lesson from this chapter is that researchers can make good partnerships outside their own universities. We had complementary skills that achieved a lot of synergy, we were able to rely on each other for different tasks while respecting and understanding each other's situations, and we benefitted from being able to discuss the research ideas between us.

The main research project

Supported by Manchester City Council, MEV was established after the 2002 Commonwealth Games to provide a range of volunteering opportunities and to develop the human legacy of the Games. It acts as a broker, feeding volunteers into events in the north west of England, and contributes an essential sector of the tourism labour force. Volunteers register with MEV and after a basic training session become members and are added to the database of prospective event volunteers. Some volunteers have been members since volunteering at the 2002 Commonwealth Games; others have joined since then. Event managers coming to the Manchester area will contact MEV, and following a process of 'vetting' the event for good practice in volunteer management, MEV will then advertise it to its database of volunteers. This allows volunteers to choose which events they volunteer for and how many. By 2009, MEV appeared to offer the best case study organisation in the UK to show how the 2012 Olympics might be linked to local volunteer development programmes, as it continued to draw on volunteers enthused by the 2002 Commonwealth Games. For instance, in 2008 around 1,500 volunteers had been involved in over 150 events – this represented some volunteers who had helped at a large number of events and some at just one or two.

Main research project objectives

The first phase of the MEV research project was funded by a Knowledge Transfer Rapid Response grant from Sheffield University of £3,442 (awarded within ten days of submission of the application) and a short project grant from Manchester Metropolitan University, initially of £1,054. The specific research questions were:

a   How many of the MEV volunteers volunteered at the 2002 Commonwealth Games?
b   For those that volunteered at the Commonwealth Games, how important was MEV in allowing them to continue volunteering?
c   What do the volunteers want from their involvement with MEV?
d   What does MEV want from the volunteers?
e   What do volunteers want from events?
f   What do event managers want from volunteers and from MEV? How is managing volunteers different to managing paid employees?

The paper described in this chapter developed from questions c and e.

Main research project methods

The programme of research addressed these questions through a pragmatic mixed method design (Tashakkori and Teddlie, 1998). All stakeholders were included and resulted in interviews with MEV managers, three focus groups of volunteers, a postal questionnaire sent to the volunteers registered with MEV, interviews with nine event managers, and an analysis of the MEV database and documentation. This case study approach allowed the research to address *how* and *why* questions of a contemporary phenomenon (Yin, 2009; Veal, 2011) using a 'case' that offered unique insights. This approach also reflected the methodological position of 'scientific realism' – that is to say, it was beneficial to combine quantitative and qualitative methods to understand what works in what circumstances (Pawson and Tilley, 1997). Developed in criminology, it is an approach to evaluation that has been very influential and is now commonly adopted in evaluation of sports initiatives. (Alternative methodological approaches to evaluation are reviewed in Nichols, 2007.) As Tilley (2000: 110) put it:

> In my particular case, realistic evaluation has provided a way of dealing with two sources of contemporary unease: about that aspect of postmodernism which casts doubt on the possibility of objective knowledge; and about that aspect of modernism that promises universal unconditional truths. Realistic evaluation ... seems to me to steer a course between the Scylla of relativism and the Charybdis of absolutism.

In other words, it is a pragmatic methodological position – avoiding the potential complete relativism of a social constructionist perspective in which individuals create their own social realities, and the inevitability of complete determinism implied by positivism. Bryman and Bell (2011) provide an excellent introduction to the philosophical assumptions underpinning these contrasting methodologies.

The research was due to be completed between May and October 2009. In practice the interviews with event managers continued into December 2009, and the final report (for which further funding was required) was written in March 2011 and published in September 2011! This illustrates that a small, easily obtained grant can fund a substantial project, but that it is easy to underestimate how long it will take, especially when all the fieldwork had to be conducted by the two researchers without sufficient funding to employ support workers. It is worth noting that the grant proposal was explicit about target journals for academic papers, the benefits for MEV and the broader benefits of disseminating the findings. The proposal also stated that the research:

> Will put us in a unique position to inform public policy on how the 2012 Olympics can link volunteers with local volunteer development programmes to create a legacy of volunteering and to work with the 2014 Commonwealth Games in Glasgow. It will improve the management of volunteers by MEV and by event managers, and will enable MEV to improve its information to volunteers and guidance to event managers.

We believe the research achieved this.

Key messages: It's important to do research that has useful outcomes – in our case, on the effectiveness of the MEV. Being able to negotiate access is critical and the organisation being researched has to see a benefit for itself.

From the main research project to the current study

The second phase of the research emerged from the first. From the interviews with MEV managers and the focus groups held with volunteers, it quickly became apparent that the rewards of volunteering were very significant, especially for the long-term volunteers. Many of these were retired, and for some of them who were still working, the rewards of volunteering seemed to be more important than those of paid work. This led us to propose an exploration of the rewards and meanings of volunteering for the regular volunteers. In-depth interviews were designed to examine the extent to which volunteering with MEV had helped volunteers move into paid work, or provided alternative rewards. These objectives were influenced by social inclusion – a dominant political agenda that strongly influenced policy within Manchester City Council, and also by the broader understanding we were gaining of the rewards of volunteering. The experience of volunteering as social inclusion became the focus of the research.

Data collection

Sampling

Although MEV had 1,500 active volunteers on its database (i.e., those who have expressed an interest and are available to volunteer), internal records showed that only 490 of the database members had actually volunteered during the preceding two years. A 'hard core' of MEV members tended to volunteer very frequently. To meet the objectives of the interviews it was necessary to sample the volunteers who had greatest experience of volunteering, and within this sample to contrast volunteers who were retired, in paid employment, or seeking paid employment. This was because those with greatest experience of volunteering would probably have been most affected (positively) by the experience. It was also necessary to contrast the experiences of those with different employment status. Interviewees were recruited either through responding to an advertisement in MEV's weekly newsletter and/or website, or through personal contact by MEV staff. In total, this approach generated 20 potential interviewees, although four of these did not attend. Sixteen individual in-depth interviews lasting 1½ to 2 hours were conducted in April and May 2010 with volunteers reflecting a range of experiences. Six interviewees had volunteered at the Commonwealth Games in 2002, and although, collectively, they over-represented this set of experiences amongst MEV volunteers, they did provide a long-term perspective of volunteering.

Process and interview guide

The interviews were all conducted in a location convenient to the interviewee, where there would be no disturbance or distraction, and the interviewee could be reassured of privacy during the interviews (offices in Manchester Town Hall or Manchester Metropolitan University). Interviewees were offered sessions in the morning, afternoon or evening.

The interviews focused on the rewards from volunteering and the relation of volunteering to paid employment. They were semi-structured by themes: an overview of the volunteer's experience with MEV; their employment status and motivations for volunteering; if they were seeking employment – how had volunteering helped this; if they were not seeking employment – how had they benefitted from volunteering; and the contribution of volunteering to the community. Within each theme there were a set of potential prompts, some of which were organised within sub-themes. Thus the interviews allowed considerable scope for developing new insights in an inductive manner from the interaction between interviewer and interviewee. A considerable range of interview skills was required (Veal, 2011; Bryman and Bell, 2011) and illustrated contrasts between Geoff and Rita's individual styles. Geoff was better at drawing the wandering and verbose respondent back to the topic of the research;

important in interviewing Andy – one of the participants (Nichols and Ralston, 2011a). Rita was better at drawing out sensitive personal issues, for example, Gloria's experiences of establishing her own sense of identity after her husband had died (Nichols and Ralston, 2011a). To a point this highlights differences in our personalities (abrupt and to the point/sensitive and sociable) but it also illustrates a tension in qualitative interviews between the more deductive approach of drawing interviewees back to the theoretical structure the researcher has brought to the research, and allowing interviewees to express themselves within their own conceptual frameworks, and hence provide the researcher with new inductive insights. There is an important theoretical point here – the distinction between a deductive and inductive approach is not clear cut. Rather, they lie at either end of a spectrum. Moreover, in conducting interviews, achieving the balance between the two requires a sensitive judgement by the interviewer. This balance will be affected by practical considerations – the interview may only be designated to last a particular time, or the interviewee and interviewer may just lose concentration. Although we were both very experienced interviewers we still learnt from each other and from reflecting on our own styles of interviewing.

The focus entirely on interviews for this part of the research was consistent with the assumption that reality is socially constructed and that to understand the world we need to understand how others experience it – the technique of *verstehen* (Bryman and Bell, 2011).

Key message: Interviewing requires particular skills and careful preparation. It is not just a conversation.

Ethical procedures

At the start of the interview the purpose of the research was explained. Interviewees were provided with a written consent form which also explained the rationale for the interviews, assured them that what they said would remain anonymous and that they could withdraw from the interview or the research at any time, and asked them if they would like to view a transcript of the interview. These procedures were consistent with the ethical guidance from our universities and had to be described in our applications for ethical approval to our departments. Our applications also had to show that we had considered risks to participants. The interviewees all gave permission for the interview to be recorded and this was used to produce transcripts. (The bulk of the budget for the research was spent on transcription.) Interviewees were reimbursed for travel expenses, provided with refreshments, and always thanked for giving up their time to take part.

Interviewees were sent transcripts of their interviews and asked if they would like any sections removed. This was important because although the interviewees' names were changed in the paper and in the research report, their distinctive circumstances might have meant they could still have been identified by other MEV volunteers or MEV staff. No interviewees asked for any changes. We felt this was as far as we could go in meeting our ethical responsibilities. We could have sent interviewees draft copies of the paper this chapter is based on, or of the report produced for MEV, asking them if they would like any changes, but it was not practical to do this. A 'bottom line' ethical test is for the researcher to put themselves in the position of the interviewee and think how they would feel in the 'worst case scenario': in this case – if other volunteers the interviewees knew recognised what they had said. This illustrates that at some points ethical behaviour is a matter of judgement rather than guided by clear procedural rules. For example, it is easy to comply with a procedure which requires transcripts of interviews to be kept confidential to the research team and destroyed after a specified period. But deciding whether a volunteer might feel harmed by something they said being reported, and that another volunteer could potentially attribute to them, even if they have been given the opportunity to edit a transcript, has to rest on the researcher's judgement. We always pondered this carefully, and in some instances have not included quotations which, although potentially very powerful at making particular points, might potentially harm the interviewee. A good rule of thumb is if one feels unsure about using anything, leave it a few days, and then go back to it.

Key message: As well as following standard university ethics procedures you may still have to exercise your own judgements.

Interview analysis, refining the focus on social inclusion

An initial bullet point summary of each interview helped us categorise interviewees into those seeking employment or other aspects of personal development through volunteering. For example, one interview was summarised as: 'Some paid work, some volunteering, looking for different work–life balance, alternative lifestyle. Volunteering has led to paid work. Likes being paid in kind to live simple life.' The NVivo package was used to identify within the transcripts where volunteering might contribute to employability, categories of experience corresponding to five basic needs fulfilled by employment, and the relation of volunteering to income (an employment reward leisure could not provide). The analysis identified where volunteering might provide an alternative lifestyle to paid employment. This analysis used 26 NVivo 'nodes' or coding categories. As often happens when using the NVivo package, this was over-complex. These codes were derived from some of the published research that we had started to apply to the analysis – specifically, the psychological functions provided by the experience of employment (Jahoda, 1981). This framework enabled us to compare the experiences of paid employment and volunteering and was used in a different paper (Nichols and Ralston, 2011c – see above). For the paper on which this chapter is based we identified the experiences of the 16 volunteers in five categories:

1   Moving into paid employment ($n = 4$)
2   Trying to move towards paid employment ($n = 2$)
3   In paid employment, but gaining rewards from volunteering too ($n = 3$)
4   Reducing paid employment and increasing volunteering ($n = 5$)
5   Not in paid employment, with no intention of moving into employment – but gaining rewards from volunteering ($n = 2$).

An example of how commentary was blended with quotations is reproduced below to illustrate a volunteer in the category of being 'In paid employment, but gaining rewards from volunteering too':

> Sandy retired from teaching in 2004. Retirement led to a greater loss of income than anticipated and a loss of social contacts: 'You suddenly found you were at home not talking, I'd go down to the shops just to talk to the girl at the counter … It was horrendous, the lack of communication …'. After 6 months she took a part-time job; the choice between this and just volunteering being determined by the need for an income. Sandy had volunteered at the Commonwealth Games, and said: 'the feeling you got during the Games was absolutely fantastic, everybody working together, everybody smiling at each other, there was a real good feel about Manchester in that time' …
>
> (Nichols and Ralston, 2011a: 908)

The use of full transcripts illustrates the ability to return to the original data and analyse it to achieve different objectives, sometimes applying a different theoretical framework. This means that when interviews are conducted sequentially, the data collection and analysis can occur in parallel – that is to say, researchers can reflect on new insights and slightly modify the interview schedule from one interview to the next. The full transcripts allow researchers to return to the original data and address a different research question. In this case, the original objectives of the research did not explicitly include examining the potential of volunteering to contribute to social inclusion, but the full transcripts allowed this to become the focus of analysis. It is also important to recognise that the process of coding, managing and analysing the data can result in fragmentation of text which can decontextualise it (see Bryman and Bell, 2011: 599).

As the research progressed our relationship with MEV developed significantly. The MEV managers had confidence in our work, and we were able to ask them to provide us with a grant of £2,000 to cover the costs of conducting and transcribing the interviews. This was an 'end of the financial year' grant – a sum of money which had to be cleared from their books by the end of March 2010, or it would be lost.

Publication

Presenting results and getting feedback

By March 2010 we had submitted an abstract based on this research to the Leisure Studies Association annual conference. The conference was due to be held in July 2010. Its theme was diversity and equality in leisure, so the focus on social inclusion through volunteering matched this. Presenting at the conference gave us a deadline to analyse the interviews and produce a draft paper; and it also gave us feedback from delegates. We have found it valuable to use conference presentations as target dates and trial runs for journal papers. However, there is very little academic capital attached to published conference presentations and there is always the danger that a publication like this might have an unacceptable overlap with a paper targeted at a journal. For this reason we have not contributed to conference publications.

The influence of the Association of Business Schools' journal rankings and the REF on journal selection

The Research Excellence Framework (REF) is the periodic process by which the UK government determines research funding to universities. The funds distributed to UK universities in this way are not a major proportion of their income, but the status associated with rankings is very important as it helps to attract more research funds, higher quality staff and students. Within a university, it is similarly very important politically for a department to maximise its ranking in relation to others. Within the REF departments can submit four papers published during the assessment period for each academic member of staff entered in the exercise. Part of the decision-making process about the contribution that an individual member of academic staff can make is linked to the perceived quality of the research outputs. The anticipated protocol is that expert members of REF Subject Sub-panels evaluating business and management research will read submitted papers and judge them on their own merits. However the Association of Business Schools (ABS) has produced a ranking of journals and a concern remains that either the ranking of the journal in which papers are published will be used as a proxy for the quality of the paper, or that this will influence heavily the judgement of the paper by the panel.

Thus the Association of Business Schools Academic Journal Quality Guide rankings (although self-perpetuating, as higher ranked journals will automatically receive more papers to choose from) are used as a key performance indicator for management school staff. This has a considerable influence on the type of research conducted in business and management.

In some universities the ABS rankings are used as a key performance indicator for staff, and have significant influence on the journals targeted and the type of research conducted. For Geoff the chosen outlets for his work became important considerations because he had been set a target of publishing four papers in journals ranked 3 or 4 in the ABS ranking in the assessment period January 2008 to December 2013. It was suggested to him that 'special issues' of journals (in which papers are clustered around a specific theme) often provide valuable publication opportunities. While ideas around social inclusion were being developed we became aware of a call for papers for a special issue of the journal *Sociology* on 'Sociology and the 2012 Olympic Games'. Listed by the ABS as a grade 3 journal, this provided an opportunity as the MEV material illustrated a potential volunteering legacy from London 2012. It was also known to be very open to the methods used in the design of the study under consideration.

The use of the ABS journal rankings as a performance indicator also influences the production of knowledge more generally because in responding to the imperative to publish in top ranking journals researchers tend to select research topics and methods which they think the top journals will be likely to accept. For example, the majority of published work on the human resource management (HRM) concept of the psychological contract in the last ten years has reflected the epistemological position that quantitative assessment and analysis based upon structured surveys characterise 'normal science', where theory testing and hypothesis disconfirmation are the focus. This reflects the perception that these methodological assumptions are favoured by the reviewers for the high ranking HRM journals. Thus, although there has been a strong body of previous work on the psychological contract based on the ontological assumption that reality is socially constructed, that qualitative methods are necessary to understand social meaning, and that an inductive approach can lead to valid results, this approach has not been favoured recently because it has been perceived as harder to publish results from such research in high ranking journals. Geoff was advised not to use qualitative methods in researching this topic for this reason (for a discussion of competing discourses in researching the psychological contract see Nichols, 2012a). Thus the perceived methodological preferences of top ranking journals may be a stronger determinant of the choice of methods than the philosophical assumptions of the researcher. However, in the case of the paper discussed in this chapter, the journal *Sociology* was very open to the methods used, which were chosen before this target journal was identified.

An implication of the use of the ABS rankings in measuring performance in management schools is that scholars of leisure, sport or volunteering who work in these schools need to engage with a management oriented academic audience to gain publication in top ranked journals. Journals specialist to the sport and leisure academic community are ranked lowly in the ABS so writing for these tends to be a lower priority. This means leisure scholars in management schools may have to strike a balance between meeting their departmental targets and having a discourse with the academic community they feel most affinity with.

Key message: Target the appropriate journal and take advantage of special issues.

Writing the paper

Having decided the target journal it is usual to search for previous papers in the same journal on a similar topic to make connections to the established knowledge. Of course, this is always easier if the target journal is known at the outset. There is also the possibility of anticipating potential reviewers, and there is recent evidence that in order to increase the number of citations in journals, journal editors frequently ask for revised papers to include new references from that same journal (Storbeck, 2012). However, as this was a special issue on the Olympic Games it was easier to write the paper without reference to other papers in this particular journal, while at the same time having to compete with anybody else who wanted to publish in this issue. Geoff's background in sociology, especially the debate over the work/leisure relationship, was helpful in being able to relate to the readership of this journal.

The presentation at the Leisure Studies Association annual conference helped us to organise the paper and define the main points we wanted to make. The structure of the results was provided by the five categories of volunteers, reported above. Before this we presented the theoretical debate of the contested nature of social inclusion. The main point – our contribution to knowledge – was that volunteering can offer a route to social inclusion which for some people is just as effective, or more so, than paid employment. This is contrary to the dominant social inclusion discourse and illustrates a potential volunteering legacy of the 2012 Olympic Games. The case studies in the paper were selected as the best examples of this.

Geoff wrote the first draft of the paper and Rita edited it. We then employed a professional copy-editor/proofreader to check the details of the presentation, help reduce the word count to the journal's specification, and put the references in the required format. The journal was strict about the word count. It was an instructive exercise to see how one could say exactly the same thing with fewer words. We submitted the paper on 23 July 2010.

Key messages: Don't try to do too much in a paper; plan a structure; engage with previous material in the journal; and pay attention to the journal guidelines.

Making revisions

The journal asked us to make revisions on 8 November 2010. This period between submission and a decision on a review is normal, especially given the summer holidays. The comments of both referees were very supportive of the paper and offered positive suggestions for improvements. This is not always the case – it is not unusual to have referees with different views. One reviewer suggested some additional material without providing references, but it was possible to write back to the journal editor to ask for these. Interesting comments from one reviewer were that we could have, 'taken the opportunity in this article to conduct a critical analysis of the dominant assumptions (and literatures on) the relationship between unemployment, volunteering and social exclusion. What this article is crying out for is a strong argument which flexes some critical muscles.'

It was not difficult to comply with this request. For example, we introduced Gorz's work (1985) providing a critique of the nature of work under capitalism. This request from the reviewer illustrates the difficult balance between offering something new and challenging to the reviewers' assumptions, and offering material which is so far from their 'normal world view' that it is rejected out of hand. This balance is described in a classic paper by Davis (1971: 309) where he makes the case that 'interesting theories deny certain assumptions of their audience. A theorist is considered great, not because his theories are true, but because they are interesting.' It is easier to achieve the acceptable balance for a particular journal if one is aware of the previous material in it, and the likely reviewer.

Contribution to knowledge

We produced the MEV evaluation report, albeit far later than we had anticipated. A specialist was employed to design the report with an attractive cover. Additional funds had to be applied for to do this, and to produce the essential 50 hard copies and electronic versions of the report. We did not realise how valuable this was going to be until we had produced it. Free copies were sent to MEV, Manchester City Council (MCC), the Glasgow Commonwealth Games Organising Committee, the London Organising Committee of the Olympic Games, other policy makers, and academics in the UK and overseas. The report was placed on the Sheffield Management School website. It was useful as a form of marketing for MEV especially 'internal' marketing as many organisations and bodies as well as people within MCC had either forgotten about MEV, didn't realise, or had taken for granted its significance as a major achievement and the strength of its legacy ten years after the Games. The report and articles became vehicles for reinvigoration, motivation and recognition for the MEV team. It supported the case for maintaining MEV during the public sector cuts and strengthened its role within the reorganised third sector section of MCC.

Impact on practice

We have also been able to include our research in our teaching. Geoff incorporates research into the legacy of the Commonwealth Games into an undergraduate module on the leisure industry and a post-graduate module on public policy through leisure. These are examples of how research informs curricula and teaching – a 'selling point' of the courses. As a consequence we have had to send several extra copies of the report to Manchester Metropolitan University Library. Distribution of results is now more important because the REF also has a measure of 'impact' – defined broadly as making a difference to the world outside academia. Yet it is not easy to measure impact – for example it may be difficult to tell if our research has made a difference to planning for volunteering at the Glasgow Commonwealth Games in 2014.

Reflection

There are things we might have done differently. In particular, we might have allowed a more realistic timescale for the main research project and budgeting in time and costs for the final report. We could have written two more journal papers for lower status journals in the ABS rankings, but those read by a larger proportion of the academic community with which we wanted to communicate. We have not yet fully exploited the data from the initial questionnaire survey of volunteers, from the focus groups with volunteers and from the interviews with event managers. The perspectives of volunteers and managers could have been juxtaposed in a similar way to the paper developed from the Newham Volunteers research (Nichols and Ojala, 2009). This was able to show a mismatch between the expectations of the two groups, illustrating the need for managers to adapt their approach.

We also presented a conference paper comparing the views of MEV managers, volunteers and event managers, and developed this into a journal paper, but after an initial rejection from a high status journal did not have time to follow it up. Another paper, examining the psychological rewards of volunteering – also based on the interviews used in the paper discussed in this chapter – is being reviewed after revision by a high status journal. It was rejected by three other journals before getting this far. We could easily have given more conference papers. This suggests that from an academic perspective, planning a much more precise link between objectives, methods, anticipated results, and output in target journals, would have been a far more effective use of our time. If our objectives had just been to publish in a particular journal, rather than to find out something that interested us and that we thought might make a positive difference to the world, we could have used our time much more effectively. However, both our academic outputs have been more inductive – they could not have been anticipated at the start of the process. Maybe it is inevitable that an inductive approach will be more time consuming.

It has been harder to achieve the outputs in higher status journals – but they have benefitted from reviewers' comments, given us more academic capital, and enabled Geoff to develop REF-returnable research outputs. The papers and presentations led to Geoff being invited to contribute chapters on volunteering to a book on the 2012 Olympics (Nichols, 2012b) and we still hope we may have an input into the 2014 Commonwealth Games. The work with MEV has opened the door to other work with Manchester City around the 2012 volunteer programme for the Manchester Olympic venue. Rita has been able to give papers in Brisbane and Tasmania and through these develop work with researchers in New Zealand evaluating the 2011 (men's) Rugby World Cup volunteer programme and potential legacy. Overall, it has been good to be able to follow our research interest and get paid for it.

Lessons for other researchers are indicated throughout the chapter. They can be categorised into the areas of: working together to create synergy; gaining access and funding; planning and implementation of research – in particular, the details of interview conduct; and publication. We have indicated where these points can be related directly to academic theory, but also where they have been influenced by our particular circumstances, such as the priorities of our institutions.

Acknowledgements

As in the paper, we would like to acknowledge the contribution of MEV volunteers and staff to the research reported in this chapter.

If you liked this chapter, you should read Chapters 5, 7 and 13, where the authors use interviews to address the given research question.

References

Bryman, A. and Bell, E. (2011) *Business Research Methods* (3rd edition). Oxford: Oxford University Press.

Davis, M.S. (1971) That's interesting! Towards a phenomenology of sociology and a sociology of phenomenology. *Philosophy of the social Sciences, 1*, 309–344. http://webserver.todaie.gov.tr/dosya/Davis_1971.pdf [accessed 20 April 2012].

Downward, P. and Ralston. R. (2006) The sports development potential of sports event volunteering: Insights from the XVII Manchester Commonwealth Games, *European Sports Management Quarterly, 6 (4)*, 333–351.

Easterby-Smith, M., Thorpe, R. and Jackson, P. (2008) *Management Research* (3rd edition). London: Sage.

Games Final Report (undated). *The XVII Commonwealth Games 2002*. Manchester, Executive Summary, E2. http://www.manchester.gov.uk/downloads/download/4399/commonwealth_games_legacy_documents [accessed 24 April 2012].

Gorz, A. (1985) *Paths to Paradise: On the Liberation from Work*. London: Pluto Press

Jahoda, M. (1981) Work, employment and unemployment, values, theories and approaches in social research. *American Psychologist*, 36, 184–191.

Nichols, G. (2007) *Sport and crime reduction: the role of sports in tackling youth crime*. London: Routledge.

Nichols, G. (2009) Case study: Newham Volunteers – London, England. In K. Holmes and K. Smith, (eds) *Managing volunteers in tourism attractions, destinations and events*. London: Elsevier Butterworth-Heinemann, pp. 225–235.

Nichols, G. (2012a) The psychological contract of volunteers – a new research agenda, *Voluntas*. Published online before print http://www.springerlink.com/openurl. asp?genre = article&id = doi:10.1007/s11266-012-9294-9.

Nichols, G. (2012b) Volunteering for the Games. In V. Giginov (ed.) *The London 2012 Olympic Games Handbook*. London: Routledge, pp. 215–224.

Nichols, G and Ojala, E. (2009) Understanding the management of sports events volunteers through psychological contract theory. *Voluntas International Journal of Voluntary and Nonprofit Organizations, 20 (4)*, 369–387.

Nichols, G. and Ralston, R. (2011a) Social inclusion through volunteering – a potential legacy of the 2012 Olympic Games. *Sociology, 45*, 900–914.

Nichols, G. and Ralston, R. (2011b) *Manchester Event Volunteers: a role model and a legacy*. University of Sheffield Management School. http://www.shef.ac.uk/polopoly_fs/1.227269!/file/MEV_2012_with_cover.pdf.

Nichols, G. and Ralston, R. (2011c) Lessons from the volunteering legacy of the 2002 Commonwealth Games. *Urban Studies, 49*, 165–180.

Pawson, R. and Tilley, N. (1997) *Realistic evaluation*. London: Sage

Ralston, R., Downward, P. and Lumsdon, L. (2004) The expectations of volunteers prior to the XVII Commonwealth Games, 2002: A qualitative study. *Event Management, 9 (1/2)*, 13–26.

Ralston, R., Lumsdon, L. and Downward, P. (2003a) *The motivation and expectations of volunteers prior to the XVII Commonwealth Games, Manchester, UK, 25th July – 4th August, 2002. Report 1: Quantitative Analysis,* International Centre for Research and Consultancy, Manchester Metropolitan University and UK Sport.

Ralston, R., Lumsdon, L. and Downward, P. (2003b) *The motivation and expectations of volunteers prior to the XVII Commonwealth Games, Manchester, UK, 25th July – 4th August, 2002. Report 2: Qualitative Analysis.* International Centre for Research and Consultancy, Manchester Metropolitan University and UK Sport.

Ralston, R., Lumsdon, L. and Downward, P. (2004) *Evaluation of volunteers' reflections on the experience of volunteering at the XVII Commonwealth Games, Manchester, UK, 25th July – 4th August, 2002. Report 3: Qualitative and Quantitative Analysis.* International Centre for Research and Consultancy, Manchester Metropolitan University, and UK Sport.

Ralston, R., Lumsdon, L. and Downward, P. (2005) The third force in events tourism: Volunteers at the XVII Commonwealth Games. *Journal of Sustainable Tourism, 13(5)*, 504–519.

Storbeck, O. (2012) Coerced citations and manipulated impact factors – the dirty tricks of academic journals, *Economics Intelligence* http://economicsintelligence.com/2012/02/25/coerced-citations-and-manipulated-impact-factors-the-dirty-tricks-of-academic-journals/ [accessed 23 April 2012].

Tashakkori, A. and Teddlie, C. (1998) *Mixed methodology*. London: Sage.

The Association of Business Schools Academic Journal Quality Guide. (2010) http://www.the-abs.org.uk/files/absfieldwintro.pdf.

Tilley, N. (2000) Doing realistic evaluation of criminal justice. In V. Jupp, P. Davies, and P. Francis (eds) *Doing criminological research*. London: Sage, pp. 97–113.

Veal. A.J. (2011) *Research methods for leisure and tourism: a practical guide* 4th edition. Harlow: Prentice Hall.

Yin, R. (2009) *Case Study Research: Design and Methods*. London: Sage.

Further reading – research methods texts

Bryman, A. and Bell, E. (2011) *Business Research Methods* (3rd edition). Oxford: Oxford University Press.

Comprehensive and detailed coverage of methods with theoretical depth, developed from a more general text on social science research.

Easterby-Smith, M., Thorpe, R. and Jackson, P. (2008) *Management Research* (3rd edition) London: Sage.

Coverage is not as comprehensive and detailed as Bryman and Bell, but includes practical considerations of the nature of management research and the politics of research.

Nichols, G. (2007) *Sport and crime reduction: the role of sports in tackling youth crime* London: Routledge. Chapter 4. 'What is "evidence" and how do we get it?'.

An introduction to contrasting methodologies in evaluation and especially scientific realism as expounded by Pawson and Tilley.

Pawson, R. and Tilley, N. (1997) *Realistic evaluation.* London: Sage.

Veal. A.J. (2011) *Research methods for leisure and tourism: a practical guide* (4th edition). Harlow: Prentice Hall.

Probably the most comprehensive text on research methods applied to leisure and tourism, with examples from these areas. Its practical approach reflects the author's considerable experience in this field.

12

EXERCISE PHYSIOLOGY

Isomaltulose improves post-exercise glycaemia by reducing carbohydrate oxidation in type 1 diabetes

Richard M. Bracken, Daniel J. West and Stephen C. Bain

Article reference

West, D.J., Morton, R., Stephens, J.W., Bain, S.C., & Bracken, R.M. (2011). Isomaltulose improves post-exercise glycemia by reducing CHO oxidation in T1DM. *Medicine and Science in Sports and Exercise, 43*, 204–210.

Article summary

Carbohydrate consumption is important for the exercising type 1 diabetes (T1DM) individual to avoid low blood glucose (i.e., *hypoglycaemia*). However, not all carbohydrates are the same! An important characteristic of carbohydrates is the *rate* at which they alter blood glucose concentrations. Carbohydrates with a rapid rate of increasing blood glucose are called 'high glycaemic' or high GI, and those that cause more gradual rises in blood glucose are called 'low glycaemic', or low GI. In this article, T1DM individuals ingested a high or low GI carbohydrate on separate occasions before treadmill running and we examined the effects of these carbohydrates on blood glucose levels and fuel use during and after treadmill running. The results demonstrated smaller changes in blood glucose after consuming a low GI carbohydrate (isomaltulose) when compared with a high GI carbohydrate (dextrose). The working mechanism appears to be related to a lower rate of carbohydrate use during running. These smaller fluctuations in blood glucose are important to the type 1 individual as avoidance of hypo- or hyper-glycaemia helps improve good glucose control and reduces risk of complications in the daily lives of those wishing to exercise safely.

Related author publications

West, D.J., Stephens, J.W., Luzio, S., Kilduff, L., Still, R., Bain, S.C., & Bracken, R.M. (2011). A combined insulin reduction and carbohydrate feeding strategy 30 min before running best preserves blood glucose concentration after exercise through improved fuel oxidation in type 1 diabetes mellitus. *Journal of Sports Sciences, 29,* 279–289.

West, D.J., Morton, R., Stephens, J.W., Bain, S.C., & Bracken, R.M. (2010). Effects of rapid-acting insulin reductions on post-exercise glycaemia in people with type 1 diabetes. *Journal of Sports Sciences, 28,* 781–788.

Personal prologue

When I (Dr Richard Bracken) joined the Department of Sports and Exercise Science at Swansea University many years ago, I presented a lunchtime talk to the College of Medicine on my PhD research that examined the effects of physical exercise and training on sympatho-adrenal activity. However, when I finished the talk, Steve Bain asked what I knew about the potential for exercise to improve the lives of those with diabetes. The question took me aback as I had, from my undergraduate days, read about the effects of exercise in the person with diabetes and (incorrectly) assumed much of the work had been completed in this area. How wrong I was! After much reading it was clear that the recommended guidelines for people with type 1 diabetes wishing to exercise appeared vague, with scant research pushing refinements in strategies to perform exercise safely. One specific aspect in need of improvement in the guidelines involved the regulation of blood glucose. Understanding the importance of glucose control during exercise in type 1 diabetes cannot be under-estimated as individuals run a daily battle to avoid low blood glucose 'hypoglycaemia' where fainting or coma might result or alternatively, with long spells of elevated glucose in the circulation 'hyperglycaemia' where cardiovascular disease, blindness, and nerve or kidney damage are accelerated. Therefore, strategies that reduce the fluctuations of blood glucose in the exercising type 1 diabetes individual are important and research into them is warranted.

Since that lunch-time talk we developed a productive research group at Swansea University examining the effects of dietary and exercise manipulations on metabolic control of those with diabetes. The research paper by West et al. (2011) is a good example of this work. Dan West was a PhD student funded by the Welsh Government to develop strategies that allow type 1 diabetes individuals to perform exercise safely. Published in *Medicine and Science in Sports and Exercise*, it represented his second study of three and examined how alterations in the type of carbohydrate might influence the glucose responses and fuel use during running in type 1 diabetes. Previous to this, low GI carbohydrates were only discussed in the context of diets and glucose control with little attention paid to carbohydrate type and pre-exercise drink. Since this paper was published more attention has been paid to the use of low glycaemic carbohydrates during and after exercise. Aside from those with diabetes, our research findings are of relevance to health care professionals who might now prescribe nutritional interventions around physical exercise with more confidence.

Key message: Your skills, knowledge and experience are valued in different disciplines than your own and create great potential for interdisciplinary research. Understanding other disciplines aids in development of new and exciting research – you may end up far from where you began!

Moving from a research problem to a research question

Hypoglycaemia or low blood glucose is a frequent occurrence in patients with type 1 diabetes mellitus (T1DM). The symptoms of hypoglycaemia include tremor, hunger, sweating and behavioural changes, cognitive dysfunction, seizures or coma and if untreated, death. Although diabetes charities like Diabetes UK endorse information statements that inform patients with T1DM on the benefits of beginning and maintaining a physical exercise programme, endurance exercise increases the chances of having a hypoglycaemic episode (Campaigne et al., 1987; Tsalikian et al., 2005). Therefore, strategies to avoid exercise-induced hypoglycaemia have received considerable attention within the literature (Campaigne et al., 1987; De Feo et al., 2006; Dubé et al., 2005; Grimm, 2005; Guelfi et al., 2005; Hernandez et al., 2000; Iafusco, 2006; Mauvais-Jarvis et al., 2003; Rabasa-Lhoret et al., 2001).

One such strategy is to reduce the amount of rapid-acting insulin that is injected before exercise. Within the existing literature, there are recommendations supporting a 10–90 per cent reduction in rapid-acting insulin in a T1DM person (De Feo et al., 2006; Campaigne et al., 1987; Grimm, 2005; Mauvais-Jarvis et al., 2003; Rabasa-Lhoret et al., 2001). Another anti-hypoglycaemic strategy is to ingest carbohydrates before exercise. Carbohydrates come in a variety of forms (mono-, di- and polysaccharides) with different characteristics. One such characteristic is the glycaemic index of carbohydrates. Low glycaemic index (LGI) carbohydrates (CHO) digest at slower rates than CHO with a high glycaemic index (HGI). Research has demonstrated lower daily mean blood glucose and reduced incidence of hypoglycaemia and reductions in glycosylated haemoglobin HbA_{1c} (the amount of glucose attached to the haemoglobin molecule) by including LGI carbohydrates into the daily diets of T1DM (Gilbertson et al., 2001; Nansel et al., 2008; Thomas et al., 2007). However, there is limited information on the post-exercise metabolic responses of T1DM after ingestion of low or high GI carbohydrates. So the aim of this study was to compare the effects of ingesting HGI and LGI carbohydrates (i.e., dextrose and isomaltulose) on metabolic and fuel oxidation responses before, during and after running in T1DM individuals.

Key message: Reviewing literature and examining practice help determine the gap into which your research question will fit.

Choice of method (Matching the method to the research question)

We wanted to examine two research questions: 1) Is the choice of carbohydrate capable of improving the blood glucose responses during and after exercise? and 2) If there was an influence of carbohydrate type on blood glucose, what was the potential mechanism explaining these differences? This demanded a controlled laboratory approach where participants performed physical exercise at the same duration and relative intensity. Factors capable of influencing the blood glucose responses such as prior exercise, diet, time of day, environmental temperature were controlled for by standardising participants for 24 hours before attendance at the laboratory as well as during and after the laboratory visit. Thus, the influence of extraneous factors was somewhat minimised in the hope it might facilitate observation of potential conditional differences, if they existed. Next, detailed schematics were discussed over several meetings and drawn up by the team where timings, blood sampling, the exercise model, severity of rapid-acting insulin reduction, amount of carbohydrate and length of recovery were quantified. This resulted in the schematic Figure 12.1.

In terms of study design, the team discussed two options: 1) Comparative; where one group of T1DM individuals consumed one carbohydrate and another group of T1DM individuals ingested the other carbohydrate; or 2) Interventional; where the one group of T1DM participants completed two trials after ingesting a different carbohydrate in each trial. The latter was the approach we adopted to further minimise inter-participant biological variability (i.e., where the magnitude of increase in blood glucose concentration after ingestion of the same amount of a CHO in two individuals will be different). Therefore, the study became a single blind, randomised trial that compared the effects of consumption of different carbohydrates in the same group of T1DM individuals. Each participant, therefore, served as their own control. 'Single blind' meant that the participants did not know what drink they were consuming, only the researchers knew this. Practicalities prevented the study becoming a double-blind study where neither the researchers nor participants knew the type of the carbohydrate solution ingested on each trial.

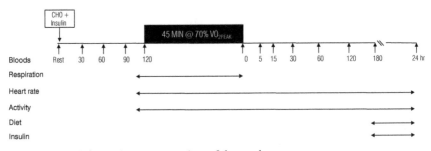

FIGURE 12.1 Schematic representation of the study

Key message: Without consideration of study design and control of experimental set-up it may be difficult to tease out conditional differences – if they exist.

Data collection

This study began a considerable number of months prior to taking the first blood sample. Development of a sound methodology occurred through a comprehensive review of the literature and scrutiny of findings of previous studies to aid in the development of a hypothesis for our study in T1DM individuals. In our experience it is vital to have a rationale that is robust and well researched as there is little point in developing a rationale only to discover that the research has already been published by another group. It is also helpful to bounce your idea off of other colleagues, as they may have a different take on your idea and their viewpoint may provide new or interesting angles to your study design. One positive point that emanated from the discussion was the need to use a low GI carbohydrate, not (as has been used in previous studies) a low GI meal. This tended to simplify the comparisons to a high GI carbohydrate. Thus, with a little further research the carbohydrate of choice for this project became isomaltulose. Isomaltulose is a disaccharide comprised of glucose and fructose and can be found in honey.

An aim should provide a tight focus for the study and it should emanate from a fully justified rationale. Our aim was a concise statement about what we needed to examine to advance the research in the area with novel findings so it was 'to compare the effects of ingesting a HGI and LGI CHO (i.e. dextrose and isomaltulose) on metabolic and fuel oxidation responses before, during and after running in T1DM individuals'.

Next, we established our objectives, namely, how we were going to achieve the aim. Although not always stated in papers our objectives were:

1   To measure and compare the blood glucose, metabolite (lactate, NEFA), and glucoregulatory hormone (insulin, glucagon, noradrenaline, adrenaline, cortisol) responses before, during and after endurance exercise;
2   To use principles of indirect calorimetry (detailed later) to measure and compare the carbohydrate and fat combustion responses before and during a continuous exercise test.

Finally, it is customary to state a (null) hypothesis, that is to say, what you think may not happen in your study. Researchers must maintain a balanced scientific and non-biased approach to examining a problem. To not state a null hypothesis would be to expect a difference in your results – which is not good science – as experimental findings demonstrating no change are equally important as those that detail large differences. So the null hypothesis in our study was 'there would be no differences in blood glucose or fuel oxidation patterns after consumption of dextrose or isomaltulose in individuals with type 1 diabetes'.

The methodology was built on the backbone of the aims and objectives of the study. This consisted of several stages: 1) ethical approval, 2) selection of participants, 3) equipment and procedures, and 4) blood sampling.

Ethical approval

Our study received favourable ethical approval from the local branch meetings of the National Research Ethics Committee (NREC), now administered under the Integrated Research Application System (IRAS: https://www.myresearchproject.org.uk/). This process entails substantial form filling and requires detailed understanding of: 1) what the rationale is for your proposed study; 2) what you are to ask your participants to do; 3) how you will care for them during your project; 4) how you will deal with them in the unlikely event of an adverse incident (including university indemnity arrangements); and 5) how you will deal with their data.

Having provided information about the project, we were also keen to demonstrate that we had sound methods for dealing with T1DM individuals in our laboratory in the unlikely event of an incident. We risk assessed our laboratory environment and the participants' experience in it during their lab visits and quantified the following major hazards:

1   *Cannulation*: Some individuals are squeamish about giving blood – even those with diabetes! This could result in fainting, and potential damage from falls. We asked each T1DM participant in advance if they were easily upset at the sight of blood, to minimise the possibility of this as a risk. All our participants were comfortable with cannulation. To obtain the blood volume necessary for the analysis of metabolites in this project a 20-gauge catheter was placed in an antecubital vein on the two experimental trials. This is an approach that minimised the stress of blood taking when compared with venipuncture – a technique that involves repeatedly inserting a needle to obtain blood samples. Clearly it is likely to be more painful than cannulation. Cannulation was performed by experienced members of the research team who received extensive training in phlebotomy (i.e., an incision in a vein) from an NHS environment.

2   *Physical exercise*: Prior to any testing, participants completed a medical questionnaire and provided their written informed consent with the option to withdraw from testing at any point. Moreover, participants were screened to exclude the presence of potentially adverse cardiovascular conditions. Notwithstanding, physical exercise causes large cardiovascular, metabolic and hormonal changes and some people may not be used to the feelings associated with performance of exercise of this nature. However, the healthy, physically active T1DM patients were recruited to perform exercise that

they were habitually used to (which is predominantly of an aerobic nature) with exercise intensities less than participants' maximum aerobic rate. Experimental laboratory work in our clinical cohort was carried out in the presence of first-aid trained and clinical personnel, with access to a cardiac crash cart (i.e., a device to electrically re-align the heart rate of a participant who has had a cardiac arrest or arrhythmia develop as a result of the stress of exercise).

3   *Hypo- and hyper-glycaemia*: An overarching theme of this project was the examination of the potential of those with T1DM to avoid hypoglycaemia following ingestion of different carbohydrates. This is to say that we would be likely to witness hypoglycaemia in the laboratory. We took steps to avoid its occurrence by: 1) defining hypoglycemia (blood glucose concentration < 3.5 mmol.L^{-1}); and 2) taking steps to rectify it as soon as it occurred, so if participants experienced a hypoglycaemic incident, a bolus of commercially available carbohydrate drink (e.g., Lucozade; GlaxoSmithKline) was administered. If participants received glucose supplementation, data from that point onward were removed from the analysis as any additional carbohydrate supplementation would have altered blood glucose in a way that differed if only the pre-exercise carbohydrate was ingested. Hyperglycaemia was defined as > 12.4 mmol.L^{-1} and if it was evident before exercise, participants were re-scheduled to another occasion when glucose levels were 7–12 mmol.L^{-1}.

After attending the IRAS/NREC meeting to discuss the study and having satisfied the panel that the risks to the participants had been suitably minimised to offer a benefit to carry out the study, we received a favourable letter of approval that enabled us to begin the trials.

Key message: Good written and oral communication skills are necessary to demonstrate the risk to benefit ratio of your study to make sure participants are properly informed and to put them at ease.

Participants

The study recruited volunteers from the Diabetes Clinics in the Abertawe Bro Morgannwg Healthcare Trust. Clinicians began the recruitment process through informal chats to those who were interested in finding out more about the research project. Written details of the study information and a reply slip were provided to the interested individuals where they could read about time commitments and details of the study (e.g., blood sampling and amount of exercise). If a volunteer returned the reply slip to the research team, a meeting with a senior member of the research team was arranged where the specific details of the project, the participants' commitment (in terms of time and effort) and potential benefits and risks of participation were outlined. At the end of this meeting participant information and contact details sheets were provided to interested parties along with a stamped-addressed envelope. Volunteers were given at least one week to return their expressions of interest for participation in the project.

Asking individuals with type 1 diabetes to perform exercise is a risk! Physical activity increases glucose uptake and tissue sensitivity to insulin so the potential for hypoglycaemia is increased. To minimise glycaemic risk we established some inclusion and exclusion criteria before selecting the participants from those volunteers who expressed an interest in partaking in the study. Volunteers needed to be free from any diabetes complications (e.g., kidney and nerve damage, blindness) apart from mild background diabetic retinopathy (damage to the retina caused by high glucose concentrations) and were not recruited if they were taking any prescribed medication other than insulin – as this would have a complicating influence on the resultant data. Medications exert a powerful influence on metabolism and exclusion of individuals that are on prescribed medications is the easiest way to control for this. Furthermore, there are different ways to administer insulin, such as with injection or by using a pump device. Most T1DM individuals are on a basal-bolus injection routine as technology and reduced cost has only in recent years begun to increase the numbers of individuals using an insulin pump meter. Volunteers were selected who were treated with a stable basal-bolus insulin regimen comprised of slow-acting insulin and rapid-acting insulin analogues for at least 3 months before the study. A long-term marker of glucose control is known as HbA_{1c} and is a measure of how much glucose is attached to a haemoglobin molecule. Non-diabetic values are ~5.0 per cent and for inclusion in the study T1DM values were included if they fell between 6.5–10.0 per cent.

Thereafter, eight individuals that passed the inclusion/exclusion criteria were selected as study participants. On each trial, participants were asked not to exercise for 24 hours before an experimental trial, and testing was rescheduled if they experienced a hypoglycaemic episode over the previous 48 hours as this has significant effect in altering low blood glucose awareness and blunts the counter-regulatory hormone (i.e., adrenaline, noradrenaline, cortisol and glucagon) responses to exercise. Participants were also instructed to maintain (and record) a similar diet and avoid alcohol and physical activity for 24 hours before each test session. On the day of each exercise trial, testing did not commence if the patients were hyperglycaemic prior to the beginning of exercise (blood glucose concentration > 12.4 mmol.L^{-1}). Patients' diets were assessed and for 48 hours prior to the main exercise trials patients followed a recommended diet plan. This plan aimed to allow individuals to consume adequate energy whilst presenting a balanced intake of carbohydrates, fats and protein that would be standardised across conditions.

Equipment and procedures

After a preliminary visit, to quantify peak rate of oxygen consumption (VO_2peak) and heart rate (HR_{peak}), participants attended the exercise physiology laboratory after an overnight fast on two occasions, at the same time (between 6 and 8 a.m.) and 7 days apart. This was to ensure participants were not still digesting foods which might influence the results. The schematic of the experimental protocol is reported in Figure 12.1.

On arrival at the laboratory, participants were seated while a catheter was inserted into an antecubital vein. Fifteen minutes later, a resting blood sample was obtained. After this, participants were given, in a randomised and counterbalanced fashion, 75 g of either an HGI dextrose or isomaltulose carbohydrate, as a 10 per cent solution. Immediately before ingestion, participants were instructed to administer their rapid-acting insulin, which had been reduced by 75 per cent into the abdomen. Once administered, participants consumed the test solution within 5 min and remained in a rested, seated position for the 120-min pre-exercise period. At 105 min, resting measures of respiration and HR were determined with the participants in a supine position. Two hours after consumption of CHO and insulin administration, a pre-exercise blood sample was obtained, and participants subsequently performed 45 min of steady-state treadmill running. HR and breath-by-breath data were collected via radiotelemetry software and analysed for CHO and lipid oxidation rates using the equations of Frayn (1983). These equations convert the values for oxygen use and carbon dioxide production into estimations of energy use and proportional use of carbohydrate and fat based on stochiometric equations. On cessation of exercise, additional blood samples were obtained at 0, 5, 15, 30, 60, 120, and 180 min after exercise. Participants remained at rest for the entire 3-hour post-exercise period, drinking water *ad libitum*. Some post-exercise blood variables were corrected for changes in plasma volume via the method of Dill and Costill (1974). This was because small molecules tend to move in and out of the circulatory system and adjusting for the change in volume of plasma in which the molecules reside is standard practice when dealing with exercise studies where large changes in blood flow occur and plasma volume decreases with sweating and evaporation of water from the body.

Blood sampling

An aliquot of blood was collected in a 4-mL Na^+-EDTA vacutainer and was analysed for HbA_{1c} by routine high performance liquid chromatography (HPLC) with cation exchange (G7; Tosoh, Theale, UK). To measure glucose and lactate concentrations we obtained a 1 mL sample of venous blood using a Ca^{2+}-heparinised syringe (to prevent the blood from clotting) then measured concentrations of our metabolic analyser (GEM3000; Instrumentation Laboratories Ltd., Croft, UK). Blood haemoglobin was also analysed (a 20-μL aliquot). Finally, a 10 ml sample was gathered and split equally into a serum separation tube (SST) and a lithium-heparinised tube that contained 200 μL of 0.1 $mol.L^{-1}$ of both ethylene glycol tetraacetic acid (EGTA) as anticoagulant and glutathione as antioxidant. Some metabolic assays require the use of serum (which is plasma without the clotting elements), so to obtain serum the sample in the SST was left to clot for 30 min in a thermoneutral environment. Plasma and serum samples were centrifuged with the resultant plasma and serum extracted and stored at –80°C for later analysis of non-esterified fatty acids (NEFA) and hormones (adrenaline, noradrenaline cortisol, and glucagon). Plasma adrenaline, noradrenaline and glucagon and serum cortisol and NEFA were measured using specific ELISA kits.

Data analysis

To improve the clarity of the changes in some metabolites with ingestion of the different carbohydrate solutions, some preliminary treatment of the blood glucose data occurred where:

a   We described the data relative to rest (see Figure 12.2). This is commonly done with data that displays large variability at rest like blood glucose changes in those with diabetes and facilitates a more refined examination of the changes in blood glucose rather than the absolute blood glucose concentration *per se*. Absolute blood glucose is the numerical glucose value within the physiological range. So non-diabetic fasted values can range from ~4–5 mmol.L⁻¹. However, fasted resting glucose concentrations in T1DM individuals are highly variable and can range from 3–16 mmol.L⁻¹! Thus, it makes more sense to express the values following CHO ingestion as changes relative to rest to determine the 'magnitude of change' rather than the actual blood glucose value under each CHO condition.

b   Area under the curve (AUC): Use of this method permits examination of time-averaged changes in blood glucose and allows for a fuller examination of blood glucose changes with alterations in treatment condition (the reader is referred to a good article on the choice of AUC technique: Brouns et al., 2005). The calculation of blood glucose area under the curve (BG_{AUC}) was

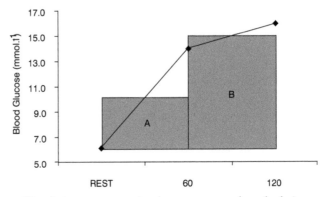

FIGURE 12.2 Blood glucose area under the curve exemplar calculation

calculated via the seminal method of Wolever and Jenkins (1988) and was subsequently time averaged. Total BG_{AUC} was averaged to mmol.L^{-1}.hour^{-1}. An example of this procedure is detailed in Figure 12.2.

Calculations (Wolever and Jenkins, 1988)

$A = (((BG_{60} - BG_{REST})/2) + BG_{REST}) \star \text{Time (min)}$
- $(14 - 6.2)/2 = 3.9$
- $3.9 + 6.2 = 10.1$
- $10.1 \star 60 = 606 \text{ mmol.L}^{-1}.\text{min}^{-1}$

$B = (((BG_{120} - BG_{60})/2) + BG_{60}) \star \text{Time (min)}$
- $(14.8 - 14)/2 = 0.4$
- $0.4 + 14 = 14.4$
- $14.4 \star 60 = 864 \text{ mmol.L}^{-1}.\text{min}^{-1}$

Total $BG_{AUC} = A + B = 1470 \text{ mmol.L}^{-1}.\text{min}^{-1}$

Statistical treatment

The aim of our study was 'to compare the effects of ingesting dextrose and isomaltulose, on metabolic and fuel oxidation responses before, during and after running in T1DM individuals'. We were interested in exploring the effects of glycaemic index on resultant blood glucose concentrations and also in exploring a working mechanism, hence the need for analysis of other metabolites. Thus, the dependent variables were blood glucose and the other metabolic variables including lactate and NEFAs; the independent variables were time and conditional treatment (i.e., dextrose or isomaltulose). Therefore, the quantitative statistical model to analyse variables was a repeated measures analysis of variance with two factors (i.e., time and treatment). We performed parametric testing on our data using the statistical package, SPSS version 16.

There are several assumptions that need to be met prior to the use of a repeated measures ANOVA statistical test, namely:

1   *The data was parametric and at interval level.* Parametric testing is normally considered to be more powerful (i.e., it can be used to detect a significant difference if one exists). However, it can only be used if the data is ratio or interval data (i.e., it offers precision in determining the differences of distances between conditions unlike less precise data such as ordinal or nominal values). Our data were classed as 'interval' because the data, when placed on a scale, tells us about the order of data points, and the size of the intervals in between data points. Some of the data were also regarded as ratio data because of a true zero point on the interval scale. For instance

glucose was regarded as an 'interval value' because we would not expect it to reduce to zero.

2   *Random sampling.* Balanced against the strict inclusion/exclusion criteria, this is difficult to achieve, however, our participant recruitment strategy aided in meeting this assumption alongside the volunteering nature of those who chose to become participants.

3   *Independence of observations.* Each participant attended the laboratory on their own with no possibility of other participants affecting another's responses.

4   *Normality of data.* Having checked our data for normality using a Shapiro–Wilk test our data were considered normally distributed (i.e., neither skewed nor kurtosed).

5   *Homogeneity of variance of the data.* This was tested by the Mauchly test to examine whether the 'sphericity' or differences between the scores had a similar variance. Examination of the Mauchly test results using our data indicated non-significant differences looking at between- or within-group data. This meant our data was sufficiently spherical to permit the use of our parametric test.

The procedure for the use of repeated measures ANOVA is detailed in the excellent *SPSS Survival Manual* by Julie Pallant (2007), which provides step-by-step instructions for the student. This type of ANOVA tests for differences in within-subject variances. Therefore, significant changes were indicated when blood glucose concentrations differed consistently within the same group of T1DM participants across time (i.e., at rest, 0, 5, 15, 30, 60, 120, and 180 min following running) and treatment conditions (i.e., under dextrose or isomaltulose). Where a main significant difference was observed we located where that difference occurred by the use of post-hoc testing (i.e., a Bonferroni test). This test allows us to control the chances of incorrectly rejecting our null hypothesis that there would be no differences in blood glucose after consumption of dextrose or isomaltulose in individuals with type 1 diabetes and re-adjusts the acceptable P-value (i.e., makes it more conservative to find a significant difference) for an indication that the results occurred due to our intervention rather than by chance. Values that were indicated following re-adjustment of an acceptable P-value were indicated in Figure 12.2 as an asterisk (i.e. ★).

Statistical power and clinical meaningfulness

In recent years there has been an increasing use of power analysis to determine the strength of statistical findings. 'Power' is the ability of a statistical test to correctly reject a false null hypothesis (Cohen 1988). Put another way, if a large enough treatment effect exists (which means the null hypothesis is false) are you able to detect it? Funding bodies often require power analysis in grant applications. It allows researchers to determine the number of participants needed to identify a statistically significantly strong finding. From a research council or charity's point of view, would they award a £100,000 grant with a 50 per cent chance of finding a statistically significant effect? It doesn't mean you would not find an effect but indicates you have not optimised the components of your research study to demonstrate a potentially significant effect. With the expense of research studies and nature of research often occurring in one time period (e.g., a final year dissertation project) limited pilot data may exist from which to work out a statistically strong research study. However, another way to determine the power of your study may be to carry out power analysis on data from other researchers with a similar research design. This was the case with this study and based on the data of Rabasa-Lhoret et al. (2001), 33 subjects were required to demonstrate an acceptably strong statistical power of 80 per cent.

In practical research and taking into consideration factors such as strict inclusion/ exclusion criteria, participants' time commitment, researchers' time constraints with respect to grant funding deadlines, equipment constraints alongside geographical ability to recruit the required number of clinical participants for completion of detailed trials, it is not uncommon to suggest that a sample size of 33 is outside the realm of available T1DM individuals. In such instances, although statistical power in our study using 8 participants was retrospectively measured as 45 per cent, the significance of the data lies in the clinical meaningfulness of the findings, namely, ingestion of a pre-exercise isomaltulose solution reduces blood glucose AUC by 21 per cent for three hours following running in T1DM individuals. Such consistent findings in each T1DM participant highlight the clinical meaningfulness of the data in spite of poor statistical power.

Key message: Reporting of statistical results from your study should also be interpreted with an understanding of the physiological or clinical meaningfulness of your data.

Data presentation

You'll remember that we wanted to examine two research questions: 1) Is the choice of carbohydrate capable of improving the blood glucose responses during and after exercise? and 2) If there was an influence of carbohydrate type on blood glucose, what was the potential mechanism explaining these differences? In our paper we laid out our results section as follows to answer these aims:

1   *Physiological responses to exercise*: the primary purpose of this reporting was to demonstrate that the participants were exercising at equal exercise intensities in each trial. We were not as much interested in the effects of exercise on blood glucose concentrations but rather we were more interested in the effects of carbohydrate ingestion on the post-exercise blood glucose responses (assuming the same amount of exercise was completed on each trial).

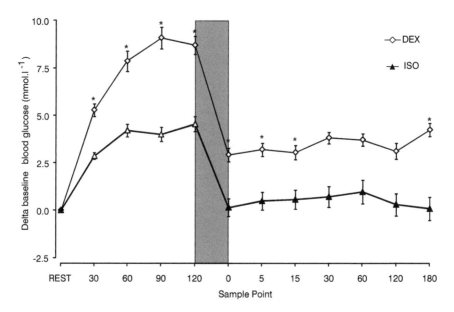

FIGURE 12.3   Blood glucose responses to ingestion of high and low glycaemic index carbohydrates at rest, during and after 45 minutes aerobic running (West et al., 2011)

2   *Blood glucose responses*: this was our primary variable for analysis and as such we spent a lot of time analysing the changes in condition and time and also the differences in the pattern of the increase, alongside the starting and recovery absolute blood glucose values. As a development of this we wrote a small section within the article that characterised the incidence of hypoglycaemia. From Figure 12.3 we expressed the data relative to resting values of each condition as this helped to visually display the subtle differences, which might otherwise have been obscured by differences in resting values.

3   *Fuel oxidation*: to go some way towards answering the second question, and as a potential metabolic explanation of the effect of isomaltulose ingestion on blood glucose and consequently its effects on whole body metabolism, we measured carbohydrate and lipid oxidation during exercise (Figure 12.4) and found that as exercise progressed T1DM participants were burning more carbohydrate after consuming the dextrose drink but were able to continue to burn some fat after consuming isomaltulose in the latter end of exercise.

Given that elevated blood glucose levels tend to suppress the use of fat during exercise, we wondered if the lower increase in blood glucose with isomaltulose (that allowed some lipids to be burned by the muscle) might allow continued release of non-esterified fatty acids (NEFA) from adipose tissue and contribute to weight loss (if performed regularly as part of a training strategy). However, although there were changes in NEFA with regards to time, there

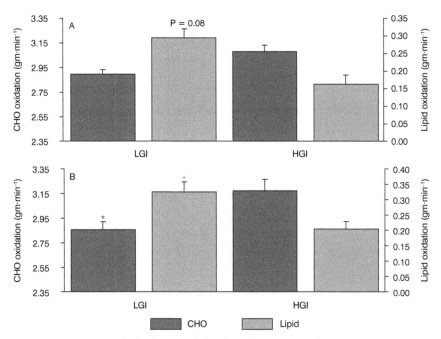

FIGURE 12.4 (A) Carbohydrate and lipid oxidation rates during 45 minutes of exercise after pre-exercise ingestion of LGI or HGI. (B) Carbohydrate and lipid oxidation rates over the final 10 minutes of exercise. Data are presented as mean ± SEM (n = 8). ★ indicates significant differences between LGI and HGI (P<0.05)

were no differences between carbohydrate conditions. An interesting finding of the study was that blood lactate was greater in the isomaltulose condition compared with dextrose at rest but this conditional difference disappeared as exercise began. Finally, we measured glucagon, adrenaline, noradrenaline, and cortisol concentrations to examine the counter-regulatory hormonal profile in an attempt to understand how blood glucose concentrations were regulated. Although there were changes in the hormones with regard to time, there were no differences across carbohydrate conditions.

Key message: Clear and accurate graphical representation of results is essential, as researchers often need to quickly assess the important aspects of your data.

Contribution to knowledge

Students need to develop a comprehensive strategy to writing a discussion of meaningfulness of their data. This involves five key points for each main finding:

1   State what you found.
2   Align your findings with other researchers' findings.
3   Explain what this result means.

4   How does your research explain a working mechanism or advance an understanding of the functioning of an accepted mechanism?
5   Where appropriate, consider research that has alternative findings and aim to reconcile the reasons why.

An example of this is located in paragraph 5, page 6 of the article's Discussion.

State what you found.

As exercise progressed, there was a greater lipid oxidation during exercise under ISO, in comparison with DEX, which became significantly greater during the final 10 min of exercise.

Align your findings with other researchers' findings.

Similar findings have been reported previously by Trenell et al. (37), who found that LGI, pre-exercise, CHO based meals increased lipid oxidation by 10% during 90 min of cycling at 70% VO2max, in comparison with isoenergetic, HGI CHO meals…

…. Relating the findings of Coyle et al. to our study, the bolus of DEX ingested before exercise may have caused a similar suppression of lipid oxidation during exercise. Moreover, combining an increase in skeletal muscle hormone-sensitive lipase activity (39) and lower glucose availability under ISO may have provided a milieu where the oxidation of intramuscular NEFA concentrations was not as suppressed, compared with DEX, during exercise. Serum NEFA concentrations did not change with exercise; an effect likely the result of a reduction in adipose tissue blood flow, with exercise intensities $\sim$70% VO_2max, reducing the removal of NEFA (18, 31). A redistribution of blood flow to adipose tissue is also the likely mechanism behind the rapid rise in NEFA concentrations after the cessation of exercise (31).

Explain what this result means.

Within our study, the increase in the combustion of lipids, with time, is possibly due to an increased mobilisation of intramuscular triglyceride stores because NEFA concentrations did not differ between conditions.

How does your research explain a working mechanism or advance an understanding of the functioning of an accepted mechanism?

A potential mechanism behind the differences in lipid oxidation demonstrated in the later stages of exercise may be related to differences in

BG concentrations between the conditions (5). Coyle et al. (5) investigated lipid oxidation, during 40 min of cycling at 50%VO2peak in non-T1DM individuals, in a fasted state or having consumed 1.4 g.kg–1 body mass of glucose. An examination of substrate oxidation revealed that an increased glucose availability and an increased glycolytic flux, and ultimately CHO oxidation, directly suppress lipid metabolism. Moreover, the increased glucose availability induced a 27% reduction in the oxidation of NEFA concentrations derived from intramuscular triglycerides.

Where appropriate, consider research that has alternative findings and aim to reconcile the reasons why.

Relating the findings of Coyle et al. to our study, the bolus of DEX ingested before exercise may have caused a similar suppression of lipid oxidation during exercise. Moreover, combining an increase in skeletal muscle hormone-sensitive lipase activity (39) and lower glucose availability under ISO may have provided a milieu where the oxidation of intramuscular NEFA concentrations was not as suppressed, compared with DEX, during exercise. Serum NEFA concentrations did not change with exercise; an effect likely the result of a reduction in adipose tissue blood flow, with exercise intensities ~70% VO2max, reducing the removal of NEFA (18, 31). A redistribution of blood flow to adipose tissue is also the likely mechanism behind the rapid rise in NEFA concentrations after the cessation of exercise (31).

So in summary, we found that blood glucose responses before, during and after exercise improve in type 1 individuals when they consume a low GI carbohydrate. In addition, we found that the consumption of isomaltulose allowed for more fat to be burned (and carbohydrate spared) during the later stages of endurance running. This suggests that the 'spared carbohydrate' is available to offset hypoglycaemia occurring following exercise. The conclusion supports the idea that low GI carbohydrates are beneficial to the person with type 1 diabetes looking to perform endurance exercise.

Key message: Your research should advance the knowledge of the area by explanation of how your data links with other research examining the same topic.

Impact on practice

Our research findings from this study, carefully carried out, result in important findings relevant to the individual with type 1 diabetes and healthcare professionals. In both groups the aim is to enable participation in exercise for health benefits whilst minimising risk associated with participation. The most important finding in this study of lower glucose values after ingestion promotes the potential for consumption of low GI carbohydrates to reduce the likelihood of hyperglycaemia which, as mentioned previously, can contribute to several long-term problems like kidney or nerve damage or blindness. Additionally, the finding that exercise decreases blood glucose may promote the use of exercise as a non-pharmacological therapy by clinically qualified staff. Finally, the stable and lower blood glucose concentrations after exercise under isomaltulose offers some confidence to people with T1DM and their healthcare professionals that low GI carbohydrates may offer greater protection against hypoglycaemia. On a more informal but nonetheless important level, translating the 'science speak' of this study to the general public occurred through our regular meetings with patient groups in Swansea where we regularly talked about the research taking place in their area and the meaning of this work for those with diabetes.

Key message: Consider the 'so-what?' aspect of your research. What does the study contribute to knowledge and who benefits from its findings? If you can't answer this, is it worth pursuing?

Reflection

This study had a number of particular strengths. Previous to this no-one had considered the idea that drink composition was as important in maintaining glycaemic control in exercising type 1 diabetes individuals as the manipulation of rapid-acting insulin. Reductions to elevated blood glucose levels without inducing a greater incidence of hypoglycaemia was an important finding of this study. Additionally, our study employed weight-bearing exercise (i.e., running) as opposed to many other research studies that looked at cycling. This is important as the blend of eccentric and concentric muscle actions in running induces different changes in insulin sensitivity following exercise compared with primarily concentric muscle actions like cycling. Hindsight is a wonderful thing, and looking back on the entire research process always reveals things we could have done differently. One such change that we have made in more recent studies is relativising the carbohydrate load to each individual participant based on body mass rather than a set amount ($g.kg^{-1}$ BM vs. g). This would ensure the same 'relative' amount of carbohydrate to each individual. There has been a wide range of recommendations for carbohydrate consumption before or during exercise in T1DM individuals that have condensed to three main strands, namely: 1) amounts based on pre-exercise blood glucose concentration (< 5.6 or < 6.7 mmol.L^{-1}, Steppel and Horton, 2003; De Feo et al., 2006); 2) amounts based on exercise duration (20–60 g every 30 min, ADA, 1997; 60 $g.h^{-1}$: Gallen, 2003); or, 3) amounts based on body mass (1–2 $g.kg^{-1}$ BM, Ramires et al., 1997; Riddell and Iscoe, 2006). We think that a combination of (2) and (3) may be a more practical approach in research studies where participants will perform exercise, as it allows the type 1 individual to better control blood glucose within acceptable margins and avoid hyper- or hypoglycaemia. However, for our study we simply wanted to know if there was a gross difference in glycaemia when participants were presented with the same amount of carbohydrate on each occasion that differed only in its glycaemic index. Our results demonstrate it did! Future studies may wish to repeat the study with relativised amounts of carbohydrate loading before exercise.

Key message: No study is perfect! However, if you carry out your work carefully, your results may allow small but progressive advancements in knowledge and may begin to inform practice.

> If you liked this chapter, you should read Chapters 2, 4 and 8 as the authors describe research processes that focus on furthering knowledge in physiology, exercise and health.

References

ADA/ACSM Joint Position Statement: Diabetes Mellitus and Exercise. (1997). *Medicine and Science in Sports and Exercise, 29,* 1–6.

Brouns, F., Bjorck, I., Frayn, K.N., Gibbs, A.L., Lang, V., Slama, G., & Wolever, T.M. (2005). Glycaemic index methodology. *Nutrition Research Reviews, 18*(1):145–171.

Campaigne, B.N., Wallberg-Henriksson, H., & Gunnarsson, R. (1987). Glucose and insulin responses in relation to insulin dose and caloric intake 12 h after acute physical exercise in men with IDDM. *Diabetes Care, 10,* 716–721.

Cohen, J. (1988). *Statistical Power Analysis for the Behavioural Sciences.* 2nd Edn. LEA Publishers, New Jersey.

De Feo, P., Di Loreto, C., Ranchelli, A., Fatone, C., Gam-belunghe, G., Lucidi, P., & Santeusanio, F. (2006). Exercise and diabetes. *Acta Biomedica, 77,* 14–17.

Dill, D.B., & Costill, D.L. (1974). Calculation of percentage changes in volumes of blood, plasma, and red cells in dehydration. *Journal of Applied Physiology, 37,* 247–248.

Dubé, M.C., Weisnagel, J., Homme, D.P., & Lavoie, C. (2005). Exercise and newer insulins: How much glucose supplement to avoid hypoglycemia. *Medicine and Science in Sports and Exercise, 37,* 1276–1282.

Frayn, K. N. (1983). Calculation of substrate oxidation rates in vivo from gaseous exchange. *Journal of Applied Physiology, 55,* 628–34.

Gallen, I. (2003). Exercise in type 1 diabetes. *Diabetic Medicine, 20,* 1–17.

Gilbertson, H.R., Brand-Miller, J.C., Thorburn, A.W., Evans, S., Chondros, P., & Wether, G.A. (2001). The effect of flexible low glycemic index dietary advice versus measured carbohydrate diets on glycemic control in children with type 1 diabetes. *Diabetes Care, 34,* 1137–1143.

Grimm, J.J. (2005). Exercise in type 1 diabetes. In D. Nagi (ed.), *Exercise and sport in diabetes* (pp. 25–43). Hoboken: Wiley.

Guelfi, K.J., Jones, T.W., & Fournier, P.A. (2005). The decline in blood glucose levels is less with intermittent high-intensity compared with moderate exercise in individuals with type 1 diabetes. *Diabetes Care, 28,* 1289–1294.

Hernandez, J.M., Moccia, T., Fluckey, J.D., Ulbrecht, J.S., & Farrell, P.A. (2000). Fluid snacks to help persons with type 1 diabetes avoid late onset post-exercise hypoglycemia. *Medicine and Science in Sports and Exercise, 32,* 904–910.

Iafusco, D. (2006). Diet and physical activity in patients with type 1 diabetes. *Acta Biomedica, 77,* 41–46.

Mauvais-Jarvis, F., Sobngwi, E., Porcher, R., Garnier, J.P., Vexiau, P., Duvallet, A., & Gautier, J.F. (2003). Glucose response to intense aerobic exercise in type 1 diabetes. *Diabetes Care, 26,* 1316–1317.

Nansel, T.R., Gellar, L., & McGill, A. (2008). Effect of varying glycemic index meals on blood glucose control assessed with continuous glucose monitoring in youth with type 1 diabetes on basal-bolus insulin regimens. *Diabetes Care, 31,* 695–697.

Pallant, J. (2007). *SPSS Survival Manual.* McGraw Hill.

Rabasa-Lhoret, R., Bourque, J., Ducros, F., & Chiasson, J. (2001). Guidelines for premeal insulin dose reduction for postprandial exercise of different intensities and durations in type 1 diabetic subjects treated intensively with a basal-bolus insulin regimen (Ultralente-Lispro). *Diabetes Care, 24,* 625–630.

Ramires, P.R., Forjaz, C.L., Strunz, C.M., Silva, M.E., Diament, J., Nicolau, W., Liberman, B., & Negrão, C.E. (1997). Oral glucose ingestion increases endurance capacity in normal and diabetic (type I) humans. *Journal of Applied Physiology, 83,* 608–614.

Riddell, M.C., & Iscoe, K. (2006). Physical activity, sport and pediatric diabetes. *Pediatric Diabetes, 7,* 60–70.

Steppel, J.H., & Horton, E.S. (2003). Exercise in the management of type 1 diabetes mellitus. *Reviews in Endocrine and Metabolic Disorders, 4,* 355–360.

Thomas, D.E., Elliott, E.J., & Baur, L. (2007). Low glycemic index or low glycemic load diets for overweight and obesity. *Cochrane Database Systematic Reviews, 18,* 1–38.

Tsalikian, E., Maurus, N., Beck, R.W., Janz, K.F., Chase, H.P. et al. (2005). Impact of exercise on overnight glycemic control in children with type 1 diabetes mellitus. *Journal of Paediatrics, 147,* 528–534.

West, D., Morton, R., Stephens J.W., Bain, S.C., & Bracken, R.M. (2010). Effects of rapid-acting insulin reductions on post-exercise glycaemia in people with type 1 diabetes. *Journal of Sports Sciences, 28,* 781–788.

West, D.J., Morton, R., Stephens, J.W., Bain, S.C., & Bracken, R.M. (2011). Isomaltulose improves post-exercise glycemia by reducing CHO oxidation in T1DM. *Medicine and Science in Sports and Exercise, 43,* 204–210.

Wolever, T.M.S., & Jenkins, D.J.A. (1988). The use of glycemic index in predicting the blood glucose response to mixed meals. *The American Journal of Clinical Nutrition, 43,* 167–172.

Websites

Integrated Research Application Service: https://www.myresearchproject.org.uk/

13

SPORT PSYCHOLOGY

Sport performers' experiences of stress and emotions

Rich Neil and Stephen D. Mellalieu

Article reference

Neil, R., Hanton, S., Mellalieu, S.D., & Fletcher, D. (2011). Competition stress and emotions in sport performers: The role of further appraisals. *Psychology of Sport and Exercise, 12,* 460–470.

Article summary

The study discussed in this chapter examined the cognitive appraisals, emotional reactions, further appraisals, and behavioural responses of athletes to the performance and organisational demands encountered within the competition environment. To achieve this, 12 sport performers (6 elite, 6 non-elite) were interviewed. The findings provided insight into the ongoing relationship (transaction) between an athlete's environment, their subsequent appraisals of the environment and the emotional and behavioural consequences. Specifically, in certain situations athletes' appraisals and negative emotions experienced were interpreted as debilitative for upcoming performance and influenced behaviour via a lack of control over these thoughts and symptoms. In contrast, examples were cited where demands experienced gave rise to negative appraisals and emotions. However, through a further appraisal of these experiences, athletes were able to interpret these thoughts and feelings as facilitative for upcoming performance, via an increase in focus and/or effort.

Related author publications

Neil, R., Hanton, S., & Mellalieu, S.D. (2009). The contribution of qualitative inquiry towards understanding competitive anxiety and competition stress. *Qualitative Research in Sport and Exercise, 1,* 191–205.

Neil, R., Fletcher, D., Hanton, S., & Mellalieu, S.D. (2007). (Re)conceptualizing competition stress in sport performers. *Sport & Exercise Psychology Review, 3,* 23–29.

Personal prologue

Rich

I became interested in sport psychology as an undergraduate student in 1999 where the focus for my final year dissertation was on the competitive anxiety responses of sports performers. This direction in my first piece of research was mainly because I felt that my own football performances had suffered due to anxiety and I wanted to explore how other performers coped when experiencing this negative emotion. This was also the topic for my MSc thesis in 2002. When reading for these projects, I became aware that the literature on competitive anxiety adopted a narrow conceptual focus in comparison to the study of competition stress and emotions. Specifically, I learnt that how individuals experience stress accounts for the demands or stressors they experience while competing or preparing to compete in sport and the evaluative thoughts (cognitive appraisals) they have about those demands. This 'process' then gives rise to a number of emotional experiences (which may include competitive anxiety) and influences behaviour (e.g., an athlete's performance). Consequently, by just focusing on anxiety I ignored the causes and consequences of this, and other, emotional responses – which limited the usefulness of the data in the real world. I therefore began reading more into the area of competition stress and emotions, and, with Dr Stephen Mellalieu, devised a PhD programme of study – Stephen later became my Director of Studies for the project. This programme was in three main stages. The first examined the stressors (i.e., demands) experienced by athletes within the competitive environment. The second stage considered the cognitive, emotional and behavioural responses to these demands. The final stage evaluated the effectiveness of an extended intervention aimed at helping performers manipulate their emotional responses experienced in relation to competitive demands. This programme of research was also supported by my second supervisor, Professor Sheldon Hanton, and David Fletcher, a fellow PhD student at the time who was conducting a parallel project in the area of organisational stress.

Stephen

My origins in sport psychology stem back to my sporting experiences and observations of the dynamics of the teams I played in and why the atmosphere surrounding these dynamics changed. Among the factors that interested me was how big matches and competitions lead people to behave in vastly different ways to when there was less pressure on the outcome. Similar to Rich, my formal entries into psychology research focused around studies of pre-competition anxiety at undergraduate and masters level. For my PhD thesis I began to study the broader emotional aspects of the pre-competition experience in elite sport and the notion that many other emotions were experienced, aside from the accepted anxiety symptoms. Equally, I was also interested in how performers deployed cognitive and behavioural strategies to manage these experiences. I had already worked provisionally with Sheldon Hanton on some pilot projects in this area for my PhD and when Rich came on board to commence his doctoral work we sought to explore the broader notion of elite performers' experiences of stress and other emotions, rather than anxiety per se, within the competition environment of sport.

Concentrating on the second stage of Rich's thesis, which is the focus of this chapter, when we considered the existing research in the area of competition stress back in 2005, there were many issues with the literature, one being that the research had not considered the entire stress and emotion process experienced by sport performers. Consequently, our aim was to explore and describe the stress and emotion process encountered by sport performers within the competitive environment. In the remainder of this chapter, we describe this research process (see also Appendix), commencing with identifying the research problem and specific research question – identifying and implementing appropriate methods – and subsequently analysing, synthesising, and representing the information gathered.

Key message: Make sure your research is of personal interest to you, it will make the whole process a lot more meaningful, enjoyable and rewarding.

Moving from a research problem to a research question

The research problem was that we wanted to gain a better understanding about sports performers' experiences of stress and emotions in and around competition. After reviewing the literature it was evident that research [in sport psychology] had advocated one of two perspectives to guide our investigation. The first approach was Lazarus and Folkman's (1984) theoretical perspective that stress was the product of a 'transaction' between the individual and the environment. Put simply, the term transaction refers to a process where an individual appraises (i.e., thinks about) the stressors (i.e., the demands) he or she encounters, with the stress response (e.g., emotions such as excitement, frustration, anxiety, and physical symptoms such as muscular tension and nervous behaviour) being the result of this transaction (see Fletcher, Hanton, & Mellalieu, 2006). The second perspective was Lazarus' (1991, 1999) more contemporary cognitive-motivational-relational theory (CMRT) that considered the emotions associated with this transaction in more detail. Specifically, the immediate emotions that are experienced as a consequence of this transaction may be positive or negative depending on whether the individual views the demands, and the consequences of not coping with these demands, as threatening, harmful, beneficial or as a positive challenge. These thoughts and emotions are then purported to influence subsequent behaviour (i.e., athletic performance).

Existing research that had adopted Lazarus and Folkman's perspective of stress in sport psychology to inform their inquiry had investigated the demands faced (e.g., Noblet & Gifford, 2002), and the evaluative thoughts and coping strategies used when experiencing these demands (e.g., Holt & Hogg, 2002). Although advocated by academics in the sport psychology literature, at this point no study had been informed by Lazarus' CMRT. Research had been undertaken that had focused on parts of the stress and emotion process, but no study had considered the entire process from the demands encountered through to athletic behaviour. Looking even more closely, at that point in time there were a number of other concerns with the existing stress and emotion research in sport psychology:

1   Few stressor research projects had considered the origin of the demands performers were experiencing. That is, whether they experienced competition-related demands (e.g., opponent ability, performing while injured, and expectations of the coach) or organisational-related demands (e.g., large crowd size, change in diet, and issues with transport to event). Consequently, no study had considered the appraisals or stress responses to the different types of demands. This distinction is important to identify as each type of demand may result in different appraisals, emotions, and behaviours – all of which may require different types of interventions.

2   No study had considered the notion of 'emotional orientation' when focusing on the stress and emotion process. Fletcher et al. (2006, in press at the time) proposed that performers interpret the emotions they experience as beneficial (facilitative) or detrimental (debilitative) towards performance. So, if performers experience negative emotions such as anger, frustration, or anxiety, then it is important to also consider whether they view the experience of these as good or bad for performance. This perspective was derived from the significant number of studies in the competitive anxiety literature that have shown some individuals view this negative emotional response as good for performance, while others view it as bad. This notion is an important addition to the stress and emotion process because if performers do view their emotional experience as good for performance, then failure to identify this further evaluative thought process may result in sport psychologists recommending an intervention that is targeted at reducing the overall emotional experience (by eliminating stressors or changing cognitive appraisals). This change in emotional state may then itself be viewed as detrimental to performance by the athlete.

Based on these issues, a clear research question was evident. We deemed it important to *illuminate* the stress and emotion process experienced by sports performers. Within this objective we sought to gain particular insight into the role of the further evaluative thought processes that sports performers have (represented by the term 'emotional orientation'). Further, we wanted to consider the perceived impact that athletes' initial cognitive appraisals and subsequent emotional experiences had on their sporting performance. Our reasons were twofold. First, from a knowledge development perspective, providing more insight into experiences of stress and emotion by considering the demands, appraisals, emotions, emotional orientation, and subsequent behaviour would offer information not yet collected in the sport psychology literature. Second, from an applied perspective, identification of the demands encountered, how they are appraised by an athlete, what the emotional responses to this demand are, whether these responses are viewed as good or bad for performance, and how they actually impact performance, would help inform practitioners about the optimal stage to target any stress management intervention. That is, whether the intervention should focus on eliminating or managing the stressors encountered, changing performers' appraisals of these stressors, deploying strategies to coping with the subsequent emotions, or adjusting behaviour.

Choice of method (Matching the method to the research question)

Given the nature of the research question, we considered a qualitative form of enquiry to be the most appropriate approach. Specifically, as we wished to illuminate performers' experiences of stress and emotions, such an approach would offer participants the opportunity to reflect and talk about their experiences of stress and emotion during competition. Previous research into the stressors encountered and coping strategies used had adopted semi-structured interviews to gather information. This was a data collection approach that normally lasted 45 to 180 minutes (see, for example, Gould, Jackson, & Finch, 1993; Holt & Hogg, 2002) and provided performers with the freedom to select the stressors they experienced and how they coped with these stressors. In comparison, adopting a closed approach through the use of questionnaires restricts information in relation to a number of 'prescribed' options identified by the researchers – an approach that would result in limited findings about the stress and emotion process. This was the main reason a semi-structured interview approach was used – interviewing performers at one point in time. Obviously, there are many other methods of qualitative enquiry that could have been used, and designs that are longitudinal in nature, but due to the time constraints of Rich conducting a PhD, we felt this was the most suitable approach.

Given the progressive nature of Rich's PhD programme, we also used the same participants that he had interviewed in his first PhD study, which had aimed to identify the broad range of demands encountered by performers during the competitive period. This was carried out to maximise 'prolonged engagement' whereby the trustworthiness of the data increases due to the participant becoming more familiar with the researcher (see Lincoln & Guba, 1985).

Data collection

Ethical issues and approval

During this stage we attempted to identify the possible social, psychological, and physical risks of harm that potential participants and Rich, as the interviewer, may have faced during data collection (i.e., interviews). The key concerns highlighted at the time of the study were that:

1   Talking about stressful experiences that the participant had endured would have brought up sensitive issues that could have caused the participant to feel anxious or distressed.
2   The participant would have deviated from the purpose of the study and discussed topics of a clinical nature – topics that were beyond Rich's competencies to discuss.
3   The interview environment was comfortable for both Rich and the participant and that the interviews could have been conducted without interference.

To help manage these issues, we proposed to provide each potential participant with a pre-interview information pack that would include a detailed voluntary informed consent form and would:

1   Highlight that participation was purely voluntary and that the voluntary informed consent form would be completed prior to interview.
2   Highlight the main purpose of the study and the types of questions they would be asked, and also inform them that they did not have to answer any question and could stop the interview at any point.
3   Inform each participant of Rich's personal qualifications and competencies and the types of topics/issues that he would not be willing to discuss due to his competencies/qualifications.
4   Inform each participant of the potential practitioners Rich could refer them to should any sensitive topics/issues be raised that were beyond his competencies/qualifications;
5   Suggest the participant identify an appropriate interview venue that would be comfortable for both Rich and the participant, and that would not be too distracting.

All this description was identified in the successful ethical approval application to the University Research Ethics Committee.

The interview guide

Prior to conducting the interviews, an individualised interview guide was developed for each of the 12 participants in order to extract in-depth information regarding their experience of stress and emotions. This was developed through the following process:

1   First, we reviewed all the stressors identified by each participant in Rich's first PhD study and listed them under 11 categories of performance stressors and 12 categories of organisational stressors (see Mellalieu, Neil, Hanton, & Fletcher, 2009). For example, 'possibility of injury reoccurring' or 'going in to tackles so soon after injury' were placed under the performance category of 'risk of injury.'

2   Under each of the 23 groups of stressors (i.e., 11 performance and 12 organisational stressors) the following questions were placed:

    i   Which from this list of stressors stand out more than the others?

    ii   Select one of the identified stressors that 'stand out' and talk to me about your experiences with this stressor.

    iii   When you experienced this stressor, what were you thinking?

    iv   Why were you thinking this?

    v   How were you feeling?

    vi   What physical symptoms were you experiencing as a result of these thoughts and feelings?

    vii   These thoughts and feelings that you experienced because of a *specific stressor*, did you view these as positive or negative with regard to your immediate performance?

    viii   Why did you view these thoughts and feelings as good/bad for your performance?

    ix   As a result of these thoughts and feelings, how did you actually behave during performance?

3   A prompt was then provided to go through the remaining 'stand out' stressors, so that they were not neglected.

Pilot interviews

Pilot interviews were undertaken to ensure: 1) the interview guide addressed the purpose of the study and that each specific question addressed what we hoped it would address; 2) all questions were understood by the participants; and 3) Rich had gained more practice in conducting interviews – refining his interview skills and techniques along the way. Two elite and two non-elite athletes were interviewed. The first and last interviews were video recorded with feedback on Rich's interviewing skills provided by Stephen and Sheldon (both of whom had considerable experience in interviewing sports performers; see e.g., Hanton & Connaughton, 2002; Mellalieu & Juniper, 2006). For example, in the first pilot interview Rich was reluctant to deviate away from the interview guide. This resulted in him 'bringing the participant back in' too forcefully and witnessing an immediate change in the participant's body language and detail of information provided (which was reinforced by the video recording). The advice was to be patient with the participants and let them move along at their own pace as the interview guide is always there to work through once the participant had finished their story. One memorable bit of advice that has stayed with Rich ever since is, 'when people talk, it's like them going on a journey, so let them feel like they've reached their destination!' A further issue identified was repetition in questions asked. Specifically, asking questions about their appraisals, emotions, and behaviours in relation to every stressor they identified became cumbersome. However, this repetitive process was important to get a good understanding of the performers' experiences, and looking back at the interview transcripts Rich did not feel that the quality of information was diminished as time went on.

Participants

The participants had come from Rich's first PhD study. They had been sampled purposefully through a procedure called maximum variation (heterogeneity) sampling. This form of sampling refers to the selection of participants who can provide different experiences based on the topic of interest, an approach used in previous research (see e.g., Hanton, Fletcher, & Coughlan, 2005). As we were interested in illuminating the stress and emotion process in sport performers, we selected men and women from a diverse range of sports. To facilitate this purposeful sampling procedure, we developed a matrix to identify the specific dimensions of the sports in which each participant competed. This matrix included whether the participant competed in a sport that was contact, non-contact, self-paced, externally paced, open skilled, closed skilled, short duration, long duration, of a fine motor nature, gross motor nature, and included a ball or included other specialist equipment – such as a racket or stick (see Table 13.1). The selection of individuals in this manner also allowed for the collection of bespoke sporting experiences that each athlete may have encountered within their context-specific setting. In addition, Patton (2002) highlighted that this method enables any common patterns (shared experiences) to emerge from investigating such a varied sample (i.e., different sports).

Regarding the use of 12 participants, similar sample sizes have been used in other studies that have adopted qualitative approaches to gather data (e.g., Holt & Hogg, 2002). This number was, therefore, deemed appropriate to gather sufficient information regarding the stress and emotion process experienced by performers across a wide range of sports, and especially because Rich had reached a point of data saturation with the 12 participants in his first PhD study. In other words, by the end of the twelfth interview nothing new was being uncovered. Arguably, new information could have been found in this study

TABLE 13.1 Matrix used to identify the characteristics of the sports that participants compete in

Participant	Gender	Sport	Sport type	Standard	Objective	Subjective	Contact	Non-contact	Racket	Ball sport	Open skill	Closed skill	Long duration	Short duration	Fine motor	Gross motor	Self-paced	External paced
Elite																		
A	Female	Rowing	Individual / Team	GB Squad	X			X				X	X			X		X
B	Female	Hockey	Team	Wales U21	X					X	X		X			X		X
C	Female	Swimming	Individual	Wales Senior	X			X				X		X		X	X	
D	Male	Snooker	Individual	Former World Champion	X			X		X		X	X		X		X	
E	Male	Rugby	Team	Welsh Regional	X		X				X		X			X		X
F	Male	Mountain Biking	Individual	International Competitor	X			X			X			X		X	X	X
Non-elite																		
G	Female	Football	Team	Southern League	X		X			X	X		X			X		X
H	Female	Surf Lifesaving	Individual	Regional	X	X	X				X			X		X	X	X
I	Female	Tennis	Individual	Regional	X			X	X		X			X		X		X
J	Male	Football	Team	National Division One	X		X			X	X		X			X		X
K	Male	Badminton	Individual	Satellite League	X			X	X		X			X		X		X
L	Male	Hockey	Team	Southern League	X		X			X	X		X			X		X

with a thirteenth participant, but we took the decision that we had enough information to address the research question.

The participants ranged in age from 19 to 56 years ($M = 23.67$, $SD = 10.32$). Six of the participants met the criteria for 'elite' standard as they had competed at major national and international championships, such as United Kingdom (UK), European, and World Championships (see Hanton & Connaughton, 2002). Based on Hanton and Connaughton's suggested criteria, the remaining six participants who completed the sample selection were of non-elite status, with standards ranging from district to UK national schools/university level. All participants provided written voluntary informed consent to take part in the study and this consent was obtained prior to the interview being conducted.

Interviews

All the interviews were conducted face-to-face, tape recorded, and lasted between 60 and 90 minutes. Telephone interviews and focus groups are alternative methods that have been used in previous studies because of the distances involved, the purpose being to gain group discussion on topics (i.e., Gould et al., 1993). However, as all the participants were within a 50-mile radius of Swansea University, and bearing in mind that Rich had only a one-study experience of interviewing, he felt that his one-to-one skills still needed developing before he could even attempt facilitating a focus group. In addition, stress is potentially a sensitive topic, not one to be shared in a group environment, such as focus groups, where the researcher's purpose is to learn and not intervene. Each interview was conducted within the time frame of the performer's competitive season and was carried out at a venue of their choice – away from the competitive environment. This approach was used to help the performer become more comfortable, allowing them to speak freely about their experiences without the worry that significant others may overhear (such as coaches, team mates etc.). Using a *semi-structured* format, each individual was led through an identical set of questions that were asked in a similar manner. However, given the semi-structured nature of the guide, ordering of questions remained sufficiently open and flexible to avoid disrupting the flow of the discussion and to allow exploration of responses to a combination of demands when the opportunity arose. Based on Patton's (2002) recommendations for conducting interviews, clarification (e.g., 'I'm not entirely sure what you mean, could you please go over that again?'), elaboration (e.g., 'Could you please explain that in more detail?'), and general (e.g., 'What effect did that have?') probes were used to investigate issues in greater depth. At the end of each section, participants were asked whether there was anything else they could add concerning what had just been discussed.

While carrying out these interviews Rich faced a number of challenges that required him to be patient and understanding with the participants and other individuals he encountered. For example, two participants cancelled and re-arranged the interviews at the last minute, while one participant finished the interview half way through due to previously undisclosed work commitments – Rich and the interviewee then had to continue two hours later at seven o'clock in the evening. The worst interruption to data collection, however, came from a colleague of one of the participants. The interview was being conducted in an office at a sports organisation and a colleague entered the office and decided it would be ok to eat their lunch with the participant. Move forward an hour and he was still there! Aside from these logistical issues, Rich still found it difficult at the start of data collection to use the large interview guide he had developed. As each participant had a lot of stressors to discuss, Rich found himself breaking the flow of the interviews by checking if he had asked for responses to all the stressors in the interview guide. This did stop by the end of the data collection as Rich developed a checklist system to 'tick off' questions for each stressor; this emphasises the importance of inexperienced interviewers conducting a series of pilot interviews until familiarity with the guide is achieved.

Key message: If conducting your first interview study, you need to know your interview guide inside and out by performing numerous pilot interviews. If you can do this, you will then focus on listening rather than worrying about what question you are going to ask the participant next. Video recording the interviews may also help with further refining interviews skills such as non-verbal communication.

Data analysis

The tapes from the interviews were transcribed yielding 400 pages of double spaced text. The transcribed interviews were then formatted for analysis in the QSR N5 (2000), the fifth version of the Non-numerical Unstructured Data Indexing Searching and Theorizing (NUD★IST) software for qualitative data analysis. This programme allowed Rich to go through the transcripts and easily identify and code quotations that represented replies to questions about stressors, the subsequent appraisals (i.e., evaluative thoughts), the associated emotional responses, emotional orientation, and actual performance behaviour, respectively. While the NUD★IST software helped to expedite the organisation of initial raw data and subsequent categorisation of the stress and emotion process, researchers can also make sense of their interview transcripts by hand (see, for example, Gould et al., 1993).

Trustworthiness

For the purpose of trustworthiness, and in line with guidelines for best qualitative practice, a reflexive journal was kept throughout Rich's PhD (see Patton, 2002). Being 'reflexive' involves self-questioning and self-understanding, an on-going examination of *what I know* and *how I know it*, with the perspective of the researcher being part of the context for the findings in a qualitative inquiry

(Patton, 2002). Adopting this approach during the entire process of this study, and Rich's PhD, he reflected upon the ways in which the data had been shaped by the research process itself. The following extract illustrates the development of Rich's understanding of why performers viewed their emotions as beneficial to performance. It provides the reader with insight into how decisions and interpretations of the data were made, and allows for evaluation of its potential influence on the subsequent study outcomes/conclusions.

> **October 20th, 2005**
> This week I have again been working through each performer's narratives and met once more with Stephen [PhD Supervisor]. What was of interest when sifting through the discussions with each performer was the explanations given for emotional orientation. That is, why the performers had viewed their emotions as facilitative or debilitative to upcoming performance. Interestingly, when emotions are perceived to be beneficial towards performance, the reasons attributed to this interpretation are due to an increase in focus or effort towards the task in hand. When emotions are interpreted as debilitative, the explanations mirror the initial appraisals given when the stressor is experienced. It is also important to note that the performers' further appraisals (i.e., of their emotions) also referred to the initial appraisals and stressor(s). From these findings, it is possible to suggest that orientation (or direction as labelled by the anxiety literature) is a representation of how performers view their emotions, initial appraisals, and experienced demands, with use of a motivational content. They do not only interpret how beneficial their emotions are to upcoming performance, but also the appraisals that caused these feeling states, and these interpretations include a motivational outcome (whether task focus, effort, or both).

Verification

This process included two stages. The first involved Stephen and Sheldon conducting an 'audit check' of Rich's analysis. They read and re-read the transcripts to become familiar with them, and then looked at Rich's analysis to see if they agreed with his 'coding' of quotations for each experience identified by each participant as 'stressors', 'appraisals', 'emotions', 'orientation', and 'behaviour'. In this particular study there was minimal disagreement with regard to Rich's interpretation of findings, perhaps because all were versed in Lazarus' idea about what stress and emotion entailed, and because the interview guide included questions that asked about each stage of the process in turn (see the example questions in the Interview Guide section of this chapter), so the responses would be in relation to what was asked (i.e., if asked about an emotion, you'd expect a response about the emotion). Where there was disagreement, Rich was challenged to explain and justify his interpretation in relation to Lazarus' theory. Once agreement was reached, data were prepared for presentation.

For the second stage, Rich's findings (interview transcripts, analysis, presentation of findings and reflexive journal) were presented to an independent researcher – an experienced sport psychologist trained in qualitative interview methods and versed in the competitive stress literature. The intention here was for the 'outside' researcher to act as devil's advocate (cf. Creswell, 1998). This allowed for further reading and re-reading of the findings and an additional opportunity for a fresh set of eyes, not immersed in the study, to question or raise concern about any interpretations or inferences made throughout the analysis. Minor concerns were raised by the independent researcher regarding the analysis, which were then discussed by the research team and resolved.

Data presentation

We aimed to illuminate the stress and emotions experienced by performers within the competition environment, and an appropriate representation of the findings was required to illustrate these experiences. In other words, a presentation format that showed the initial stressor(s) identified the subsequent appraisals, emotions, emotional orientation, and performance behaviour. The majority of previous research into competition stress had used hierarchical frameworks to either display the different stressors or coping strategies adopted by athletes (see, for example, Fletcher & Hanton, 2003; Holt & Hogg, 2002). Such an approach was deemed inappropriate for our study, as we were interested in representing the entire stress and emotion process, step by step. Alternative approaches to presenting qualitative data had been adopted in competitive anxiety research. These offered more of a sequential representation of data, and have be termed 'causal networks' (see Hanton & Connaughton, 2002). Visual representations are advocated when the purpose of the study is to represent relationships between variables (such as stressors and coping strategies) or provide explanations for such relationships in a particular context, or over a prolonged period of time (see, for example, Hanton & Connaughton, 2002). As the stress and emotion process is sequential, in that one part has implications for the next (starting with the stressors encountered, the appraisals and associated emotional responses, further appraisals – or emotional orientation – and then behaviour), we decided to present this process through single-case causal networks. This was a logical decision because by representing the process step by step we would be able to illustrate to the reader how Lazarus' perspective on stress and emotions can inform an easy, sequential understanding of performers' specific competitive stress experiences. Figure 13.1 illustrates this entire process in five stages. First, two performers' experiences of encountering both organisational and performance demands in the same situation are reported. Next in the process are their initial appraisals (represented as 'cognitions') and the associated emotions experienced. Third, the figure illustrates the

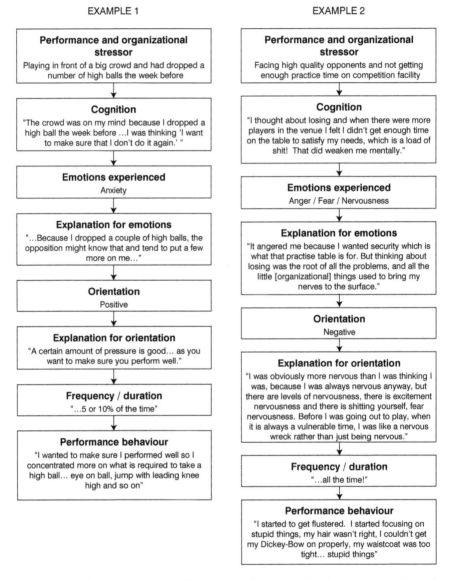

FIGURE 13.1 Responses to a performance and organizational stressor experienced simultaneously

performers' explanations for why they felt these emotions and the orientation of the emotions (i.e., whether they were viewed as good or bad for performance). Then they provide their explanations for the orientation (i.e., which include insight into the further appraisals through representing what the performer was thinking at this stage of the process). Finally, the eventual behavioural outcome is indicated (i.e., how the performer behaved during competition). We included quotations from the performers to offer the reader insight into what they had indicated they were actually experiencing at each stage of the process.

In total, five figures were presented in the published manuscript, encompassing 10 examples of performers' experiences of stress and emotions. The figures gave examples of when performers encountered performance stressors, organisational stressors, multiple performance stressors, multiple organisational stressors, and a mixture of performance and organisational stressors in one situation. Within each figure, the two examples gave an illustration of where a performer viewed his or her emotional experience as either facilitative (i.e., beneficial) or debilitative (i.e., detrimental) towards performance. We also provided a narrative around the figures that briefly described each step of the athletes' experiences of the stress and emotion process for the reader. This approach was adopted to increase the understanding for the reader about what we were presenting and to allow the reader to get a feel for the context of performers' experiences of stress (see Creswell, 1998; Patton, 2002 for a discussion on narrative representations).

Contribution to knowledge

As with all discussions, it is important to identify how the study contributed to knowledge by comparing the data with those of previous research, and by illustrating how the findings from our study can be utilised by sport psychologists in real-world settings. With regard to furthering knowledge, in the article we emphasised that our study added to existing research by being the first to illuminate the stress and emotion process using the conceptual approach advocated by Lazarus (1999). Indeed, we showed that athletes face a diversity of demands, and have differing cognitive appraisals and emotions in relation to these demands as a consequence. These emotions also have varied performance consequences dependent on whether the athlete views the emotions as good or bad for performance. We emphasised that the findings seemed to suggest that this 'emotional orientation' was pivotal for enabling successful stress management and subsequent performance. For example, when negative emotions were viewed as beneficial to performance, athletes were motivated to do well and increased their effort and concentration on the task in hand. When negative emotions were viewed as detrimental to performance, a continuation of the negative appraisals that caused those emotions in the first place remained, leading to poor sporting performance.

Impact on practice

From an applied perspective, the findings highlighted the importance of practitioners understanding the entire stress and emotion process the performer experiences during competition. In particular, if a practitioner focuses solely on the stressors encountered by performers, the appraisals of these stressors, or the emotions experienced during competition, then the practitioner is only assessing 'part of the picture'. Consequently, the practitioner may mistakenly attempt to reduce an athlete's emotional state when it is not needed, as through closer examination of the whole process (that includes emotional orientation) this emotional state may have been viewed as beneficial to performance. Within the manuscript we therefore advised practitioners to consider the entire stress and emotion process and, where performers view their emotional experiences as debilitative to upcoming performance, to adopt cognitive (evaluative thought) restructuring techniques to change the way they 'think' about their emotional experiences. We have recently shown that such an approach can be successful in changing the emotional orientation of performers who view their emotional states as detrimental for their performance (see Neil, Hanton, & Mellalieu, 2013).

Reflection

In Section 2 (Choice of method) we suggested that the contribution to knowledge of previous research in our topic of study was restricted because few researchers had considered the entire stress and emotion process experienced by sports performers. It was therefore important to conduct the study to further knowledge and inform applied practice. On reflection, however, we acknowledge that a number of measures could have been implemented to strengthen the study and that its design may have taken a different form. Focusing on the former, to improve the validity of the findings we could have presented our interpretations of the interviews conducted to the performers for verification. This is important and something that we now do in every study we conduct. By offering participants the opportunity to scrutinise interview transcripts, and our interpretations of their responses, we increase the authenticity of qualitative findings presented to the reader. This seeks to ensure that our interpretations are representative of what the performers have actually stated. In addition, to offer further insight into performers' experiences, more visual representations of the stress and emotions reported could have been provided in the manuscript. Journal page length restrictions limit what authors can include, however, we did initially seek to be more creative in representing the stress and emotion process – an endeavour we as a team are still working on – due to the complexity of capturing the process. Every stressful experience is unique, encompassing numerous demands, different appraisals, emotions, and behaviours. To represent what people are experiencing in a visual format is somewhat challenging. For example, in other research we have opted to overlook visual representation of the stress process and give insight into performers' experiences through their own quotes within the narrative. Through this approach we feel we are able to portray a more comprehensive story about the stress-related experiences of sports performers.

A further obvious limitation with the study is its retrospective nature. If we had provided the performers with the actual interview guide before meeting with them, then his may have prompted memory recall and improved the detail of the accounts given by the interviewees. As a consequence of these reflections on the research process at the time, we now always provide the interviewee with the actual interview guide prior to interview. For verification purposes we also aim to provide the participant with the interview transcript, any interpretations of findings, and the results section of the subsequent manuscript it contributes to prior to submitting to a journal.

Focusing on what we could have done differently, we identified in Section 3 (Choice of method) that other methods of data collection could have been adopted (i.e., focus groups or longitudinal approaches, such as participant diaries). We chose to use face-to-face interviews in order to build Rich's own skills of interviewing and because this approach was more realistic given the time constraints on conducting a full-time PhD. Due to the confidence gained from undertaking this study, we have subsequently used other qualitative approaches to investigate the competition stress process (e.g., video-assisted self-confrontational interview) and we continue to reflect on what went well during data collection and why, and what we can do differently to improve both knowledge and our competencies as researchers.

> If you liked this chapter, you should check out Chapter 9 that conducts a quantitative approach to furthering knowledge within the sport psychology field and Chapters 5, 7 and 11 that describe a research process where interviews are used as the data collection method.

References

Creswell, J.W. (1998). *Qualitative inquiry and research design: Choosing among the five traditions.* London: Sage.

Fletcher, D., & Hanton, S. (2003). Sources of organizational stress in elite sports performers. *The Sport Psychologist, 17,* 175–195.

Fletcher, D., Hanton, S., & Mellalieu, S.D. (2006). An organizational stress review: Conceptual and theoretical issues in competitive sport. In S. Hanton & S.D. Mellalieu (Eds.). *Literature reviews in sport psychology* (pp. 321–374). Hauppage, NY: Nova Science.

Gould, D., Jackson, S.A., & Finch, L.M. (1993). Sources of stress in national champion figure skaters. *Journal of Sport and Exercise Psychology, 15,* 134–159.

Hanton, S., & Connaughton, D. (2002). Perceived control of anxiety and its relationship with self-confidence performance: A qualitative explanation. *Research Quarterly for Exercise and Sport, 73,* 87–97.

Hanton, S., Fletcher, D., & Coughlan, G. (2005). Stress in elite sport performers: A comparative study of competitive and organizational stressors. *Journal of Sports Sciences, 23,* 1129–1141.

Holt, N.L., & Hogg, J.M. (2002). Perception of stress and coping during preparations for the 1999 women's soccer world cup finals. *The Sport Psychologist, 16,* 251–271.

Lazarus, R.S. (1991). *Emotion and adaptation.* New York: Oxford University Press.

Lazarus, R.S. (1999). *Stress and emotion: A new synthesis.* New York: Springer.

Lazarus, R.S., & Folkman, S. (1984). *Stress, appraisal, and coping.* New York: Springer.

Lincoln, Y.S., & Guba, E.G. (1985). *Naturalistic inquiry.* Newbury Park, CA: Sage.

Mellalieu, S.D., & Juniper, S.W. (2006). A qualitative investigation into experiences of the role episode in soccer. *The Sport Psychologist, 20,* 399–418.

Mellalieu, S.D., Neil, R., Hanton, S., & Fletcher, D. (2009). Competition stress in sport performers: Stressors experienced in the competition environment. *Journal of Sports Sciences, 29,* 729–744.

Neil, R., Fletcher, D., Hanton, S., & Mellalieu, S.D. (2007). (Re)conceptualizing competition stress in sport performers. *Sport & Exercise Psychology Review, 3,* 23–29.

Neil, R., Hanton, S., & Mellalieu, S.D. (2009). The contribution of qualitative inquiry towards understanding competitive anxiety and competition stress. *Qualitative Research in Sport and Exercise, 1,* 191–205.

Neil, R., Hanton, S., Mellalieu, S.D., & Fletcher, D. (2011). Competition stress and emotions in sport performers: The role of further appraisals. *Psychology of Sport and Exercise, 12,* 460–470.

Neil, R., Hanton, S., & Mellalieu, S.D. (2013). Seeing things in a different light: Assessing the effects of a cognitive-behavioral intervention upon the further appraisals of golfers. *Journal of Applied Sport Psychology, 25,* 106–130.

Noblet, A.J., & Gifford, S.M. (2002). The sources of stress experienced by professional Australian footballers. *Journal of Applied Sport Psychology, 14,* 1–13.

Patton, M.Q. (2002). *Qualitative research and evaluation methods* (3rd Edn). Newbury Park, CA: Sage.

QSR N5 [Computer software] (2000). Melbourne, Australia: Qualitative Solutions & Research Pty Ltd (QSR).

Appendix: Research Process Flow Chart

No.	Stage	Detail
1	Research problem	To gain a greater understanding about performers' experiences of stress in sport.
2	Research question	To illuminate sport performers' experiences of stress and emotions, informed by Lazarus' Cognitive-Motivational-Relational Theory of Emotions
3	Choice of method	Qualitative approach to provide in-depth information
4	Data collection	Face to face interviews to identify experiences of stress and emotions in relation to predetermined stressors
5	Data analysis	Deductive approach, culminating with trustworthiness and verification procedures
6	Data presentation	Single-case causal networks to illustrate each step of the stress and emotion process
7	Contribution to knowledge	First study to illuminate stress and emotion process
8	Impact on practice	Opportunity for practitioners to intervene at different stages of the stress and emotion process

INDEX